Defoe

&

CASUISTRY

Defoe

&

CASUISTRY

BY

G. A. STARR

PRINCETON, NEW JERSEY
PRINCETON UNIVERSITY PRESS

1971

Copyright © 1971 by

PRINCETON UNIVERSITY PRESS

LCC: 75-113010

ISBN: 0-691-06192-0

This book has been composed in Linotype Granjon

Preface

CASUISTRY: *That part of Ethics which resolves cases of conscience, applying the general rules of religion and morality to particular instances in which "circumstances alter cases," or in which there appears to be a conflict of duties. Often (and perhaps originally) applied to a quibbling and evasive way of dealing with difficult cases of duty.* OED

Nearly all of Defoe's fictional works cause us to identify imaginatively with characters whose actions we regard as blameworthy. At the same time that they compel sympathy, his heroes and heroines evoke moral judgment, and our two responses are often sharply opposed. Several critics have previously noted the paradox; this monograph seeks to elucidate it by examining the influence of traditional casuistry on the subject matter, narrative technique, and ethical outlook of Defoe's writings. The affective problem is posed concisely by Angus Ross, who says of Crusoe, "He knows his disobedience is wicked. So does the reader: but he is drawn on by Defoe to sympathize with Crusoe. . . . the reader is not held at a distance and forced to judge. . . . 'So,' we say, 'if I had been Crusoe, I should have behaved.' "[1] What draws us on to sympathize with Crusoe—and with the more patently "wicked" Moll Flanders and Roxana as well—is in large part Defoe's casuistical emphasis on intention and qualifying circumstances. In terms of overt behavior, we respectable readers are remote from such characters, but there is no such distance between

[1] Introduction to *Robinson Crusoe* (Baltimore, 1965), p. 15.

Preface

their motives and ours. The difference in our circumstances therefore serves to explain, and to bridge the gap between, our dissimilar outward careers. Moreover, the differences between their situations and ours are shown to be largely accidental: this too keeps us from adopting a complacently superior stance, and from passing rigorous judgment on Defoe's erring heroes and heroines.

This is not to say that Defoe forbids us to judge his characters, or that he asks acquittal for one and all. Both their prosecutor and defender, he tends to seek a verdict of guilty, but also a suspended sentence and even, in some cases, a full pardon. The reader, of course, is both judge and jury, which may be why there is so much of what Ian Watt calls "forensic ratiocination" in Defoe's fiction.[2] Details that appear to be introduced for their psychological, social, or economic import, or for the sake of narrative realism, frequently involve covert appeals for sympathy as well; their function is not only descriptive or analytic, but also rhetorical. Some of them call in question the conventional assumptions and values which ordinarily shape our judgment, and attempt to make us judge more favorably than we otherwise would, given the outward facts of a case. More often, it is the tone rather than the substance of our judgments that they induce us to modify; they insist that reprehensible as a character may be, he merits our compassion, not our contempt. Lionel Trilling has called the traditional English novel "the literary form to which the emotions of understanding and forgiveness were indigenous, as if by definition of the form itself."[3] Recent critics preoc-

[2] *The Rise of the Novel* (London, 1957), p. 85.

[3] "Manners, Morals, and the Novel," in *The Liberal Imagination* (Garden City, 1953), p. 215. Trilling's two preceding sentences seem to me equally applicable to Defoe's fiction. The greatness and practical usefulness of the novel, he maintains, "lay in its unremitting work of involving the reader himself in the moral life, inviting him to put his own motives under examination, suggesting that reality is not as his

vi

cupied with irony have tended to lose sight of such emotions in the experience of reading Defoe: this study tries to reaffirm their importance, and to trace the part that casuistry plays in eliciting them.

The chapters that follow are not wholly concerned, however, with the impact that casuistry has upon Defoe's reader. They also examine the role of seventeenth-century casuistical divinity in the genesis of his writings, for it was a significant element in Defoe's artistic as well as intellectual background. Casuistry furnished some of his most characteristic subject matter: many of its traditional cases of conscience turn up as letters to the editor in his periodicals, as matrimonial, mercantile, and religious predicaments in his conduct manuals, and as crucial episodes in his novels. Moreover, the casuistical tradition affected Defoe's attitudes toward these cases of conscience. Neither natural law, divine law, positive law, nor expediency is a touchstone by which Defoe decides all ethical problems. He takes up or sets aside each of these sanctions as the occasion demands, and his moral outlook gains much of its flexibility, independence, and vigor by refusing steady allegiance to any single legal or moral code. Casuistry acknowledges the existence and value of such codes, but comes into play when their scope or meaning is obscure, or when their obligations conflict—as is generally the case in Defoe's fictional works. "His characters live in a moral twilight," Martin Price observes,[4] and it is in an ethical no-man's-land (to

conventional education has led him to see it. It taught us, as no other genre ever did, the extent of human variety and the value of this variety." Tony Tanner has recently made a similar point; the novelist, he says, can effect "a kind of redistribution of our sympathies," which involves "understanding forms of life which hitherto one had rather casually considered as axiomatically alien" ("Realism, Reality, and the Novel," a symposium in *Novel: A Forum on Fiction*, ii [1969], 208-09).

[4] *To The Palace of Wisdom: Studies in Order and Energy from Dryden to Blake* (Garden City, 1964), p. 270.

vary the image) that casuistry flourishes—and Defoe seems most at home. As Spiro Peterson has demonstrated, Defoe makes extensive use of contemporary canon and common law, and Maximillian Novak has shown that natural law also figures prominently in his writings;[5] my object is not to minimize Defoe's indebtedness to such systems, but rather to suggest that he invokes them, as they serve his turn, in a thoroughly unsystematic fashion. Defoe has not rejected what Watt calls "a transcendental scheme of things" only to put in its place some mundane but equally schematic conception of life.[6] It is largely by eschewing the schematic, whether in its worldly or otherworldly versions, that Defoe manages to register (if not always to resolve) so many of the moral tensions and complexities of his characters' careers. He is aware that life is infinitely various, that every new situation poses new problems, and that these problems must be dealt with on their own terms. For him, as for earlier English casuists, cases of conscience are not matters of idle speculation, but the very stuff of daily existence. Experience is a constant challenge, since action involves choice and choice involves responsibility. At the same time, each new challenge must be met afresh, since circumstances alter cases. Commonplace situations thus take on moral significance, even an air of adventure; and the adventure is of a distinctly modern kind, in that casuistry offers the tentative in place of the final, the probable in place of the certain. In part, then, this is an essay in the history of ideas, which investigates the casuistical background of Defoe's view of life as intensely problematic; and in part it is a study of the influence of seventeenth-century case divinity on Defoe's choice of specific ethical problems as material for prose fiction.

[5] "The Matrimonial Theme of Defoe's *Roxana*," *PMLA*, LXX (1955), 166-91; *Defoe and the Nature of Man* (Oxford, 1963).
[6] *The Rise of the Novel*, p. 80.

Preface

Insofar as it is concerned with what Defoe made of this material as well as where he got it, this monograph is also formal in orientation. Defoe's narrative techniques can be illuminated by examining the adaptation of certain principles and methods of casuistry in his writings. Particularly noteworthy is the relation of casuistry to Defoe's handling of character and action. With respect to character, casuistry is as concerned with the manner in which a man arrives at his decisions as with what he ultimately chooses, as concerned with the motives that influence action as with the eventual actions themselves. It thus rests on an assumption that something definable as conscience or consciousness is at the core of individual identity—and like the French language (*conscience*), it virtually equates the two terms. On this view, a man can be characterized by his outward behavior only if all his grounds for it are taken into account, and from this position it is a very short step to the belief that characterization consists of the analysis of consciousness. It would be an exaggeration to say that any of Defoe's characters embody this principle consistently, for he often employs other ways of presenting them. To some extent they simply *are* what they *do*, and to this extent they differ little from the traditional figures of roguery, voyaging, and romance. Yet for all that they do and undergo, Defoe's heroes and heroines spend a great deal of time weighing their actions, and through this process we come to know and care much more about them than about any of their seventeenth-century predecessors.

The main effect of casuistry on the action of Defoe's imaginative works is to dissolve it into a series of discrete episodes. Casuistry was not the sole source of fragmentation in Defoe's stories, yet its assumptions about experience probably reinforced episodic tendencies inherent in certain literary genres (such as criminal biography) upon which he drew, as well as in his own improvisatory method of composition.

Preface

The continuity of each character's struggle breaks down into a sequence of local crises, each somewhat isolated from those that precede and follow it, and I think we can regard such plotting (or nonplotting) as the expression of a casuistical conception of life without implying that it is peculiar to casuistry, or that it is Defoe's only mode of analyzing experience. Watt remarks that between Defoean episodes there is "an inordinate number of cracks," and although Defoe's having "worked piecemeal, very rapidly, and without any subsequent revision" may be chiefly responsible for "discontinuities" in plot, Defoe's casuistical sense of life's intrinsic discontinuities probably contributed to the same effect.[7] Whatever larger thematic coherences his books may have, individual episodes tend to be connected chronologically, not causally, and far from helping to organize them into a sustained narrative, casuistry appears to be one of the factors responsible for their disjointedness. Within the individual episode, however, casuistry often afforded Defoe both his subject matter and a distinctive way of treating it. Many scenes are not only based upon traditional cases of conscience, but organized internally in ways that reflect the casuistical method of posing and resolving moral dilemmas. There is a constant marshalling of motives and sanctions, choices and circumstances, precedents and hypothetical analogues; although this procedure can jeopardize any larger pattern or design a book may have, it can also supply a kind of minimal consistency between episodes, and can give each of them a fullness and complexity lacking in earlier fiction.

About the casuistical tradition itself, one or two preliminary remarks are in order. I shall often speak of seventeenth-century English casuistry as if it were a homogeneous body of thought, and to a considerable extent this is justified: between Anglican and Puritan casuists there was a striking community of

[7] *The Rise of the Novel*, pp. 100, 99.

methods and assumptions. A full account of the subject, however, would have to bring out the individual character of the various casuistical manuals as well as their similarities. The marked differences of mind and spirit between Jeremy Taylor and Richard Baxter, for instance, are reflected in the very styles of the *Ductor Dubitantium* and the *Christian Directory*. To speak of "traditional casuistry" is not to deny that diversity exists, but simply to stress a remarkable degree of uniformity. In *Defoe and Spiritual Autobiography*, I maintained that the leading religious ideas in Defoe's fiction were commonplaces of the English Protestant tradition, not merely crotchets of his much-discussed Dissenting milieu. That study dealt more with spiritual than moral aspects of Defoe's religious background—with theories of man's relation to God rather than to his fellow man—and concluded that Defoe's attitudes were less exclusively Puritan than they are commonly taken to be. The casuistical writings of such Puritans as William Perkins, William Ames, and Richard Baxter, on the one hand, and of such Anglicans as Bishops Hall, Sanderson, and Barlow, on the other, seem to me to bear out this argument in the moral sphere as well. Not only does agreement greatly outweigh disagreement between these authors, but disagreement does not necessarily follow sectarian lines.[8] One object in citing Anglican as well as Nonconformist divines is to suggest once again that Defoe's Puritanism (and for that matter post-Restoration Puritanism itself) is a complex problem which calls for further exploration, not a settled historical fact on which interpretations

[8] See John T. McNeill, "Casuistry in the Puritan Age," *Religion in Life*, xii (1943), 83: "It is not, I think, justifiable, to attempt a clear separation within [casuistical literature] between Anglican and Puritan strains. To a large degree each writer uses his own judgment, and where the particular opinions of predecessors are evaluated there is little or no evidence of party alignment . . . differences in severity and laxity, in conservatism and modernity, cannot safely, in my opinion, be related to the ecclesiastical cleavage."

of his life and works can profitably be based. A second object has to do with casuistry rather than Defoe. Casuistry has become so completely identified with the continental Jesuits whom Pascal attacked, and so generally discredited, that one must stress the number and variety of English authors who put a high value on it throughout this period. Although casuistry had from the beginning an equivocal reputation, my citations should indicate that its constructive side was recognized by some of the ablest divines of the seventeenth century.

Of the five books discussed here in some detail, four were published in 1722, Defoe's *annus mirabilis*. If my chief concern had been to trace the history of Defoe's involvement with casuistry, I would have examined his own early controversial and journalistic writings as fully as John Dunton's *Athenian Mercury*, his *Family Instructor* and *Conjugal Lewdness* as fully as *Religious Courtship*, his commercial career and *The Compleat English Tradesman* as fully as any of the novels. But it is the novels that interest me most, and rather than using imaginative works to illustrate a historical thesis, I have tried to shed light on the novels themselves by showing how Defoe drew on the materials and methods of traditional casuistry for his own purposes.

Graduate fellowships at Princeton made possible the research on which this monograph is based; a fellowship from the American Council of Learned Societies enabled me to write it; and a grant from the University of California assisted me in revising the manuscript for publication. I am grateful to these institutions for their support, and to the editors of the *Journal of the History of Ideas* for permission to reprint here some passages from my article on the *Athenian Mercury*.

Throughout this project I had the benefit of Professor Louis A. Landa's advice and encouragement; Professors John Preston and Eric Rothstein were kind enough to comment

Preface

on parts of the original draft, and in its final stage I received very helpful suggestions from Professors Ian Watt and Spiro Peterson. It is only fair to add that their interpretations of Defoe often differ from mine (and from one another's: if reading Defoe helps one to appreciate "men in their infinite plurality,"[9] so too, in its way, does criticism of one's own work by fellow scholars whom one respects). My many colleagues and students at Berkeley are also to be warmly thanked for their help, and for giving me a sense of community amidst our diversity. I dedicate this study to them, and particularly to Stanley Fish, Frederick Crews, and Julia Bader.

[9] The phrase is Hannah Arendt's, from *Men in Dark Times* (N.Y., 1968), p. 31.

Contents

From Casuistry to Fiction

THE CASUISTS *have become a by-word of reproach, but their perverted spirit of minute discrimination was the shadow of a truth to which eyes and hearts are too often fatally sealed: the truth, that moral judgments must remain false and hollow, unless they are checked and enlightened by a perpetual reference to the special circumstances that mark the individual lot.* George Eliot, The Mill on the Floss

ONE

Casuistry has always had both positive and negative aspects. As "the art of cavilling with God" and a set of "rules for the breaking of rules," casuistry has frequently and deservedly been a target of ridicule; as "a by-word for hypocrisy and dishonesty," it has been an object of dismay; yet it has also been prized, with equal justice, as a way of examining and resolving difficult moral problems.[1] Today casuistry tends to be regarded as at best ludicrous, at worst sinister: one must therefore stress at the outset that for all its abuses, casuistry also has its uses, and that moralists have long recognized its

---

[1] The first phrase is from the *Journal des Savans* of March 30, 1665, quoted in Pierre Bayle, *A General Dictionary, Historical and Critical,* ed. John P. Bernard, Thomas Birch, John Lockman, *et al.,* 10 vols. (London, 1734-38), VII, 196; the second, from Charles F. D'Arcy, *A Short Study of Ethics,* 2nd edn. (London, 1901), p. 218; the third, from Benjamin Jowett's "Casuistry," in *A Collection of Theological Essays from Various Authors,* ed. George R. Noyes (Boston, 1857), pp. 312-13. In all subsequent footnotes the place of publication, unless otherwise indicated, is London.

1

potentialities for good as well as evil. In *The Rambler*, Johnson acknowledges that casuistry is "useful in proper hands," even though it "ought by no means to be carelessly exposed, since most will use it rather to lull than awaken their own consciences";[2] and in *Clarissa*, Richardson's hero and heroine offer striking paradigms for the two aspects of casuistry. Both are expert casuists, but Lovelace uses casuistry to quiet his scruples, evade responsibility for his actions, and palliate his baseness, Clarissa to seek moral integrity amidst conflicting duties and complex circumstances.

In the writings of Defoe and his contemporaries, the terms "casuist" and "casuistry" are often but not invariably used in a derogatory sense. Those who could see in *"Unerring Nature, still divinely bright,/ One clear, unchang'd, and Universal Light"* were apt to dismiss casuistry as fundamentally inimical to truth and virtue.[3] But those who believed that nature's light had been dimmed by man's fall, or who were skeptical about theories of an innate moral sense, were inclined to regard casuistry as a precarious but necessary enterprise. Defoe himself perceived the dangers and shortcomings of casuistry, yet he was too distrustful of "impulse" and "inclination"— too convinced of the banefulness of everything spontaneous and instinctive in fallen man—to find congenial the moral intuitionism gaining ground in his day. Not that I suppose he was attracted to casuistry on purely philosophical grounds; his personal background and temperament probably con-

[2] No. 13 (May 1, 1750), *Yale Edition of The Works of Samuel Johnson*, ed. W. J. Bate and Albrecht B. Strauss (New Haven, 1969), III, 73.

[3] Alexander Pope, *An Essay on Criticism*, ll. 70-71 (Twickenham Edition, ed. E. Audra and Aubrey Williams [New Haven, 1961], I, 246-47); cf. the vision of "skulking *Truth* to her old Cavern fled,/ Mountains of Casuistry heap'd o'er her Head," and of *"Morality*, by her false Guardians drawn,/ *Chicane* in Furs, and *Casuistry* in Lawn" (*The Dunciad*, Bk. IV, ll. 641-42, 27-28; Twickenham Edition, ed. James Sutherland [New Haven, 1965], V, 407-08, 342-43).

tributed at least as much to his interest in the subject. Like St. Paul, he seems to have imagined an objector always at his elbow, demanding that he account for himself. His social class and education, his commercial disasters, his years as agent and publicist of various ministries, his experience of prison and pillory, and the sheer fact of his being a Dissenter, all provoked him to ceaseless review and redefinition of the grounds he judged, acted, and (frequently) suffered on. He and his varied personae feel compelled to explain themselves—to spell out not only what they are doing but why—and in this respect they show a marked family resemblance. Confronted on the one hand with novel and trying predicaments, and on the other hand with inherited rules of conduct that often seem irrelevant, contradictory, or inequitable, Defoe and his characters alike are naturally drawn (if not driven) to casuistry. Finding themselves at odds with the existing legal and moral order, they are preoccupied with law and morality, and seek to adjust traditional codes to their own aberrant situations, needs, and values. Defoe appears to have believed that in such perplexities one must rely chiefly on one's own conscience. But he also recognized that conscience is prone to negligence and error, and must therefore be exercised and instructed constantly. To these legitimate tasks casuistry had long addressed itself.[4]

Because Defoe was aware of the positive functions of casuistry as well as its hazards, his explicit references to the subject display considerable ambivalence. "I had no Casuists to

[4] It has been suggested that emphasis on strengthening the layman's own moral powers marks the main departure of English casuistry from its Roman Catholic antecedents: "The teacher's business now became, not to prescribe the outward conduct, but to direct the inward thought; not to decide *cases*, but to instruct the *conscience*. . . . attention had hitherto been bestowed mainly on the former word; it was now transferred to the latter" (William Whewell, *Lectures on the History of Moral Philosophy in England* [1852], p. 3).

resolve this Doubt," Roxana laments during one of her periodic bouts of troubled conscience; nevertheless she manages to allay her misgivings without the help of "any of the *Romish* Clergy," the traditional exponents (in English eyes) of casuistry *in malo.* Yet she regains her composure by stifling rather than searching her conscience—"Lethargick Fumes doz'd the Soul," as she puts it—for she proves to be an untutored master of what Defoe once called *"Playing-Bopeep* with God Almighty."⁵ If casuistry amounted to no more than this, neither we nor Defoe need have read esoteric treatises to be familiar with it, since the tendency to rationalize misdeeds is timeless and universal. But on other occasions Defoe uses the term without any such connotations. "Strangely surprised" by one of Friday's questions about God and the Devil, Robinson Crusoe confesses that "though I was now an old man, yet I was but a young doctor, and ill enough qualified for a casuist, or a solver of difficulties." In the course of resolving Friday's doubts, Crusoe becomes adept at the kind of casuistry which had been recommended and exemplified in the writings of a century of English divines. In his hands, as in theirs, casuistry is a heuristic mode: "in laying things open to [Friday], I really informed and instructed myself in many things that either I did not know, or had not fully considered before, but which occurred naturally to my mind upon my searching into them for the information of this poor savage." In other respects Crusoe may be an "absolute lord and lawgiver," but his responses to Friday's "serious inquiries and questions" are remarkably free from dogmatism; discovery rather than dictation is the order

⁵ *Roxana*, ed. Jane Jack, Oxford English Novels (1964), pp. 68, 69; *An Enquiry into the Occasional Conformity of Dissenters* (1698), in *A True Collection of the Writings of the Author of the True Born English-man* (1703), p. 315.

4

of the day, and Crusoe's probing is casuistical in the best sense.[6]

The main arguments for and against casuistry have remained constant for three hundred years, and can be readily summarized. Many critics contend that casuistry obscures lines of duty that are intrinsically straightforward, and substitutes legalistic quibbling for the clear light of conscience.[7] Others charge that casuistry incapacitates man for the ordinary business of life, not only by raising scruples at every turn, but also by making him helplessly dependent for their resolution on the expertise of a clerical adviser.[8] Some protest that casebooks of the Jesuit type, far from enabling man to avert sin, actually put evil suggestions in innocent minds; still others maintain that casuistry caters to man's weaknesses, and makes for moral laxity.[9] Such complaints, first lodged by Luther and

[6] *Robinon Crusoe*, in *Romances and Narratives of Daniel Defoe*, ed. George A. Aitken, 16 vols. (1895), I, 243, 245, 269, 246.

[7] Jeremy Taylor observes with regret that "what God had made plain, men have intricated"; see the Preface to *Ductor Dubitantium* (1660), ed. Alexander Taylor, in *Whole Works*, ed. Reginald Heber, rev. Charles P. Eden, 10 vols. (1852), IX, xii. Cf. Martin Thornton, *English Spirituality: An Outline of Ascetical Theology According to The English Pastoral Tradition* (London and N.Y., 1963), pp. 245-46, and H. R. McAdoo, *The Structure of Caroline Moral Theology* (1949), p. 74.

[8] Misgivings on this score were to be summed up in the nineteenth century by Thomas De Quincey in "The Casuistry of Duelling," *Uncollected Writings*, ed. James Hogg, 2 vols. (1892), II, 65-66, and by Benjamin Jowett in "Casuistry," *A Collection of Theological Essays*, pp. 307-09. For seventeenth-century views, see Thomas Wood, *English Casuistical Divinity during the Seventeenth Century* (N.Y., 1952), pp. 55-56.

[9] On the former issue, see Taylor's Preface to *Ductor Dubitantium*, pp. vi-vii, xi, and De Quincey's "Casuistry of Duelling," pp. 67-68; on the latter, see Robert South, "An Account of the Nature and Measures of Conscience," in *Twelve Sermons Preached upon Several Occasions*,

brilliantly charged home by Pascal, eventually comprised the
prevailing view of casuistry.[10] During the seventeenth century,
however, casuistry also found a host of advocates. John Selden,
for instance, advises that casuistry is one of the "four things
a Minister should be at"; casuists, he says, "may be of admirable use, if discreetly dealt with, though among them you
shall have many leaves together very impertinent."[11] And
George Herbert speaks for many fellow Anglicans when he
declares, in his survey of "The Parson's Accessary Knowledges," that "He greatly esteemes also of cases of conscience,
wherein he is much versed."[12] In their visitation charges,
various prelates prescribe the study of casuistry for the clergy
of their dioceses. Thomas Sprat, better known today as historian of the Royal Society than as bishop of Rochester, is
typical in maintaining that "the being a sound and well-
experienced casuist is . . . a most excellent qualification towards all the other ends of your ministerial office; there being
no kind of skill or proficiency in all your theological studies
that more becomes a divine of the Church of England, whose
highest spiritual art is to speak directly from his own conscience to the Consciences of those under his Pastoral care."[13]
In memoirs of churchmen of the period, a skill in casuistry

3rd edn. (1704), pp. 440-41. Both objections are central in Pascal's
Lettres Provinciales (1656-57); in other lesser-known but able continental attacks on the Jesuits, such as Nicolas Perrault's *La Morale
des Jesuites* (Mons, 1667; English translation by Ezerel Tonge, 1679);
and in Bayle's *Dictionary*, art. "Sanchez," IX, 45-49.

[10] Other grounds for recent disapproval of casuistry are mentioned
by Benjamin Nelson in the *Encyclopaedia Britannica* (1963), art. "Casuistry"; there is also a useful survey by R. M. Wenley in the *Encyclo-
pedia of Religion and Ethics*, ed. James Hastings (N.Y., 1925).

[11] *Table Talk*, ed. S. W. Singer (1890), pp. 95-96.

[12] *A Priest to The Temple*, in *Works*, ed. F. E. Hutchinson (Oxford,
1959), p. 230.

[13] Visitation Charge, 1695, quoted in John H. Overton, *Life in the
English Church, 1660-1714* (1885), p. 333; Overton cites Stillingfleet
and Gardiner to the same effect.

is often singled out for special praise: thus it is said of one provincial vicar that "his known abilities in resolving cases of conscience drew after him a great many good people, not only of his own flock, but from remoter distances, who resorted to him as a common oracle, and commonly went away from him intirely satisfied in his wise and judicious resolutions."[14] Puritan commendations of casuistry are equally common and emphatic.[15] In short, there appear to have been as many who admired casuistry as loathed it, as many who practiced it as shunned it.

The historically ambivalent status of casuistry can perhaps be further indicated by a brief comparison with rhetoric. Between casuistry and rhetoric there are interesting substantive affinities; what concerns us here is chiefly the equivocal reputations of the two terms. Seventeenth-century attacks on rhetoric contain parallels to many of the complaints against casuistry already mentioned, and the lines of defense were also similar. Casuistry rests on the axiom that "circumstances alter cases"—the principle that every ethical problem must be approached on its own terms and decided on its own merits; rhetoric, on the principle that every occasion demands its own mode of expression. Casuistry and rhetoric thus share a

[14] John Scott, Preface to John March's *Sermons Preach'd on Several Occasions* (1693), quoted in Appendix to *Memoirs of the Life of Mr. Ambrose Barnes*, ed. W.H.D. Longstaffe, Surtees Society Publications, Vol. L (Durham, 1867), 442. Similar praise of William Perkins, Robert Bolton, and William Whately can be found in Samuel Clarke's *Marrow of Ecclesiastical History* (1654), pp. 851, 926, 931. Defoe was to report to Harley that he passed for "an Oracle" among the clergymen of Edinburgh, who attended him "night and Morning . . . to Answer their Cases of Conscience" concerning the Union (*Letters*, ed. George H. Healey [Oxford, 1955], pp. 139-40).

[15] See *Life of the Rev. J. Angier* in *The Whole Works of the Rev. Oliver Heywood*, 5 vols. (Idle, 1826), 1, 561-64; cf. Gordon S. Wakefield, *Puritan Devotion: Its Place in the Development of Christian Piety* (1957), pp. 111-29; and John T. McNeill, "Casuistry in the Puritan Age," in *Religion in Life*, XII (1943), 76-89.

responsiveness to experience, an adaptability to changing situations, which is in one sense a great virtue; yet this very suppleness has often been seen as their most sinister quality, since it apparently permits them to serve ill purposes as readily as good ones. In the view of their enemies, both casuistry and rhetoric are tools that the just can dispense with, but which the unjust characteristically rely on; to be good, in this view, one's words and actions alike should be spontaneous and uniform, not calculated and variable. Indeed, the term "sophistry" probably occurs as frequently in denunciations of casuistry as in attacks on rhetoric: as a synonym for whichever of the two is under censure, "sophistry" has always linked casuistry and rhetoric in the minds of their opponents. In recent years, however, the term "rhetoric" has been rescued from longstanding and powerful negative associations, and now enjoys considerable prestige, whereas it is still the case that "in popular estimation, no one is supposed to resort to casuistry but with the view of evading a duty."[16] Although this one-sided conception of casuistry has been countered in several valuable exploratory studies,[17] the full-scale history which might effectively rehabilitate the subject has not yet appeared.[18]

For our purposes, the precise contours of seventeenth-century casuistical divinity matter less than its contributions to

[16] Jowett, "Casuistry," *A Collection of Theological Essays*, p. 313.

[17] Most notably George L. Mosse's *The Holy Pretence: A Study in Christianity and Reason of State from William Perkins to John Winthrop* (Oxford, 1957). Although the term "casuistry" is never used, J. L. Austin's paper "A Plea for Excuses" is an illuminating inquiry into everyday casuistry, particularly its language (*Philosophical Papers* [Oxford, 1961], pp. 123-52.

[18] Thomas Wood's *English Casuistical Divinity during the Seventeenth Century* deals mainly with Jeremy Taylor, but this work and a more recent essay on "Seventeenth-Century Moralists and the Marital Relationship" (*Trivium*, 1 [1966], 67-87), offer promising specimens of the monumental history of English practical divinity on which Professor Wood has long been engaged.

8

From Casuistry to Fiction

Defoe's ethical outlook, his fictional subject matter, and his narrative techniques. The task of tracing these lines of influence is hampered by the lack of an adequate history of casuistry, but it is greatly facilitated by the existence of a work which provided an important link between Defoe and the earlier casuistry—John Dunton's *Athenian Mercury*.[19] Although this pioneering periodical of the 1690's deserves to be better known for a variety of reasons, it is significant for the present study primarily as a medium through which traditional casuistry found its way into Defoe's fiction.[20]

The nature and extent of Dunton's debt to his casuistical precursors can be determined only by comparing his *Athenian Mercury* with their manuals of cases of conscience, but there are prior indications that such a debt exists. In the first place, the original subtitle of the paper is revealing: *The Athenian Gazette: or, Casuisticall Mercury, resolving all the most nice and curious questions proposed by the ingenious of either sex.*[21] Dunton was to supplement the *"Casuisticall"* with the

[19] 20 vols. (March 1690–June 1697); reprinted as *The Athenian Oracle: Being an Entire Collection Of all the Valuable Questions and Answers In The Old Athenian Mercuries*, 3rd. edn., 3 vols. (1706), with *A Supplement To The Athenian Oracle: Being A Collection Of the Remaining Questions and Answers . . . To which is prefix'd The History of the Athenian Society, And an Essay upon Learning* (1710). Subsequent quotations from the *Athenian Oracle* are identified as *"A.O.";* the *Supplement* is referred to as Vol. iv of the *Athenian Oracle*, since it was issued and bound as such through the 1728 edition; the original *Athenian Mercury* is cited by volume, number, and question (e.g., *"A.M.,* x, x, 10").

[20] The *Athenian Mercury* is discussed briefly as a forerunner of the *Tatler* and *Spectator* in such studies as George S. Marr's *The Periodical Essayists of the Eighteenth Century* (New York, 1924), pp. 14-15; Bertha-Monica Stearns has examined its role as "The First English Periodical for Women," *MP*, xxviii (1930), 45-59; and its editor is the subject of an attractive sketch by Peter Murray Hill in *Two Augustan Booksellers: John Dunton and Edmund Curll* (Lawrence, Kansas, 1958).

[21] *Gazette* was immediately dropped from the title, probably because of difficulties with the proprietors of the official publication of the

historical, the philosophical, the mathematical, and the poetical, but we have here a hint that the *"nice and curious questions"* themselves, the manner of *"resolving"* them, or perhaps both, were initially regarded as belonging to the familiar domain of casuistry.

A second piece of evidence is to be found in Dunton's *Life and Errors*, where he undertakes to "oblige the reader with a true Discovery of the Question-Project." The relevant passage is worth quoting, for it suggests that the project was inspired by a case of conscience which troubled Dunton himself:

> I had receiv'd a very *flaming Injury*, which was so loaded with Aggravations, that I cou'd scarce get over it; *my Thoughts were constantly working upon't,* and made me strangely uneasy, sometimes I thought to make Application to some *Divine*, but how to conceal *my self* and the *ungrateful Wretch*, was the Difficulty. Whilst this perplexity remain'd upon me, I was one Day walking over St. *George's-fields*, and Mr. *Larkin*, and Mr. *Har*[r]*is* were along with me, and on a suddain I made a Stop, and said, Well Sirs, I have a Thought I'll not exchange for Fifty Guineas; they smil'd, and were very urgent with me to DISCOVER it, but they cou'd not get it from me. The first rude *Hint* of it, was no more than *a confus'd Idea of concealing the Querist and answering his Question.*[22]

By guaranteeing the anonymity of querists, Dunton hoped to elicit *"nice and curious questions"* which his readers were reluctant to pose to divines.[23] To be sure, not all the cases dealt

same name. In his "History of the Athenian Society," Charles Gildon offers a more fanciful pretext for altering the name: see *A.O.*, IV, 24.

[22] *The Life and Errors of John Dunton Late Citizen of London; Written by Himself in Solitude* (1705), sigs. [R7ᵛ]-[R8ʳ].

[23] In a prefatory note to the first volume of the collected *Oracles*, the

with in previous generations by Sanderson, Hall, and their clerical colleagues had been tamely decorous; nor were Dunton and his associates, on the other hand, now free to print whatever they pleased.[24] But times were changing, so that a case which once might have been raised more or less publicly in a "scruple shop,"[25] or privately in a conference with some grave divine, was now brooded over—*"my Thoughts were constantly working upon't"*—in helpless, agitated isolation.[26] The question project may have originated, then, as an

---

project is said to have as its design *"to remove those Difficulties and Dissatisfactions, that shame, or fear of appearing ridiculous by asking Questions, may cause several Persons to labour under, who now have Opportunities of being* resolv'd in any Question, *without knowing their Informer"* (*A.O.*, I, 1).

[24] See several of the rules laid down for prospective querists: "II. *That none send obscene Questions, as not fit to be answer'd by any that pretend not to as great Debauchery as the Senders of them.* IV. *Nothing, the Answer of which may be a Scandal to the Government, or an Abuse to particular Persons.* V. *Nothing that may be destructive to the Principles of Virtue and sound Knowledg"* (*A.O.*, IV, 23). In practice, the Athenians were wariest of political controversy. Three decades later, readers of Nathaniel Mist's *Weekly Journal* were invited to submit "such Questions as are pertinent, decent, and diverting, ——neither dangerous as to Party, doubtful as to Religion, or Scandalous as to Virtue"; Mist—whose leading writer at the time was Defoe—promises "to give such Satisfaction as may lye in his Way, and do his utmost to direct and oblige his Friends" (Feb. 13, 1720; see William Lee, *Daniel Defoe: His Life, and Recently Discovered Writings*, 3 vols. [1869], II, 201 [cited hereafter as "Lee"]).

[25] On the "scruple shop," the undergraduate nickname for a weekly public conference established at Oxford in 1646 to resolve cases of conscience, see Robert Barclay, *The Inner Life of the Religious Societies of the Commonwealth* (1876), p. 185. Richard Baxter reports that "Every Thursday evening my neighbours that were most desirous and had opportunity met at my house, and there one of them repeated the sermon, and afterwards they proposed what doubts any of them had about the sermon, or any other case of conscience, and I resolved their doubts" (*Autobiography*, ed. J. M. Lloyd Thomas [1931], p. 77).

[26] But cf. the *Spectator* for Nov. 12, 1714, in which *"J.C.* who proposes a Love-Case, as he calls it, to the Love-Casuist, is hereby desired

opportunity for the mute inglorious Duntons of the 1690's to voice their problems and obtain the kind of guidance long afforded by the clergy.[27]

The background of the collaborators on the Athenian project affords a third kind of evidence. John Dunton was a son-in-law of the Bartholomean Samuel Annesley, whose *Morning-Exercise at Cripplegate* comprised a series of casuistical sermons by the major Nonconformist divines of the 1660's and 1670's; several large quarto collections were issued over a period of twenty years, and Dunton himself published one of them.[28] Samuel Wesley and Daniel Defoe also contributed to the *Athenian Mercury*,[29] and both were trained for the ministry in famous dissenting academies. Wesley was subsequently to take orders in the Church of England and write against these very academies, and Defoe was in his own words "first . . . set a-part for, and then . . . set a-part from the Honour of that Sacred Employ."[30] But both probably had

to speak of it to the Minister of the Parish; it being a Case of Conscience" (ed. Donald F. Bond, 5 vols. [Oxford, 1965], v, 115-16).

[27] Dunton claims to have received questions from such distinguished personages as Sir William Temple (*Life and Errors*, sig. S3), but the bulk of those printed purport to be from middle-class readers. The genteel querists tend to have lost their lands, to have been left unprovided as younger brothers, or to be otherwise in a declining state (cf. *A.O.*, II, 279, 418, 477; III, 303). The laborers, apprentices, and servant-girls are mainly intent on bettering themselves, and seek advice as to ways and means (cf. *A.O.*, II, 202-03, 305, 311, 404-05; III, 239).

[28] *A Continuation of Morning-Exercise Questions and Cases of Conscience, Practically Resolved by sundry Ministers, In October, 1682* (1683). The *Morning Exercises* are discussed briefly by John T. McNeill in "Casuistry in the Puritan Age," p. 82.

[29] For Wesley's role in the project, see *Life and Errors*, sigs. [R8ᵛ]-S1. Apart from an ode "To The Athenian Society" signed "D.F." (*A.O.*, II, sigs. [A3ʳ]-[A3ᵛ]), the extent of Defoe's participation is problematical; see John Robert Moore, *Daniel Defoe: Citizen of the Modern World* (Chicago, 1958), p. 232.

[30] *Review*, fac. ed. Arthur W. Secord, 22 vols. (N.Y., 1938), VI (Oct. 22, 1709), 341.

an early grounding in casuistical divinity, since the practical works of Perkins, Ames, and Baxter are known to have been standard texts in their academic curricula.[31] Richard Sault, whose specialties in the *Athenian Mercury* were science and mathematics, also appears to have been qualified to handle casuistical questions, whether or not he actually did so.[32]

Finally, scattered through the text are references to the classic manuals. These are not as frequent as the actual borrowings, yet they do confirm the Athenians' familiarity with the major documents of English casuistry, and their consciousness that the question-project lay within a recognizable tradition. At one point, for instance, the querist is instructed to "Read Mr. *Perkins's Case of Conscience*," and supplied with chapter and page; on at least two occasions he is referred to a "Famous Case in Bp. *Sanderson*"; and once he is sent to "Bishop *Barlow's Posthumous Works*," when the Oracle modestly protests that "because of that great Esteem that that Learned & great Casuist has justly merited from all Sober and Ingenious Persons, I seem to distrust my own Judgment in the point."[33]

---

[31] See Lew Girdler, "Defoe's Education at Newington Green Academy," *SP*, L (1953), 573-91, and H. McLachlan, *English Education Under The Test Acts: Being The History Of The Non-Conformist Academies 1662-1820* (Manchester, 1931), pp. 76-80, 303.

[32] Except for a few details about Sault's last years, the *DNB* adds nothing to Dunton's account of him in the *Life and Errors*, sigs. [P5^v]-[P7^r], [R8^v]-S1, and Gildon's half-bantering remarks in the "History" (*A.O.*, IV, 16); but see also the character of "Joachim Dash, Mathematician" in [Elkanah Settle], *The New Athenian Comedy* (1693), pp. 8-9, 12, 20, and Letter LXIII in [Charles Gildon], *The Post-Boy Robb'd of his Mail: Or, The Pacquet Broke Open*, 2nd edn. (1706), pp. 156-57.

[33] *A.O.*, III, 273; II, 233; III, 351; II, 56. The diffidence of the final passage becomes less remarkable when we recall that Thomas Barlow's *Genuine Remains* were published by Dunton. Barlow is also cited at II, 206.

13

Earlier in the century Joseph Hall had divided into four "Decades" his *Resolutions and Decisions of Divers Practical Cases of Conscience, in Continual Use Amongst Men* (1648). His four categories are "Cases of Profit and Traffick," "Cases of Life and Liberty," "Cases of Piety and Religion," and "Cases Matrimonial."[34] All four kinds appear in the *Athenian Mercury*: the first and last far outnumber the second and third, and "Cases Matrimonial" are commonest of all. Bishop Hall had observed that "amongst all the heads of case-divinity there is no one that yieldeth more scruples than this of marriage," but that "it were pity that so many should, in that estate, be necessary."[35] To the Athenian Society, such abundance was scarcely a cause for regret: on the contrary, it proved the very life-blood of the project. By examining specific cases, we can see most clearly how Dunton and his colleagues adapted and modified traditional casuistry.

The relationship can be traced first of all in the very substance of the questions, apart from the form in which they are presented. The matrimonial queries, for instance, cover a great variety of topics, including incest, separation, and divorce; the obligatory force of rash vows; the efficacy of oral and otherwise irregular contracts; and the extent of parental power over the choice and rejection of mates. Some of these matters obviously extend beyond the domain of casuistry. Whether incest, for instance, is a *malum in se*, and whether it is lawful or expedient for certain close relatives to marry, are

[34] Richard Baxter's *Christian Directory* (1673) is divided into four rather different parts: "Christian Ethics (Or Private Duties); Christian Economics (Or Family Duties); Christian Ecclesiastics (Or Church Duties); Christian Politics (Or Duties To Our Rulers and Neighbours)" (*Practical Works*, ed. William Orme, 23 vols. [1830], II-VI). Other arrangements of cases differ still further from that of Hall; his is cited as a lucid and comprehensive pattern, not an invariable one.

[35] *Resolutions and Decisions*, in *Works*, ed. Philip Wynter, 10 vols. (Oxford, 1863), VII, 408, 367; cf. Taylor, *Ductor Dubitantium*, in *Whole Works*, X, 500.

problems that interested canonists and civilians as well as casuists. What places a question within the special domain of casuistry is the fact that it is a case of conscience: whether hypothetical or actual, it is someone's practical moral dilemma, not merely a topic of abstract speculation. This point can be illustrated by putting off for a moment the discussion of "Cases Matrimonial," and observing that virtually anything, from deposing kings to dissecting dogs, can pose a case of conscience. One of the Athenians' correspondents reports:

> *I am mightily addicted to the Study of Anatomy, I have dissected many Dogs and other Animals alive, not out of any design of cruelty; but, I protest, purely out of a design to be perfect in that excellent Study. . . . I desire to know, whether it is a Sin to put those Creatures to such Tortures, as they must needs suffer in live Dissections . . . to further my own Knowledge in particular, and the good of Mankind in general, my Study being Physick. I shall be Impatient till I hear your Answer to this Question, which however Inconsiderable it may seem to you, has made so deep an Impression on my Thoughts, that I am grown very Melancholy about it.*[36]

Although this is clearly a case of conscience, it should be equally clear that the moral problem of cruelty to animals can be discussed—as it began to be during this period—without being cast into the form of a case of conscience, and thus in a manner having little to do with casuistry.[37]

[36] *A.M.*, vi, xxvii, 11. In Aesop, dogs themselves grapple with such questions as whether promises made under duress are binding: see Fable 119, of "A Dog and a Wolf," which Roger L'Estrange labels "a kind of a *Dog-Case of Conscience,*" in *Fables, of Aesop and Other Eminent Mythologists: With Morals and Reflections,* 6th edn. (1714), p. 136.

[37] See the *Tatler,* No. 134 (Feb. 16, 1710), ed. George A. Aitken, 4 vols. (1899), iii, 109-14; cf. also *Original and Genuine Letters sent*

From Casuistry to Fiction

On the other hand, certain cases of conscience recurred so frequently in the casuistical literature that their very topics became intimately associated with casuistry. As *"Inconsiderable"* (or "low") as the preceding question in subject matter, but standing in a long casuistical tradition, are such *Mercury* cases as the following: *"Having lately bought an Horse vouch'd to me for a sound one, and upon tryal find him otherwise,——Query, whether I am obliged to discover his faults unask'd to him that shall buy him of me?"* (*A.M.*, III, xxi, 6). Among the "Cases of Profit and Traffick" pondered in nearly every manual of casuistry, one finds the question "Whether is the seller bound to make known to the buyer the faults of that which he is about to sell."[38] To call attention to this tradition is not to challenge the genuineness of the horse-vending query submitted to the Athenian Society—like many other classic cases of conscience, this question must have arisen often in the actual life of the period[39]—but merely to suggest that in its formal deliberations on these everyday problems, the *Mercury* was heir to a considerable body of earlier casuistical discussion. Still other predicaments could scarcely have been common among Dunton's readers, and yet had ample precedents in the literature of casuistry. One man, for instance, who learns that he has by mistake married

to the Tatler and Spectator, During the Time those Works were publishing, ed. Charles Lillie, 2 vols. (1725), I, 25-29.

[38] See Hall, *Resolutions and Decisions*, in *Works*, VII, 277-79; cf. Baxter, *Christian Directory*, in *Practical Works*, VI, 308.

[39] One seventeenth-century diarist records similar misgivings about selling some horses: he had instructed his agents "to speak truth, neither denying nor using any means to conceal any Fault: Only I doubted I was not sufficiently careful to have the Buyers acquainted with all I knew my self. . . . Yet I could not learn the Buyers were damag'd, nor say that they paid too dear; and good Men laugh'd at my Scruples, professing themselves would do as I had done" (*Some Remarkable Passages in the Holy Life and Death Of the late Reverend Mr. Edmund Trench* [1693], p. 42).

his own daughter, inquires whether he is obliged to reveal this fact to her; he fears that the news will kill her, and that their children will also suffer greatly from the scandal. Bizarre and unlikely as such a case may sound, it had been discussed with somber relish by Taylor and Hall, who had found it in earlier continental manuals.[40] Both Anglican and Puritan casuists had confessed—if at times grudgingly—their indebtedness to Roman Catholic writings,[41] and although the Athenians acknowledge no such mentors, there may be occasional traces of them.[42] But whatever the actual range of the Athenians' reading, the content of many questions suggests a familiarity with traditional casuistry.

Far more important, however, is the way the *Athenian Mercury* presents its questions. The most notable innovation

[40] *A.O.*, II, 183; Taylor, *Ductor Dubitantium*, in *Whole Works*, IX, 149; Hall, *Resolutions and Decisions*, in *Works*, VII, 410-14; see the discussion of the first Virginian episode in *Moll Flanders*, p. 134 below.

[41] In the preface to *Ductor Dubitantium*, Taylor laments that his countrymen are unprovided with casuistical treatises, and are "forced to go down to the forges of the Philistines to sharpen every man his share and his coulter, his axe and his mattock" (*Whole Works*, IX, v). William Ames had employed this very image (from 1 Sam. 13) to deplore the same situation a generation earlier, in his *Conscience With The Power And Cases thereof* (1643), sig. B. Cf. also Baxter's "Advertisement" to the *Christian Directory*, in *Practical Works*, II, viii.

[42] In the ninth book of his *De Matrimonia*, for instance, Tomás Sanchez inquires "An liceat sponsis de futuro delectari in cogitatione copulae habendae, vel viduis in cogitatione habitae tempore matrimonii." In the *Athenian Mercury*, a young man who has for some time "*made Honourable Love to a young and Beautiful Lady*" finds that a strong imagination leads his "*revolving Thoughts to anticipate what's yet to come,*" and inquires whether "*the last Transport of Thought can be a Sin?*" (*R. P. Thomae Sanchez Cordubensis, E Societate Jesu, De Sancto Matrimonii Sacramento Disputationum*, 3 vols. [Venice, 1754; first edn. 1602-05], Lib. IX, Disp. xlvii, III, 243-44; *A.O.*, I, 497). The writings of Sanchez were known in England: his opinions are cited by Hall, *Resolutions and Decisions*, in *Works*, VII, 367.

17

is that most cases are posed in the first person singular; the actual or supposititious querist addresses the Athenians *in propria persona*. Even if all the letters printed were genuine, which I doubt,[43] Dunton and his colleagues could have transcribed them into the third person: this had been the practice of earlier divines, and is sometimes followed by the Athenians. The decision to allow querists to speak for themselves had important consequences, to be considered shortly, but another feature of the questions should be noted beforehand, since its effects are closely connected with those of first-person narration. I refer to the sheer abundance of detail in the presentation of cases. This constitutes an extension of traditional practice, rather than a departure from it. Casuistry had long embodied the principle that every relevant circumstance must be taken into account in resolving a case of conscience; indeed, it had been charged at times with an excessive concern for seemingly marginal and trivial factors. But if a tendency towards circumstantial realism had been inherent in the entire casuistical method, it was nevertheless exploited by the Athenians to an unprecedented extent.

Through the use of first-person querists who report their predicaments in detail, the *Athenian Mercury* creates char-

[43] See Defoe's *Commentator*, No. xv (Feb. 19, 1720): *"Do you believe these People really receive all the Letters they publish? Not one in Fifty of them. But it is a Way of Writing, that has mightily obtained of late Years, and is found to be of singular good Use."* There is documentary evidence, however, that various letters printed in the *Spectator* were based on ones submitted by readers, and that the editors received many others which were not used: see Bond's Introduction, i, xxxvi-xliii, and *New Letters to the Tatler and Spectator*, ed. Richmond P. Bond (Austin, 1959). As for the queries printed in the *Athenian Mercury*, there was some suspicion at the time that *"the Bookseller proposes and answers most of the Questions therein contained"*; the Society neither denies nor confirms this charge, but maintains that "if our Papers have any thing useful in them, it matters not whether the Bookseller [Dunton] be taken for the Author of them or not" (*A.M.*, xv, xvii, 2).

acters, settings, and actions that surpass those in the traditional manuals both in vividness and complexity. The Athenian Society says of the writer of the following letter that "her *Character* and Quality . . . might have been guess'd at without much *difficulty*, by her way of *Spelling* and *Writing*":

> *I Have been in Love this three Years, almost to Distrection——i have had one Child by him i Love so dear, he is very sevil to me, but visits me very seldom, unless I send to him, and then he is angerry, then am i one ten thousand Racks. . . . i have been advised by all my Friends never to see him more, i have strived to do it, but can't. . . . Now Gentillmen, I beg your Answer what I must do in this Cease, leave him i never can; all I desire is, that he will never marry unless it is to me, or Else never forsake me, for if he do, I shall sartainly murder my self. I bags your Advise in your next Mercury——thus bagging your pardons, I hope you will give a charitable anser. . . .* (*A.M.*, ix, iii, 1).

Here the correspondent's social and psychological "*Character* and Quality" are vividly suggested, but there is little of the self-awareness or moral perplexity that gives so many *Mercury* queries their vitality. In the following case, for example, the woman grasps the moral implications of her behavior, although she alleges extenuating circumstances; her case has additional interest in that it reappears, considerably amplified but not greatly altered, first in Defoe's *Review* and later in the opening episode of *Roxana*:

> *Q. I'm a Gentlewoman of a small Fortune, and Married to a Man who . . . left me with a Charge of Children, and went to another Country, without making the least Provision either for them or me—Nor will his Friends look on us, and I've been already very chargeable and*

19

*troublesome to my own, who are now grown as Cold
as his: A Gentleman now Importunes me very much to
be his Mistress, who I know Loves me passionately, and
will provide for me and them. I desire your Advice what
I were best do, Whether I must lay my Children to the
Parish; for Begging won't maintain us, and Stealing is as
bad as Whoring? Or how I ought to behave my self for I
can find no Means, but either to yield to this Temptation;
or see my Children starve? I know I ought not to do the
least Evil that Good may come of it; but yet of two Evils,
we must chuse the least: An Answer to this would both
oblige and quiet, your, &c.*[44]

This woman's nature is a curious mixture of piety and
worldly prudence. The combination occurs more strikingly
in some of Defoe's fully developed characters, but it is shared
by a number of querists in the *Athenian Mercury*. It is most
evident in what Hall had labelled "Cases of Profit and
Traffick," for as Defoe was to remark in the *Review*, "People
are very willing to have their Profit and their Conscience go
together."[45] Such mingling of mundane self-interest and lofty
morality is a much-discussed feature of the period, and need
not be dwelt on here; it should be noted, however, that the
literature of casuistry offers no evidence that this tendency
was peculiarly Puritan or middle-class, as is frequently main-

[44] *A.O.*, III, 350-51; cf. *Review*, II (Apr. 14, 1705), 70-71.

[45] *Supplement* (Nov., 1704), p. 17; Defoe is accounting for the fact
that "These sort of Money Cases of Conscience, have always something
of Interest attends them." In a similar vein Archbishop Sharp observes
that what "has given Occasion to the Discussion of so many Cases of
Conscience" is the fact that men "have a great Mind to *serve* their
Pleasure and their *Ambition*, and their secular Ends, and yet to *serve
God* too; and this puts them upon tampering and trying to reconcile
these interests together" (John Sharp, "Rules for the Conduct of Ourselves," preached in April 1690, in *Fifteen Sermons Preached on Several Occasions*, 7th edn. [1738], p. 215).

tained. At all events, it is an ambivalence to be found in many of the *Mercury* queries on love and marriage, as well as those on profit and traffic.

Complexities of characterization can also arise when the querist recounts or anticipates mischief but is unwilling or unable to recognize it as such. The case that follows is presented in the third person, but offers revealing points of contrast with the preceding one: "*Q. A Gentlewoman that has a Husband who used her* barbarously, *makes her go in danger of her Life, and keeps a Whore, refusing to live with her, but making her work* for her Bread, *having the offer of a single Gentleman that will* maintain *her very well*: *Whether it be any* Sin *to* accept of his kindness?" (*A.M.*, v, xiii, 2). The Athenians remark at once that "Here are several ambiguous words in this Question, which must be explained before we can go any further," and eventually demand, "Why all this fine clean Language to wrap up that broad word WHORE, with which she so fairly *brands* one that is kept by her Husband, when about to bring her self into the same Circumstances: Is't any *Case of Conscience* whether a Woman ought to turn Whore because her Husband is a Whoremaster?" Other querists reveal even more about themselves through their very obtuseness. There is the man who has promised two different women that he will marry them after his present wife dies, and is troubled only by doubts as to which one he should marry.[46] There is the woman who has exchanged similar "*Vows and Protestations*" with a married man, but reports that "*he has disoblig'd me so highly, that out of Revenge I wou'd now marry*," and only wants to know whether such promises need restrain her.[47] And there is the

[46] *A.O.*, I, 372-74; a virtually identical case is considered at III, 306-07.
[47] *A.O.*, IV, 244-45; a precedent for this query and the preceding one is to be found in Robert Sanderson's "Case of Unlawful Love," in *Works*, ed. William Jacobson, 6 vols. (Oxford, 1854), v, 88-103.

woman whose seducer, a charming but poor man, is willing to marry her; a wealthy but less attractive man has also proposed to her, and she is *"wrack'd with Confusion"* only as to which suitor is preferable.[48] In such cases the querist incriminates himself unwittingly, and ignores or evades the real issue of conscience. The Athenians make this quite explicit in their answers, often with considerable irony at the querist's expense, but the content of the question has already enabled the reader to discover it for himself. In other words, it is not left altogether to the Athenian respondents to settle these perplexed cases, or to point the moral of these curious tales. The reader is made to resolve them in his own mind, and the effectiveness of any given question depends largely on its ability to engage and exercise his conscience.

All this would appear to reduce the relative importance of the responses, but they are no less interesting than the questions, and reveal just as much about the relationship between the *Athenian Mercury* and traditional casuistry. The answers tend to consist of two distinct parts, a discussion of general principles and a determination of the case at hand. Cases of conscience had always demanded both, but one or the other had usually received greater attention. In the *Athenian Mercury* a certain balance is struck: an immediate dilemma will be referred to its theoretical context, yet the specific case is not lost sight of amidst ethical speculation. There are ex-

[48] *A.O.*, III, 325-26; cf. *Review*, I (Sept. 19, 1704), 243, for the case of a young lady whose seducer is willing to marry her: she cannot decide whether *"I had better have a Knave, for a Spark, or a Fool for a Husband."* The same case arises over the Dutch merchant's offer of matrimony in *Roxana*, and over the hero's second marriage in *Colonel Jack*. William Perkins had seen knavery in the second alternative as well: "It is an vnseemely thing for a man to make promise of mariage to such a woman, as hath been formerly deflowred. . . . Nay, I adde further, that a contract made with such a one, as himselfe hath before deflowred, is by the law of God vnlawfull' ("Of Christian Oeconomie, or Houshold gouernment," in *Workes*, 3 vols. [1616-18], II, 680).

ceptions, but by and large the Athenians set an admirable example for later moralists in the periodical essay and the novel. An interest in the concrete and particular *case* goes hand in hand with a concern for its wider implications of *conscience.*

When they come to weigh cases, the Athenians invoke at least four distinct norms: divine law, natural law, human or positive law, and expediency. It is difficult to generalize about the use of these principles in the *Athenian Mercury*, but two points can be made. In the first place, there are a number of cases in which the lawfulness of an action is vindicated, but its inexpediency is regarded as a decisive obstacle. The *"Condescention of a Protestant Lady to the Conjugal Request of a Romish Gentleman,"* for instance, is not unlawful, but is discountenanced by a long recital of its *"signal inconvenience[s]."*[49] On the other hand, though an action may thus be condemned as inexpedient even when natural, divine, and human laws do not forbid it (or are silent), the converse is not true: expediency is never a sufficient argument *for* doing what any of the three laws prohibits.[50] In the second place, no consistent hierarchy obtains among the

---

[49] *A.O.*, I, 169-70; for other determinations of this case, see the discussion of *Religious Courtship*, p. 44 below. Joseph Hall remarks that "A wise and good man will not willingly trespass against the rules of just expedience, and will be as careful to consider what is fit to be done as what is lawful" (*Resolutions and Decisions*, in *Works*, VII, 408). William Perkins frequently invokes the same standard, saying of one or another practice that though it "is not expresly forbidden in the word; yet it is agreeable to the rules of expediencie and decencie" that it be avoided ("Of Christian Oeconomie," in *Workes*, II, 680). The basis for such reasoning is St. Paul's "All things are lawful unto me, but all things are not expedient" (I Cor. 6:12).

[50] Expediency is seldom simply a matter of self-interested calculation: for this the more usual term is "policy." Expediency is associated rather with what L'Estrange calls such "Niceties" as "Honour, Decency, and Discretion, Humanity, Modesty, Respect, &c." (*Fables, of Aesop*, p. 234).

three forms of law, but some common patterns are discernible. The Athenian Society appeals to natural law either to reinforce or to supplement the laws of God and England; only the querists appeal to natural law *against* the precepts of divine and human law, and allege it as a higher authority. Mischief of all kinds is defended by querists as conforming to a law of nature; the Athenian response tends to be that on many questions natural law has been superseded by divine and human enactments, and is itself obscure and contradictory on almost every point but self-preservation.[51] The Athenians show considerable sympathy for the victims of harsh ordinances, but refuse to endorse violations of them in the name of natural law. In their hands casuistry is humane, but does not encourage "Playing-Bopeep" either with God or the civil authorities.

That tolerance and flexibility need not imply laxity is borne out by a typical group of cases concerning bigamy. The issue is one of particular interest: it was to arise prominently in *Moll Flanders* and *Roxana*, and two scholars have recently discussed it in terms of one or another of the sanctions I have mentioned.[52] In the query that follows, for instance, the

[51] See *A.O.*, ii, 74-75, in response to an inquiry *"Whether Retaliation in cases not otherwise unlawful, be not according to the Law of Nature"*: " 'Tis no easie matter to know what the Law of Nature is: The best way to discover it is by what seems to come nearest it, namely the Law of Nation[s], or the common usages, and consent of mankind . . . but indeed this is very narrow, there being not many Cases wherein all the World agree, and the Law of Nature; supposing we think, a state of Nature, and what this is, there may be also some difficulty in discovering, some making it a State of War, . . . others thinking with Reason, that such Persons mistake corrupted Nature, for Nature true, genuine and unsophisticate, or indeed making their own Nature the Standard of all others."

[52] For the bearing of canon and common law on Defoe's treatment of his heroines' many marriages, see Spiro Peterson, "The Matrimonial Theme of Defoe's Roxana," *PMLA*, lxx (1955), 166-91, esp. pp. 172-75;

From Casuistry to Fiction

Athenian Mercury anticipates the dilemmas of Moll and Roxana over remarriage:

> *One of a Sanguine Complexion being marryed to a Husband, who soon after went upon a Trading Voyage for* Virginia, *intending to return back in a Years time, but hath been absent from her for above these Eight Years; neither hath she received any Letter from him in all the time, and not knowing whether he be dead or alive, but by uncertain reports, she desires to be inform'd whether she may lawfully marry another Man?*

To this the Athenians reply,

> The Law provided formerly *seven Years*, after which it suppos'd the Man dead, but since *Navigation* and *Commerce* are so well settled, a less time is requir'd, because Advices arrive much sooner and more certain than formerly; if she means by *lawfully*, according to our *Law*, she may Marry another, but we can't Promise her *Free by the Law of God*, which no where makes such an Exception. We have several Instances of this Nature. . . . [we] desire her to secure the *Quiet of her Conscience*, and advise with the *Ecclesiastick Authority*, since the other gives her the Liberty she wants.[53]

The lawfulness of remarriage is shown to be a more complex question than the query itself would indicate, since two distinct sanctions are insisted upon. In a sense, the Athenians complicate the matter rather than resolve it: they acknowledge that common law allows the proposed marriage, but warn that the spiritual courts may invalidate it, and advise her to con-

---

for the pertinence of current theories of natural law, see Maximillian E. Novak, *Defoe and the Nature of Man* (Oxford, 1963), pp. 96-103.

[53] *A.M.,* IV, vii, 3; cf. IV, xxiv, I.

25

sult "the *Ecclesiastick Authority*" beforehand.[54] We may doubt
whether a querist "*of a Sanguine Complexion*" would be altogether satisfied by this response, and if the lady were to
appear in a work by Defoe, we would not be surprised if she
ventured into the match, armed with the law of man against
her scruples about the "*Law of God*." In the *Athenian
Mercury*, such a marriage is not prohibited, but a formidable
obstacle is placed in its way. Together with this caution in
the substance of the answer, there is a notable absence of anything dogmatically prescriptive in its tone.

Difference of opinion within the Athenian Society also
fosters a tone of judicious moderation. Although no consistent attempt is made to characterize the Society as a group
of distinct individuals, there are occasional debates and
changes of mind among the Athenians, and these help to
create an air of open-minded deliberation. Defoe was to make
similar use of this device in the *Review*: the pretense that
questions are being answered by a "Club" of learned men
allows him to do justice to opposing sides of a question, and
to reach his conclusions in a seemingly inductive manner.
Thus it is not a mere ruse to give greater authority to Defoe's
single-handed pronouncements, but serves to keep the advice
eventually given from seeming hasty or peremptory.

When the facts warrant it, the Athenian Society can be very
forthright in its decisions. One lady discovers that her hus-

[54] The ecclesiastical authorities themselves regarded this as a difficult
question. Perkins had argued that if the husband "be absent either
because he is in captiuity, or vpon malice, or feare, or any such like
cause; the wife must rest in the expectation of his returne, till she hath
notice of his death"; if she lacks such notice, "some haue thought that
it behooueth her to expect his comming againe for the space of foure
yeares; others of fiue; some of seauen, some of tenne yeares; after which
time, she is free, and may marry another man" ("Of Christian Oeconomie," in *Workes*, ii, 688; cf. Baxter, *Christian Directory*, in *Practical
Works*, iv, 167; among Anglicans, see Hall, *Resolutions and Decisions*,
in *Works*, vii, 398-99).

band is already married to another woman, parts from him, is courted by another man, and writes to inquire whether she can lawfully remarry. She adds that her first husband has married a third wife in the meantime. The Society abruptly declares, "Your *Marriage* to this *Great Turk of a Husband*, that keeps such a *Seraglio* of *Women*, must be *void*, because by our *Laws* a Man can have but one *Wife* at *one time*, nor (we think) does the *Christian Law* allow any more: Consequently you are not in *Bondage* in that *Case*, but may embrace any *fair Offer* that's made you."[55] When a question is posed "*Whether Polygamy were lawful to the Jews*," the Athenians do take into account the law of nature, just as they invoke the standard of expediency when asked "*If Polygamy were again introduc'd, whether wou'd it bring more* Trouble *or* Pleasure *to Mankind?*" (*A.O.*, I, 8; I, 503). But these are historical and speculative questions, not cases of conscience, and although the Athenians hold that polygamy is unnatural as well as inexpedient, they appeal to neither standard in answering the two queries on bigamy cited previously. What the situation may have been among the Jews, or might prove to be if the custom "*were again introduc'd*," would be relevant to the practical decisions of an English Christian only if the laws of Christianity and England were silent about the matter, which they are not.[56]

It remains to consider briefly the effects of the question project on subsequent literature. The influence of the *Athenian*

[55] *A.O.*, III, 337; the Society does caution, however, that "you ought not to impose upon your new *Servant*, but let him know what a sort of a *Widow* you are, if he's yet ignorant of it."

[56] Such considerations regain a degree of relevance if such a man is placed in a non-Christian, non-English setting—a marginal locale in which several of Defoe's characters find themselves. But it is a mistake to assume, or to represent Defoe as assuming, that the law of nature takes automatic priority over the law of God even under such circumstances.

Mercury on the writings of Defoe will be noted from time to time in later chapters, but this is an appropriate point to mention the clearest instance of direct contact, and also to consider briefly the impact of Dunton's journal on other works of the early eighteenth century. On the most elementary level, there is the matter of overt adoption of the Athenian question-and-answer device. Critics have long recognized that the "Advice from the Scandal Club" and the later *Supplements* in Defoe's *Review* are modelled on the *Athenian Mercury*.[57] In fact, Dunton himself complained that "[Defoe's] answering Questions Weekly put a stop to my 'Monthly Oracle' . . . for most are seized with the Athenian Itch, and chuse rather to be scratched *Weekly*, than stay till the *Month* is out for a perfect cure."[58] Defoe was not the only interloper, however. While the original *Athenian Mercury* was still in existence, it had a short-lived rival in the *London Mercury*, continued as the *Lacedemonian Mercury* (Feb.-May 1692); and there was at least one later attempt to exploit "the Athenian Itch," entitled *The British Apollo, Or, Curious Amusements for the Ingenious* (Feb. 1708-May 1711).

Although letters from readers were an important feature of both the *Tatler* and the *Spectator*, neither journal gave cases of conscience as prominent a place as they had found in the *Athenian Mercury*. The *Tatler*'s Mr. Bickerstaff is "an excellent casuist," who occasionally resolves classic cases in the traditional manner,[59] and the *Spectator* has its "Love-Casuist,"

[57] See Paul Dottin, *Daniel De Foe* (Paris and London, 1924), pp. 129-30; James Sutherland, *Defoe*, 2nd edn. (1950), pp. 123-24.

[58] "It is strange," Dunton continues, "that such a first-rate Author as Daniel De Foe should be so barren of new Projects, that he must interlope with mine" ("A Secret History of The Weekly Writers," from *The Whipping Post* [1706], reprinted in *Life and Errors*, ed. John B. Nichols, 2 vols. [1818], II, 423-24).

[59] See No. 20 for May 26, 1709, where the question is one of divorce for impotence; Steele advises the distressed wife that "in case of infirmity, which proceeds only from age, the law gives no remedy" (I,

whose task is "giving Judgment to the Satisfaction of the Parties concerned, on the most nice and intricate Cases which can happen in an Amour."[60] But on the whole, Steele and Addison seek to show that morality is a broad, well-lit, well-posted highway without sharp turnings or steep grades; the tortuous, obscure, and uneven path of casuistical ethics is therefore alien to the essential spirit of their writings. At the same time, it is characteristic of both authors that casuistry should be treated as at worst something superfluous and faintly ridiculous—as a kind of equivalent in the realm of ethics to Sir Roger de Coverley in the social or political sphere. But the popular taste for casuistical journalism was unaffected by the gentle mockery of Addison and Steele, as is shown by the number of cases of conscience which they themselves continued to receive from readers. As late as 1725, Charles Lillie issued two substantial volumes of letters which Addison and Steele had not seen fit to use;[61] their publication testifies not only to the enduring prestige of the *Spectator*, but to the steady public demand for casuistical reading matter—a demand which has kept advice-to-the-lovelorn columns alive to this day.

Even more influential than its question-and-answer format, however, was the actual content of many of the *Athenian Mercury*'s queries. Although Defoe probably knew some of

---

166-69). English casuists had been unanimous on this point (e.g., Hall, *Resolutions and Decisions*, in *Works*, vii, 399-400; cf. also *Conjugal Lewdness* [1727], pp. 69-70). Elsewhere Steele tends to introduce cases of conscience as points of departure for more general discussions—as in No. 98 for Nov. 24, 1709—or as occasions for drollery, as in No. 228 for Sept. 23, 1710 (ii, 328-30; iv, 167-68).

[60] The Love-Casuist appears late in the paper's life, in numbers written by Budgell and Tickell: see No. 591 for Sept. 8, 1714, No. 614 for Nov. 1, 1714, No. 619 for Nov. 12, 1714 (v, 22-23; v, 98; v, 115-16).

[61] See n. 37 above (*Original and Genuine Letters*); among the twelve pages of subscribers are "Mr. Daniel De Foe" and "Mr. Daniel De Foe junior."

the earlier casuistical manuals at first hand,[62] the *Mercury* is
nevertheless a more immediate and likelier source for certain
cases incorporated in the *Review*, especially since their circumstantial, epistolary presentation to a learned "Club" or "Society" had no other precedent. Dunton's periodical seems to
have been regarded as a convenient storehouse of lively and
occasionally risqué casuistical subject matter, and a number
of its cases turn up in writings of the period other than Defoe's.
An apprentice reports to the Athenians his discovery that
*"my Mistress entertain'd an unlawful Amour, with a Gentle-
man who lodg'd in our house,"* and asks whether he is not
"bound in Conscience to . . . divulge the matter?" In 1726
another apprentice, the hero of a novel by William Rufus
Chetwood, learns of his master's wife's adultery and has the
same difficulty deciding whether he is obliged to inform his
master.[63] Examples could be multiplied, and although one can
never be certain that Dunton's journal is the sole or specific
source of such material—Chetwood could have encountered
the apprentice's case of conscience in *The British Apollo* or
in the earlier casuistical writings of Sanderson or Hall[64]—the
immediate popularity and frequent reprinting of the *Athenian*

[62] In *Conjugal Lewdness*, for example, Defoe acknowledges his indebtedness to Jeremy Taylor, who had inquired three-quarters of a
century earlier whether the virtue of chastity is called for within marriage (pp. 51-56; cf. Taylor's *Holy Living* [1650], Ch. 11, Sect. iii, in
Whole Works, 111, 55-68). William Perkins had maintained that "euen
in wedlocke excesse in lusts is no better then plaine adulterie before
God," and defended as "the iudgement of the auncient Church" the
principle that "intemperance, that is, immoderate desire[s] euen between man and wife are fornication" ("Of Christian Oeconomie," in
Workes, 11, 689). This thesis is the ideological point of departure for
Conjugal Lewdness—a title Defoe probably chose as a catchy oxymoron,
but which he eventually makes into a virtual tautology.

[63] See *A.M.*, viii, xi, 5; cf. also *A.M.*, vii, i, 5; *The Voyages and Adventures of Captain Robert Boyle, In several Parts of the World*, pp. 3-7.

[64] See *The British Apollo*, Supernumerary Paper No. 5 (Aug. 1708),
p. [4], for the same case; Hall, *Resolutions and Decisions*, in *Workes*,

Mercury make it reasonable to suppose that other writers knew and used it. Indeed, even unsympathetic witnesses testify to the durability of the Athenian vogue, for the *Mercury* and its cases of conscience were not only adapted but parodied widely in the literature of the period. The *Spectator*'s "Love-Casuist" has already been mentioned; in Captain Alexander Smith's *Complete History of the Highwaymen* (1716), there is a leering discussion of a case which is said to have been "a month's theme, or more, for the Athenian Society, at that time of day, to resolve";[65] and burlesques of Athenian questions and answers turn up for years in unexpected places.[66]

However important the *Athenian Mercury* may have been as a source or transmitter of casuistical subject matter, its em-

---

VII, 314-16, on the question "Whether, and in what cases, am I bound to be an accuser of another"; *ibid.*, pp. 413-14 on the question "How far we may or ought to make known the secret sin of another." For the influence of such queries on other novelists, see Natascha Würzbach's useful introduction to *The Novel in Letters: Epistolary Fiction in the Early English Novel 1678-1740* (Coral Gables, 1969), pp. xx, xxiii-xxiv.

[65] Ed. Arthur L. Hayward (1926), p. 196. Cf. also Settle's *New Athenian Comedy*, n. 32 above.

[66] A 1734 collection of criminal trials says of a convicted felon named Philip Storey that "While he was under Condemnation, his Conscience was puzzl'd with a scruple not very common with Men of his Profession. He had taken it into his Head that the most heinous offence a Man could be Guilty of, was Sacrilege, thereupon was very inquisitive to know whether picking Pockets in a Church was a species of that Crime or not. To this the Ordinary of *Newgate* (who was a profound Casuist) answer'd affirmatively. *Picking Pockets in a Church*, says that Ghostly Father, *is certainly one sort of Sacrilege, and may perhaps be more offensive in the sight of God, than what is generally call'd by that Name, because it may possibly deter some from frequenting God's Temple, or make those who are there, so cautious and uneasy for fear of losing their Money, as to take their thoughts off from Heaven, and damp their Devotion . . . Now stealing the Vessels or Ornaments of the Church can have none of these effects, and consequently picking Pockets there must be the greater Sin*" (*Select Trials . . . at the Sessions-House in the Old-Bailey . . . From the Year 1720, to 1724* [1734], p. 79).

ployment of casuistical methods probably made an even greater contribution to early eighteenth-century literature. In Dunton's periodical, highly diverse ethical dilemmas are resolved through detailed consideration of the relevant circumstances and sanctions; as a consequence, each case of conscience becomes something of an episode, and each querist is more or less fully realized as a character. Such a technique was obviously adaptable to prose fiction, although it was better suited to portraying and assessing character than to organizing a sustained narrative. Owing to the assumption that life is composed of a series of cases of conscience, each of which must be decided on its own merits, the casuistical method tends to dissolve narrative into a series of discrete episodes. It is not my contention that there ever existed such a thing as a "casuistical novel," or that Defoe ever attempted to write one, but rather that the paratactic structure of such books as *Moll Flanders, Colonel Jack,* and *Roxana* is in part ascribable to Defoe's habit of approaching experience casuistically, case by case. Each hero and heroine passes through numerous self-contained scenes, often based directly on traditional cases of conscience, and even when conscience plays little part in a character's deliberations, the internal shape of an episode will often preserve the case-stating, case-resolving pattern. There is a similar absence of direct causal linkage between scenes in *A Journal of the Plague Year,* although the progress of the plague provides a loose chronological and geographical structure, and in Defoe's conduct manuals, where the primary aim is a full and persuasive treatment of moral problems, there is still less concern with novelistic plotting.

TWO

My initial object has been to show that John Dunton's *Athenian Mercury* effectively developed and popularized various features of seventeenth-century casuistical divinity, and thus served as a valuable intermediary between the writings of Perkins, Taylor, and Baxter, and those of Defoe. In the transmutation of traditional cases of conscience into the materials of prose fiction, Defoe's so-called conduct manuals represent the next significant stage. To this class belong *The Family Instructor* (1715-18), *Religious Courtship* (1722), *A New Family Instructor* (1727), and one or two other similarly titled works. Chronologically, the casuistical portions of the *Review* appear midway between the *Athenian Mercury* and Defoe's first novels, and as subsequent discussion of the novels will indicate, the *Review* adumbrates many of their cases of conscience. Formally, however, the *Review* does not seem to me to have appreciably altered or improved upon Dunton's successful formula for casuistical journalism, whereas the conduct manuals do mark a distinct advance. The pages that follow will therefore trace what becomes of the traditional methods and materials of casuistry in these conduct manuals; and since later discussions of *Moll Flanders* and *Roxana* will be particularly concerned with matrimonial casuistry, it will be appropriate to give special attention to *Religious Courtship*, which contains a number of classic "Cases Matrimonial." What one finds in the conduct manuals is that cases of conscience are investigated in "purer" form than in the novels. Defoe is more detached from the people whom he puts in casuistical predicaments, and more intent on the moral principles which character and action alike are designed to illustrate. As a consequence, cases of conscience can be presented and resolved somewhat more straightforwardly than is usually possible in the novels, where various factors—notably Defoe's imaginative involvement in the fate of his heroes and heroines —complicate the presentation, and sometimes prevent any final resolution, of the same traditional dilemmas.

Before turning to *Religious Courtship*, we should briefly consider the features which the conduct manuals share with one another and with the novels, as well as the differences between them. Benjamin Franklin first noted their common use of "Narration and Dialogue,"[67] and there are many other similarities: a comparable attainment of circumstantial realism through concrete detail; an analogous preference of exhaustiveness to conciseness, of reiteration to understatement, of plainness to elegance; and (more generally) the same focus on bourgeois characters winning material and spiritual victories in demanding environments. What, then, are the differences? As the very term "conduct manual" would suggest, critics have felt that a fundamental distinction of intent separates this genre from the novel. As long ago as 1895, George A. Aitken argued that the story exists for the sake of the moral in the conduct manuals, and vice versa in the novels; he saw the two types of work as closely connected, and maintained that the novel emerged from the conduct manual through a reversal of priorities on Defoe's part.[68] Although not all subsequent scholars have granted the conduct manuals such a decisive role in Defoe's literary development,[69] Aitken's line

[67] Speaking of Bunyan in his *Autobiography*, Franklin says that "Honest John was the first that I know of who mix'd Narration and Dialogue, a Method of Writing very engaging to the Reader, who in the most interesting Parts finds himself as it were brought into the Company, and present at the Discourse. Defoe," he goes on to say, "in his Cruso, his Moll Flanders, Religious Courtship, Family Instructor, and other Pieces, has imitated it with Success" (ed. Leonard W. Labaree, *et al.* [New Haven, 1964], p. 72). All quotations from *Religious Courtship* (1722) refer to the second edition of 1729.

[68] In Aitken's words, the change "was one of degree rather than kind. The difference lay chiefly in the prominence now given to the story, which took the leading place, hitherto occupied by the moral" (Introduction to *Romances and Narratives*, 16 vols. [1895], I, xxix).

[69] See Arthur W. Secord, *Studies in the Narrative Method of Defoe* (Urbana, 1924), pp. 16-17. According to Secord, Aitken's thesis exaggerates the importance of the conduct manuals in the genesis of Defoe's

of demarcation between the two genres has not been challenged; its main drawback, of course, is the difficulty of determining whether "the moral" or "the story" was uppermost in Defoe's mind in any given work of fiction. There are moments in all the conduct manuals when the story takes on a momentum of its own, or at any rate is shaped by other than moral interests, just as there are moments in all the novels when moral impulses clearly dominate the narrative. None of the conduct manuals, however, offers as much sustained storytelling as any of the novels; Defoe never focuses on a single individual, as he always does in the novels, but on small groups of people bound together by blood, marriage, or professional relationships. The result is that each conduct manual contains a series of short narratives which exemplify various responses to the same cases of conscience. The novels are no less episodic, but their fragmentation is offset by the constant presence of a first-person narrator, chronicling experiences which are mostly his own; in the conduct manuals the narrator is sometimes a participant but more commonly a chance observer, less interested in connecting scenes than in commenting on them individually.[70] Thus the persistence of a single voice, which gives a minimal coherence to even the most disjointed of Defoe's novelistic plots, is absent in the

---

prose fiction, and correspondingly slights the influence of other genres, such as voyage and criminal literature.

[70] The role of the narrator varies from one conduct manual to another, and even to some extent within single works. At the beginning of *The Family Instructor* (1715-18), Defoe's first major venture in the genre, short dialogues are held together with extensive authorial notes; as the work progresses, dialogues grow longer and are linked by short narrative passages. Authorial comment is curtailed and relegated to the end of parts—each "Part" of the book is subdivided into "Dialogues" —as Defoe appears to grow more confident of having made his meaning clear, either through the action or through the speakers' own comments on it.

conduct manuals, and the lack of it prevents "the story" from developing as we should expect it to in a novel.

But the conduct manuals are no more failed novels than the novels—in which Defoe partially relaxes his emphasis on the exemplary episode, and allows a single character to give an unbroken account of his vicissitudes—are failed conduct manuals.[71] The primary task of *Religious Courtship*, for instance, is to show the necessity, as the extended subtitle puts it, *of Marrying Religious Husbands and Wives only, Of Husbands and Wives being of the same Opinions in Religion with one another*, and *of taking none but Religious Servants*. But the important thing is that these "necessities" be proven, not merely asserted as they are on the title page; and what makes Defoe's demonstration interesting is that despite the dogmatic air of their initial assertion, these propositions are generated within the text in a seemingly inductive fashion. No other device plays a greater part in creating this effect than the dialogue method. This is usually spoken of as a means simply of achieving narrative realism or of enlivening dry precepts, but its functions in *Religious Courtship* are more subtle and varied. Through dialogue we are persuaded that the speakers are groping their way toward principles of behavior, not serv-

[71] That apologues and other didactic fictions cannot be regarded as novels *manqués*, but must be seen as obeying generic requirements of their own, is convincingly argued by several recent commentators on *Rasselas*. See Bertrand H. Bronson, "Postscript on *Rasselas*" in *Rasselas, Poems, and Selected Prose* (New York, 1958), p. xvi, on Johnson's work as a "philosophical dialogue"; Gwin J. Kolb, Introduction to *Rasselas* (New York, 1962), pp. v-vi; and especially Sheldon Sacks, *Fiction and the Shape of Belief* (Berkeley and Los Angeles, 1964), pp. 49-60. One advantage of the term "conduct manual" over "apologue" as a description of these works of Defoe is that it suggests the rootedness of the theoretical and didactic—the "manual" aspect—in actual behavior—"conduct." Moral issues here are not speculative but firmly practical; it is as if Defoe had altered Socrates' maxim to read, "The unlived life is not worth examining."

36

ing as mere mouthpieces for the author's predetermined views. Without claiming that they engage in full-fledged dialectic, one can maintain that through their discussions various characters gradually arrive at solutions of the cases of conscience confronting them. It is the very gradualness of this process, punctuated by doubts, tentative judgments, and changes of mind along the way, which allows an inductive spirit to prevail, and gives the eventual attitudes of Defoe's characters such persuasiveness as they possess. To put it another way, conduct manuals attempt to make characters (and by extension, readers) arrive with an air of discovery at what the author knew in the first place: one way Defoe achieves this in *Religious Courtship* is by making various people discuss cases of conscience aloud. In their casuistical periodicals, both Dunton and Defoe posit a collective entity—an Athenian *Society* or a Scandal *Club*—within which there can be difference of opinion; this helps to create an atmosphere of open-minded deliberation. Cases of conscience are thus explored in a stochastic, not a peremptory manner. The family discussions in *Religious Courtship* represent an extension of the same device, with the members of the group given more specific and distinct identities, and their views more fully articulated and qualified in the give-and-take of dialogue. Defoe himself may finally be "The Family Instructor," but he is careful to keep from delivering the instruction *ex cathedra*, or even from above. Rather, he is fond of making it move in the opposite direction; and instead of fathers, husbands, and masters laying down the law to children, wives, and servants, it is "from the mouths of babes" that wisdom most commonly —and most convincingly—comes. The native woman who converts Will Atkins in *The Farther Adventures of Robinson Crusoe* is one well-known instance of a pattern characteristic of all the conduct manuals: the slave, the child, the youngest sibling, the apprentice, the unlettered peasant, and the savage are Defoe's favorite spokesmen.

We can best illustrate some of these generalizations by turning directly to *Religious Courtship*. The first part deals with what the title page calls *The Necessity of Marrying Religious Husbands and Wives only*, but in the text this is posed as a question rather than an assertion. The youngest of three sisters is courted by a man who has everything to recommend him but religion. He is no atheist, but religion is "a Road he had never travell'd" (41); his worldly upbringing makes him one of those who "would choose a Wife first, and then choose his Religion" (42). The problem is whether the girl ought to marry him all the same: not a subject, one might suppose, capable of interesting most modern readers. Nevertheless, this central question takes on considerable dramatic force through an accumulation of peripheral questions. Each of the latter might have been the essential question in a different context, for most are based on traditional cases of conscience; yet their chief role here is to involve the characters in a maze of conflicts and anxieties, without which any prolonged treatment of the central issue would be lifeless.

Prior to the beginning of the action, for instance, the girls' dying mother had laid down two "Maxims in the Choice of their Husbands," the first of which was *"Never to Marry any Man, whatever his Person or Fortune might be, that did not at least, profess to be a* Religious Man" (3). These are represented several times as "injunctions" on the part of the mother, and elsewhere as "promises" on the part of the girls; the question becomes, how far are such deathbed injunctions or promises binding on the daughters? A related question arises in connection with the father, a passionate man who makes various oaths and vows about banishing and disowning his daughter if she refuses to comply with his wishes and marry her suitor. One recent commentator represents

Defoe as holding that all vows are sacred, however rash, but neither he nor his casuistical predecessors went quite this far.[72] Robert Sanderson's "Case of a Rash Vow Deliberately Iterated" may be taken as a typical resolution of this problem;[73] his view that such oaths are *not* binding is echoed in several of Defoe's works.[74]

Behind both of the preceding questions lies a more general one, which had formed a staple of the seventeenth-century casuistical manuals and was to be crucial to the opening

[72] See Maximillian E. Novak, *Defoe and the Nature of Man* (Oxford, 1963), pp. 99.

[73] See Sanderson's *Works*, ed. William Jacobson, 6 vols. (Oxford, 1854), v, 60-74: "A Gentleman of good estate hath issue one only Daughter, who, placing her affections upon a person much below her rank, intendeth Marriage with him. The Father, hearing of it, in great displeasure voweth, and confirmeth it with an Oath, that if she marry him, he will never give her a farthing of his estate. The Daughter notwithstanding marrieth him: after which the Father sundry times iterateth and reneweth his said former Vow. . . . *Quaere*: Whether the Father's Vow so made, and so confirmed and iterated as abovesaid, be Obligatory or not?" Sanderson's opinion is that "the Vow was Rash, and is not at all Obligatory." See the *Athenian Mercury*, vii, ii, 2; viii, v, 5.

[74] What Defoe did believe is that such vows, whether kept or not, necessarily plunge those making them (as well as those against whom they are made) into terrible difficulties, and must issue either in repentance or general misery. In *The Family Instructor*, several stories are told about rash vows and their aftermath. One man stalks out of his house in a rage, and wishes "it might fall on his Head if ever he came into it again," but later makes the following reflections, which Defoe evidently regards as sound: "I have sinn'd greatly in making this rash Vow, but I must continue to sin as long as I live, if I keep it; I'll cast myself upon GOD's Mercy and ask Pardon for my Sin, and venture the Consequence" (Vol. ii [1718], p. 210). In *Applebee's Journal* a husband who signs himself "Furioso" describes a similar predicament: "This horrid Case" concerns an oath made twenty years earlier by the separating spouses, never to see each other again; they had cursed one another heartily, and now, two decades later, are afraid to come together "for fear the House should fall upon our Heads" (Mar. 27, 1725; Lee, iii, 369-71).

volumes of *Clarissa*: namely, the extent to which parents can legitimately determine whom their children are to marry. *Religious Courtship* contains Defoe's fullest exploration of this topic. Like John Harlowe, the father in this book is an autocrat who manages to "hurry and terrify his Children so with his Fury and his Passions, that they are afraid to see him, and ready to swoon when they hear he is coming to them" (103); and like John Harlowe, this man assumes that it has "been always the Right of Fathers to give their Daughters in Marriage," and cites Old Testament texts to justify his patriarchal pretensions. But he is advised by his own sister that neither "the Laws of God or Man give Parents that Authority now," and that "there is a great Difference between your negative Authority and your positive Authority in the Case of a Daughter" (98-99). This conventional distinction grants both father and daughter a veto power: the girl cannot choose her own husband, nor can the father choose one for her, without the other's consent.[75] The youngest daughter therefore appeals to established principles, which Richardson's heroine would likewise invoke, in telling her father, "If I was going to marry any one you did not like, it was, no doubt, in your Power to command me not to do it, but I cannot think you ought to command me to marry any Man against my Will" (28). Despite her painful awareness that "there is a powerful Force in a Father's Command," whether or not that command is just, she nevertheless believes that "as I am

[75] See *Conjugal Lewdness* (1727), in which Defoe says that "The Limits of a Parent's Authority, in this Case of Matrimony, either with Son or Daughter, I think, stands thus: The Negative, I think, is theirs, especially with a Daughter; but, I think, the Positive is the Childrens" (p. 170). For earlier defenses of the right of children to reject matches proposed by their parents, see Jeremy Taylor, *Ductor Dubitantium*, ed. Alexander Taylor, in *Whole Works*, ed. Reginald Heber, rev. Charles P. Eden, 10 vols. (1852), x, 496; Richard Baxter, *Christian Directory*, in *Practical Works*, ed. William Orme, 23 vols. (1830), IV, 196.

sure I am right, I must do my Duty, and trust Providence; if my Father does not do the Duty of his Relation to me, I'll pray to God to forgive him" (33, 34).[76]

A hazard here is that the girl will seem priggishly willful, but Defoe sees the danger and takes various precautions against it. For one thing, all the arguments for her marrying the man are given their full weight. Before she is able to discover her suitor's want of religion, his "very agreeable Person" and his "engaging Conduct" have "made some Way into her Affection," and eventually "she not only has a Respect for him, but really loves him" (115). Defoe develops with some skill the girl's struggle between love and principle; the "poor young Lady" is so afflicted by her plight that—like Moll Flanders during her Colchester *crise de coeur*—"she fell very sick with it, and it was fear'd she inclined to a Consumption" (116). In the second place, any feeling we might have that the girl exaggerates the importance of religion is neutralized by making the father callously reiterate this very charge; through his sneers at her "canting Scruples" and "fine-spun Notions" it is suggested that there is nothing trifling or arbitrary about her misgivings (28, 111). On the other hand, sympathetic characters like the aunt praise the girl's conscientiousness as "the noblest

---

[76] William Perkins had maintained that "the parent is the principal agent and disposer of the child" in matrimony, but adds that "although his authoritie be not so great as that the child is to be forced and compelled by him; yet the reuerent and dutiful respect which the child ought to beare towards him, ought to be a strong inducement, not to dissent, or renounce his aduice, without great and waighty cause. Yea, the child must indeauour by al manner of dutifull carriage to ouercome, or at least to mitigate his parents seuerity in that behalfe" ("Of Christian Oeconomie, or Houshold gouernment," in *Workes*, 3 vols. [1616-18], II, 695). Cf. Hall's similar response to the question "Whether the authority of a father may reach so far as to command or compel the child to dispose of himself in marriage where he shall appoint," *Resolutions and Decisions*, in *Works*, ed. Philip Wynter, 10 vols. (Oxford, 1863), VII, 380-82; cf. also *The Ladies Library*, 3 Vols. (1715), II, 29.

Resolution that ever I heard of, since the Story of St. *Catharine*" (98). Also effective is the way the reality of the girl's own immediate predicament is heightened by the introduction of other, imaginary ones. Her "actual" case, of course, is itself only hypothetical, invented by Defoe to convey his notions of religious courtship; but by making the actors in it discuss still other cases as hypothetical, Defoe strengthens our belief in the genuineness of their own. This is a recurrent strategy in *Religious Courtship*; the characters have such active imaginations that we tend to forget that they and their cases of conscience are themselves imaginary. Their inventiveness conceals (yet in another sense testifies to) that of Defoe.

Most important, however, is the fact that many lines of communication remain open, and that the question can be canvassed from many points of view. What becomes so oppressive and fatal in the Harlowe household—Clarissa's gradual isolation from her family, their growing imperviousness, and her growing desperation—is adumbrated here in a temporary estrangement between father and daughter. But the tragic potentialities of the situation are curbed, partly by the fact that even when the principals are not in direct contact, third parties keep the circuits of discussion unbroken, and partly by the fact that the father, for all his intransigence on matrimonial questions, is by no means a complete ogre, so that the possibility of his being sooner or later amenable to reason is also kept open. Similarly the suitor, despite a breezy aloofness towards religion at the outset, is shown as a victim of the genteel miseducation which Defoe was to deplore in *The Compleat English Gentleman*, rather than of ill-nature: he is endowed with enough modesty and sense to seem reclaimable, and we are not surprised when a poor but pious tenant of his—whose role resembles that of Colonel Jack's slave-tutor in Virginia—becomes his spiritual father and sets in motion his conversion. Defoe never presents a reformed rake as an ideal husband, but he is rather partial to weaned worldlings.

The sheer indefatigability of all these talkers gives us confidence in the eventual success of their negotiations,[77] but for Defoe's purposes it is also important that the two high-principled daughters be able, as an acquaintance says of one of them, "to run down a whole Society of Doctors in these Points." It is not enough that they be innocent as doves: they must also have enough serpentine wisdom to make us confess, as does one potential objector within the story, "I have not been able to open my Mouth against one Word she says" (146).

The second part of the book concerns the middle daughter, whose history, Defoe claims, is "no less fruitful of Instruction than the other, tho something more tragical." This girl "would not trouble herself, when it came to her Turn, what Religion the Gentleman was of, or whether he had any Religion or no, if she had but a good Settlement" (183); she therefore ventures to the altar without determining beforehand whether her suitor, a rich merchant, has been tainted with Popery during his long residence in Italy. Not until long after the wedding does she realize that her husband's valuable paintings are objects of a superstitious devotion, that his exotically furnished closet is a private chapel, and that his con-

[77] In *The Family Instructor*, the conflict of wills within a family is allowed to reach its tragic conclusion, but this outcome is compatible with the point Defoe is making about how a family ought to be governed. In *Religious Courtship*, if his interest had been centered on the question of paternal rather than filial conduct, he could have kept the father tyrannically inflexible, made "a Consumption" consume the daughter, and so on, with no loss of edifying effect. But since he is intent on recommending the daughter's exemplary behavior, and is unwilling to defer its reward to an uncertain afterlife (as Richardson had the temerity to do in *Clarissa*), he eventually unites her with her now-worthy suitor.

fidential secretary is a disguised priest. She is eventually "delivered" from this fatal mismatch by her husband's death, and in this part of the book, the tearful widow and her more prudent sisters discuss the dire consequences of failing to recognize "the necessity of husbands and wives being of the same opinions in religion with one another." This monitory tale, which balances the other exemplary ones, rests on a case of conscience which nearly every seventeenth-century English casuist had discussed: that is, whether Protestants are justified in marrying Roman Catholics.[78] The question had usually been resolved more or less as it is here: such marriages are not sinful, but are attended with such "signal inconveniences" that they ought to be avoided.[79] Yet the episode is not really an attack on Roman Catholicism; Defoe lets the Papist put his best foot forward, so as to show that even when both spouses grant one another complete liberty of conscience, and all sectarian friction is happily avoided, a difference in religious opinion is nevertheless bound to generate "Sighs and sad Hearts," and "No Kindness, no Tenderness, no Affection can make it up" (258, 257).

On the other hand, the Papist is not idealized, either. Defoe wants to show a girl who, though in a sense innocent, comes to grief through a lack of her sisters' serpentine pru-

[78] Typical is "The Case of Marrying with a Recusant" in Sanderson, *Works*, v, 75-80; the *Confession of Faith* of the Westminster Assembly of Divines (1643) declares that "such as profess the true reformed religion should not marry with infidels, Papists, or other idolaters" (Chap. xxiv, Par. iii [Edinburgh, 1877], p. 102), but the Canons of the Church of England contain no such provision.

[79] See *A.M.*, vii, xix, 4; xvii, i, 5; xiii, xv, 6; and v, ix, 8, where the Athenian Society prefers to leave this question "to the decision of all Learn'd and Casuistical Divines," and modestly concludes that "tho we have given our [negative] Opinion, we desire you not to rely on it, unless confirm'd by the Approbation of some of *our Bishops*, for 'tis a matter of great Moment, that pretends to the decision of an Interest in both Worlds."

dence. He therefore puts in the mouth of the Papist several equivocations which she ought to see through (or at least question), but blithely accepts at face value. Thus in recounting the gradual stages by which she learned of her husband's Catholicism, she says that one day as he was entering his closet "he made an extraordinary low Bow towards that Place where the Candlesticks stood: Indeed I took no notice of it at first, for I verily thought he had stoop'd for some thing, but when he carry'd the Candlesticks in again he did the same, and that gave me . . . some Idea of this being an extraordinary Place, tho I did not know what; and I very innocently ask'd him this foolish laughing Question; My Dear, you are mighty mannerly to your empty Rooms, you bow as if the King was there; he put it off with a Smile, and an Answer that was indeed according to *Solomon, Answer a Fool in his Folly,* My Dear, says he, 'tis our Custom in *Italy.*" "He was no Fool," the eldest sister observes, "what he said was very true" (251-52). Richard Baxter had declared, in his *Christian Directory,* that "If I find a man in an ignorance or error which I am not bound to cure . . . I may either be silent, or speak darkly, or speak words which he understandeth not, (through his own imperfection,) or which I know his weakness will misunderstand: but I must speak no falsehood to him."[80] " 'Tis our Custom in *Italy*" would appear to satisfy Baxter's criteria of truthfulness, but what Defoe stresses in this passage is the girl's gullibility, rather than the ethical status of the man's words. On another occasion the Papist resorts to a still more dubious amphibology. While the courtship is still in progress, the bride-to-be reports that "accidently speaking about Religion, he declared he was a Member of the Church of *England,* as by Law establish'd." Her eldest sister replies, "Well, you are an easy Lady; a little Matter satisfies

[80] *Practical Works,* iii, 509.

you; I should presently have said, I hope, Sir, you mean the Protestant Church of *England*; Why, [do you] not imagine, the Roman Catholicks think the Popish Church is the only Church of *England* that is establish'd by Law?" At this the unwary young lady is aghast: "Sure, Sister, you take all the World to be Hypocrites and Cheats; I never can suspect any Gentleman, that bears the Character of an honest Man, would set up to impose upon me with such equivocal Speeches; why I never heard such a vile Distinction in my Life."[81] We need not enter into the legitimacy of the man's ruse here, since the subject of mendacity is discussed in an Appendix below. The point is that whether or not this equivocation is a "vile Distinction," we see that the girl's dovelikeness is extremely vulnerable, and the contrast with the other sisters suggests that her naïveté is blameworthy, however charming.[82]

The two scenes just discussed also illustrate the effectiveness of Defoe's dialogue, the nuances of which keep the central topic—whether Protestants should marry Roman Catholics—from becoming drearily tendentious. The same may be said of graphic detail. In the *Review*, Defoe's Scandal Club had considered the case of a Protestant lady wearing a crucifix,

[81] P. 191; cf. Pascal's Jesuit on such equivocations: "In social intercourse and intrigues," he says, "one of the most embarrassing problems is how to avoid lying, especially when one would like people to believe something untrue. This is where our [Jesuit] doctrine of equivocation is marvelously helpful, for it allows one 'to use ambiguous terms, conveying a different meaning to the hearer from that in which one understands them oneself,' as Sanchez says" (*Provincial Letters*, trans. A. J. Krailsheimer [Baltimore, 1966], p. 140). But cf. also n. 17 to Appendix below.

[82] In *Applebee's Journal* for Sept. 16, 1721, Defoe cites a relevant text (Prov. 27:12): "*The Prudent Man foreseeth the Evil, and hideth himself; but the Simple pass on and are punish'd*" (Lee, II, 430). More severe is the remark earlier in *Religious Courtship* that "if we are deceived, it may be our Unhappiness, but will not be our Fault; *but if we neglect* the Caution, it may be a double Misery, by its being our Sorrow, and our Sin too" (p. 15).

46

and had reprimanded her for it.[83] Here the husband gives his wife a diamond cross, "worth above six hundred Pounds," and for five pages the widow discusses with her father and sisters the difficulties that this gift caused. These difficulties are not exclusively moral ones; or rather, the genuineness of the moral problem is established partly through the vivid presentation of prosaic, non-moral *realia*. The father points out that Protestant ladies in Italy all wear crosses, but avoid any religious contretemps by putting them out of sight. The daughter replies, "I did so. . . . I lengthen'd the String it hung to, that it might hang a little lower, but it was too big, if it went within my Stays, it would hurt me; nor was it much odds to him; for if he [her husband] saw the String, he knew the Cross was there, and it was all one" (270). The homely realism of such passages may border on the bizarre, but various comparable scenes indicate that Defoe's imagination was at work in this book, not merely his urge to instruct, and they help to make palatable precepts which might have been only wearisome.

According to the title page, the final portion of *Religious Courtship* concerns the necessity *"of taking none but Religious Servants,"* but this is actually displaced by the more general question of recommending servants. This problem recurs elsewhere in Defoe's writings and in contemporary literature; a century later, in fact, Thomas De Quincey was to single out, as typical of "the many cases of conscience daily occurring in the common business of the world . . . the case which so often arises between master and servant, and in so many varieties of form—a case which requires you to decide between some violation of your conscience, on the one hand, as to veracity, by saying something that is not strictly true, as well

---

[83] *Review*, 1 (July 18, 1704), 171-72.

as by evading (and that is often done) all answer to inquiries which you are unable to meet satisfactorily . . . or, on the other hand, a still more painful violation of your conscience in consigning deliberately some young woman . . . to ruin, by refusing her a character, and thus shutting the door upon all the paths by which she might retrace her steps."[84] This is the same dilemma that exercises the characters in *Religious Court-ship*, but Defoe attaches decisive importance to one factor which De Quincey neglects. He anticipates De Quincey's view that to deny an unsatisfactory servant a recommendation may be to plunge her into even more mischievous courses. But he insists that the alternative—to give bad servants good charac-ters, and to evade inquiries which would handicap the servant if answered truthfully—involves not only a violation of one's own conscience, but also an injury to the prospective employer. Defoe's stress on this latter consideration may reflect his own middle-class bias, and it is true that when he discusses the servant problem his tone sometimes becomes more petulant and alarmist than usual. But his assessment of the matter in the closing pages of *Religious Courtship* is both judicious and humane, and from a literary standpoint his manner of treat-ing it is as significant as his conclusions.

The following dialogue between an aunt and her two nieces epitomizes several of the techniques already mentioned. The first niece takes what she imagines to be a charitable position: "We are loth to hinder poor Servants; for to take away their Character is to take away their Bread." But the second niece replies, "We may say the same of a Thief, or a House-breaker, when we find them in our Houses or Gardens, and take them even in the very Fact: We are loth to ruin them for it; that it was Necessity forc'd them to do what they did, and if we have them committed, they will be hang'd or trans-

[84] "The Casuistry of Duelling," in *Uncollected Writings*, ed. James Hogg, 2 vols. (1890), II, 71.

ported; nay the Argument is stronger, because the Injury done may have been trifling, and the Punishment there is Loss of Life, which we may be loth to be concern'd in." "You carry the Case a great deal too high," protests the first niece, "I cannot think they are alike." But the aunt finds the analogy valid, and supports it with further arguments:

> If I take the Thief, and give him up to the Law, he is undone, and his Life must pay for it; and 'tis a sad Thing for me to let a poor Fellow be put to Death or transported for robbing me of a Trifle. But on the other Hand I am to consider, (1) I am oblig'd by the Law to do it; that it is not I that put him to Death, but the Laws of his Country, and his own Crime is the Cause of it; and I am an Offender against that very Law, and in some sense a Confederate with him, at least an Encourager of him in his Crime, if I omit it: But which is more than that, (2) By my perhaps unseasonable and indeed unjust Compassion, I become accessary to all the Robberies he shall be guilty of after it; because if I had done as the Law directed me, I had put him out of a Condition to rob or injure any other Person (343-44).

The first thing to note here is that instead of moral principles being laid down and enforced, the use of dialogue allows a more inductive spirit to prevail. These people do not seem to be merely acting out assigned parts in an ethical game whose every move and eventual outcome have been settled beforehand. In the second place, an issue that might at a glance seem trifling is shown to have serious and extensive implications. On the one hand, the servant problem is metaphorically associated with thievery and housebreaking—hanging matters; on the other hand, legal and moral sanctions are invoked which are at once weighty and far-reaching. Defoe thus establishes the total context of his original problem by investing it not only with further concreteness through analogies, but also greater generality through abstractions. This pattern, at once ethical and rhetorical, is highly characteristic of him—especially of his way of resolving cases of conscience in the conduct manuals; for as I suggested at the beginning of this chapter, both his methods and his results tend to be "purer" in these works than in the novels. Finally, this scene further illustrates Defoe's awareness of the interrelatedness of ethical issues. For these characters the immediate question, about recommending bad servants, can properly be solved only by taking into account its distinctive circumstances as well as its practical and theoretical ramifications. Critics of casuistry have always objected to such a complex procedure, and Defoe himself knew its pitfalls and abuses, but in such instances as this he clearly regarded it as not only legitimate but also necessary. In the novels, as we shall see, various factors can render it impracticable. Instead of wise old aunts and precociously prudent sisters to discuss their cases of conscience with, the heroes and heroines are either alone, or are thrown together with midwives, fortune-hunters, and highwaymen. Instead of the leisure for casuistical deliberation which the "middle station of life" permits, the heroes and heroines of the novels find themselves hurried along by events, and in some cases seem enabled to reflect on their actions only by the very rise in fortune which has already permitted them to change their actions. Perhaps most crucial of all, the novelistic heroes and heroines tell their own stories, and this makes for an imaginative involvement on Defoe's part—and ours—which (as I shall suggest in the following chapters) often qualifies to the point of reversal the kind of judgments typified by the title page of *Religious Courtship*.

A Journal of the Plague Year

E VEN when no ethical question is involved, Defoe's characters tend to state their problems in a way that reflects the formal outlines of a case of conscience. "The fear of being swallowed up alive," says Crusoe, "made me that I never slept in quiet; *and yet* the apprehension of lying abroad without any fence was almost equal to it. *But still*, when I looked about and saw how everything was put in order, how pleasantly concealed I was, and how safe from danger, it made me very loth to remove."[1] In these anxious musings conscience plays no part, but the weighing of counterpoised circumstances is adapted to the form of a traditional case of conscience. The sentence structure conveys a sense of deliberation-in-progress—of groping uncertainly towards a difficult decision—that is characteristically (though not exclusively) casuistical. The frequency of such connectives as "but," "yet," "nevertheless," "still," "however," "on the other hand," "on second thoughts," gives the most mundane predicaments of Defoe's heroes and heroines an air of dramatic tension. A constant balancing of alternatives not only lends significance to dilemmas of all kinds, but puts an emphasis on the process of choosing which at times obscures the substance of the choice eventually made. Motives tend to rival deeds, intentions to vie with acts, as objects of focal interest and importance.

[1] *Robinson Crusoe*, in *Romances and Narratives of Daniel Defoe*, ed. George A. Aitken, 16 vols. (1895), 1, 90; italics mine.

By hedging each assertion with counterstatements or uneasy qualifications, Crusoe conveys his apprehensiveness as forcibly as by the content of his remarks. His final words do not bring the sequence of thoughts to a definitive conclusion, nor could a decision either to move or to stay dispel retroactively the misgivings he has already expressed. This pattern too is characteristic of the handling of serious ethical questions in Defoe's novels. Except when a character has become so hardened in a course of behavior as to act out of habit rather than choice, his overt deeds will be preceded by a marshalling of his circumstances and motives, and those of everyone around him. Such hopes and fears, doubts and convictions, incentives and restraints, will vary in intrinsic weight and in relevance to the character's actual situation; between them, but on a far greater scale, there will often be the same contrariety that we find within the sentence from *Robinson Crusoe*. One effect of this has already been suggested: our attention is shifted from the ultimate act to the various factors that influence it. But the multiplicity and mutual contradictoriness of these factors have a further effect: a character becomes in some sense the sum of them all—the motives he fails to act on as well as those he finally endorses. When he describes himself as feeling or wanting or believing one thing *and yet* another *but still* another, he embraces all three, mutually exclusive as they may seem. What appear to be rejections are actually accretions; the process is *in*clusive, not *con*clusive.

In a useful discussion of "Some Aspects of Defoe's Prose," Bonamy Dobrée observes that Defoe's more aristocratic contemporaries wrote "with a tone of authority, with the calm and sometimes infuriating assurance of a dominant class," whereas Defoe's prose "seems to miss calm assurance, especially after the humiliation of prison and pillory." "We are sensible," Dobrée adds, "that Defoe is arguing with equals:

Swift is informing his reader with the voice of authority."[2] In *A Journal of the Plague Year*, Defoe maintains an air of "arguing with equals," but this quality can perhaps be better accounted for in affective than in genetic terms—as the book's way of persuading readers of the validity of various "*Observations or Memorials*," rather than as an expression of the author's personality or middle-class background. In the *Journal*, Defoe uses the materials and methods of both history and novel, partly for the sake of veracious and vivid narration, and partly for forensic purposes. Among the "novelistic" traits that serve as means to forensic ends, the characterization of the narrator is possibly most important, and will be examined in the pages that follow; a similar case could be made for many of the "historical" features of the book, such as its use of contemporary edicts and documentary records.[3] By showing what has happened, Defoe not only establishes the

[2] In *Pope and His Contemporaries: Essays Presented to George Sherburn*, ed. James L. Clifford and Louis A. Landa (Oxford, 1949), pp. 171-72, 179. Cf. also John F. Ross, *Swift and Defoe: A Study in Relationship* (Berkeley and Los Angeles, 1941), pp. 109-24, and *passim*.

[3] Defoe's use of the Bills of Mortality has been regarded as a pioneering instance of statistically based historiography, and there is no doubt that Defoe intended such materials to give an impression of rigorous accuracy; like the itemized bookkeeping in his novels, these quantitative data in the *Journal* help to suggest the narrator's scrupulous fidelity to fact. But that Defoe's object is as much rhetorical as scientific is indicated by his skepticism towards the "official" figures, especially when they fail to bear out his own position on one or another disputed issue—e.g., "The Weekly Bills are the only Evidence on the other side, and those Bills were not of Credit enough, at least with me, to support an *Hypothesis* or determine a Question of such Importance as this" (ed. Louis A. Landa, Oxford English Novels [1969], p. 205; all further references are to this edition). On the importance of the Bills of Mortality in determining the temporal and geographical structure of the *Journal*, see F. Bastian's valuable article, "Defoe's *Journal of the Plague Year* Reconsidered," *RES*, n.s. xvi (1965), 161-62, and Landa's masterly Introduction to the Oxford English Novels edition, pp. xxxviii-xxxix.

53

possibility of its happening again, but employs matters of fact to gain acceptance for what are at best matters of belief. To ascertain and reveal truths about a past plague is not his only goal; it is also an important means to another goal, which is to persuade readers to adopt a certain attitude in face of a new plague, and towards life's dangers and perplexities in general. The apparatus of history, in other words, serves to reinforce the author's opinions by conferring on them the status of experienced verities. At the same time, it lends them greater urgency by shifting the context of enquiry from the novel's realm of hypothesis to history's domain of actuality.

Both as a character within the *Journal* and as an interpreter of the past, Defoe's "H. F." tries to maintain an outlook that is at once reasonable and religious. In their immediate responses to the plague, as well as in their subsequent writings about it, many of the narrator's contemporaries had fallen into superstition on the one hand and atheism on the other. Defoe's spokesman tries to distinguish himself from earlier clerical writers, whose uncritical zeal might savor of "ignorance and enthusiasm" to readers of the 1720's,[4] but he is equally wary of the materialism and infidelity associated with the medical profession. He must avoid "preaching a Ser-

---

[4] Bastian cites *God's Terrible Voice in the City* (1667), by the dissenting minister Thomas Vincent, as one "highly declamatory and emotional account" ("Defoe's *Journal* Reconsidered," pp. 162-63); and Landa observes that by Defoe's day "only an occasional writer was willing to defend the extreme position that the plague is an extraordinary, direct, and immediate interposition of the deity, an intervention in or suspension of the laws of nature" (Introduction, p. xxi). Elsewhere Defoe proposes to write "without any canting Expressions, or straining of Words, without any pharisaical Gingle, or the odious Hypocrisie of a pretending Sanctity," and H. F.'s religiosity is tempered by the same considerations (*Mist's Journal*, April 5, 1719, in William Lee, *Daniel Defoe: His Life, and Recently Discovered Writings*, 3 vols. [1869], II, 31).

mon instead of writing a History," yet "a Discourse full of learned Simplicity" will be no less ridiculous and even more blameworthy, inasmuch as it is worse to slight than to exaggerate God's role in human affairs.[5] To establish an anonymous saddler as a more reliable commentator on the plague than the physicians and divines whose treatises on the subject were already in print, Defoe has to invest his narrator with authority; at the heart of his method is a constant vacillation, the very reverse of "calm assurance."

"I cou'd give a great many such Stories as these," a typical sentence begins, ". . . which in the long Course of that dismal Year, I met with, *that is* heard of, and which are very certain to be true, or very near the Truth; that is to say, true in the General, for no Man could at such a Time, learn all the Particulars."[6] Here the qualifying phrases tone down assertions rather than opposing them with equally emphatic counterassertions, and testify to H. F.'s care in sorting out hearsay and speculation from fact. This technique sometimes suggests the narrator's determination to do justice to differing opinions: many passages have the form, "I am, verily, perswaded that . . . some have been critical enough to say, that . . . I dare not affirm that; but this I must own, that . . ."[7] Sometimes

[5] Pp. 247, 75. In *The Consolidator* (1705), Defoe says, "Physicians are generally Atheists, and Atheists are universally Fools" (p. 29). Although H. F.'s tone is usually respectful rather than ironic, the same principle is implicit in much of the *Journal*, and now and then becomes overt, esp. at p. 246. As Landa points out, however, many medical tracts did acknowledge that the plague came from God, even though they tended to concentrate on natural causes once they had "paid [their] respects to the theological view": see his remarks on Nathaniel Hodges (whose work Defoe is known to have used), Sir Richard Blackmore, Diemerbrock, and Boghurst, Introduction, pp. xx-xxii.

[6] P. 52; cf. pp. 116, 162, 201.

[7] Pp. 178-79; "the general Notion . . . went about . . . tho' I cannot say, but there might be some Truth in it too, but not so general as

it makes clear that H. F. is open-minded but by no means credulous: "I cannot say, but that . . . and I think . . . and I have heard that . . . but I must say I believe nothing of its being so common . . . nor did it seem to be so rational."[8] And sometimes it shows that the narrator can be trusted to take a reasonable position on controverted questions: "I will not undertake to say, as some do, that . . . but this I may say, that . . ."[9] This guardedness is crucial to H. F.'s intended self-image. "It is much to the Satisfaction of me that write," he declares late in the book, "as well as those that read, to be able to say, that every thing is set down with Moderation, and rather within Compass than beyond it" (238). In other words, Defoe's object in making so many modifications and concessions is often to win credit for his narrator's scrupulous veracity, for his command of conflicting data, and particularly for his good judgment. Discussions of the book that stress its narrative realism tend to overlook the latter point, but in my opinion Defoe is just as concerned with persuasively interpreting the plague as with graphically recreating it.

This is to say that he conceives of the plague not only as a series of events to be brought to life, but also as a series of questions to be answered. How did the plague begin? Could

---

was reported" (p. 54); "This I believe was in Part true, tho' I do not affirm it: But it is not at all unlikely, seeing . . ." (p. 214).

[8] P. 83; cf. such phrases as "I cannot say with Satisfaction what I know is repeated with great Assurance, that . . ." (p. 78); or the sequence "It was reported, that. . . . But as I cannot easily credit any thing so vile . . . I can only relate it and leave it undetermined" (p. 63).

[9] P. 211; cf. the discussion of the fate of quacks: "Some fancied they were all swept off in the Infection to a Man . . . but I cannot go that Length neither; that Abundance of them died is certain, many of them came within the Reach of my own Knowledge; but that all of them were swept away I much question; I believe rather, [that many of them fled]. . . . This however is certain, not a Man of them appear'd for a great while" (p. 240).

it have been anticipated? What was God's role in it? How was it spread? Was there any way to prevent or avoid it? What was the best way to treat it? Did it help to shut up houses? Or to keep fires burning indoors and out? What finally brought the plague to an end? Such questions not only provide structural units for the greater part of the *Journal*, but they give the book its intensely purposeful spirit. The narrator is always attempting to resolve one or another difficulty: in recounting what happened, he is generally laying out facts that call for explanation, or charting out the range of practical and theoretical responses which those facts elicited from him and his contemporaries. Stories of what people did and thought, however striking in their own right, are presented as so many hypothetical answers to whatever question is under consideration at the moment; as materials, in other words, which serve to define or defend H. F.'s own position on a given question, and which the reader is invited to weigh as critically, as sympathetically, and as earnestly as if he were in the same circumstances.[10] As previous commentators have noted, the *Journal* is astutely topical: it appeared at a time when the plague was raging in Provence, and the possibility of its reaching England was widely feared. Critics have also suggested that by dramatizing the horrors of 1665, the *Journal* lent implicit support to the government's controversial anti-plague measure of 1721, an embargo on shipping from the

[10] "It was [Defoe's] interest as well as his inclination," Bastian maintains, "to deal almost exclusively in facts"; a more accurate view of Defoe's preoccupations, in my opinion, is that (as Bastian elsewhere observes) "He was continually led away into the discussion of some generalization or opinion, so that the work became an uneasy compromise between a narrative and a commentary" ("Defoe's *Journal* Reconsidered," pp. 166, 169). But why an "uneasy compromise"? The two aims are not conflicting but complementary, so that the *Journal* becomes rather "history ordered and infused with an interpretation" (Landa, Introduction, p. xxxix).

Mediterranean.[11] But besides addressing a leading issue of the day and justifying a policy of those in power, the *Journal* is history-with-a-purpose in a more basic sense. Like the fact of isolation in *Robinson Crusoe*, the plague poses a series of vital questions, which H. F. and his fellow Londoners are forced to grapple with. In his own life, the reader may face no more threat of finding himself in a plague-stricken city than of finding himself shipwrecked on a desert island, but in both cases he is compelled to put himself in the predicaments described. Yet the process does not end in a vicarious experience: this is rather a way of inducing the reader to re-examine his own habitual assumptions and values, and to embrace an attitude compounded as the narrator's is of rationality and piety.

The narrator's dilemma as the plague approaches illustrates some of these generalizations. It is not the earliest instance of uncertainty in the book—conflicting hypotheses begin jostling one another in the very first sentence—but the scene is worth examining in detail because it is so complete a specimen of the Defoean case of conscience, and so typical a treatment of practical and speculative as well as ethical questions in the *Journal*. The problem is first presented as the narrator's: "I now began to consider seriously with my Self, concerning my own Case, and how I should dispose of my self; that is to say, whether I should resolve to stay in *London*, or shut up my House and flee, as many of my Neighbours did." Whatever more abstract or theoretical issues it may raise, the topic is rooted firmly from the outset in an actual case. Immediately, though, H. F. generalizes his predicament: his next words are, "I have set this particular down so fully, because I know

[11] See Paul Dottin, *Daniel De Foe et ses Romans* (Paris and London, 1924), p. 586; John Robert Moore, *Daniel Defoe: Citizen of the Modern World* (Chicago, 1958), p. 320; Manuel Schonhorn, "Defoe's *Journal of the Plague Year*: Topography and Intention," *RES*, n.s. XIX (1968), 396-97.

58

not but it may be of Moment to those who come after me, if they come to be brought to the same Distress, and to the same Manner of making their Choice and therefore I desire this Account may pass with them, rather for a Direction to themselves to act by, than a History of my actings, seeing it may not be of one Farthing value to them to note what became of me" (8). This sentence makes explicit the aim to involve the reader spoken of earlier: the narrative is to be regarded not as "History" but as "Direction," and its "value" is held to consist in its potential utility to those "brought to the same Distress." The emphasis on engaging the reader is unmistakable, yet the process would appear to be more crudely didactic than my previous remarks suggested. It is not only H. F.'s ultimate decision to stay in London, however, that is offered as exemplary, but also the "Manner of making [his] Choice"; he eventually advises that the wisest policy is to flee the plague, so that in offering readers "a Direction to themselves to act by," he is not prescribing a decision but recommending a mode of deliberating. This mode bears the marks of traditional casuistry.[12]

We already know from the title page, of course, what the narrator's eventual decision will be, since the book is "Written by a CITIZEN who continued all the while in *London*." But this knowledge does not lessen the drama of the pages that follow, in which he recounts the mental conflict that preceded his decision. Indeed, he presents the various considerations that influenced him in such a way that the difficult process of choosing, rather than the substance of the eventual choice, becomes the episode's center of gravity. Thus he ranges competing motives and obligations on either side of the question, so as to show that he has compelling reasons both to leave and

---

[12] For evidence that the question of fleeing the plague had been regarded as a significant case of conscience for two centuries, see Landa, Introduction, pp. xxix-xxxiii.

stay. For instance, he declares that "I had two important things before me; the one was the carrying on my Business and Shop . . . and the other was the Preservation of my Life" (8). No explicit judgment as to the relative weight of the two is required: the sheer fact of their juxtaposition establishes a degree of equivalence between them. The question of God's role in the plague poses further difficulties. For a time, H. F. leans towards the position that since any such visitation is "a Stroke from Heaven" and "a Messenger of his Vengeance," and since God has both the power and the "undisputed Right" to preserve or destroy his creatures as he pleases, man's best and only course is to go calmly about his business, trusting entirely to divine protection, and acquiescing passively in whatever God wills. The narrator's brother, however, associates this doctrine with *"Turks* and *Mahometans,"* and suggests that despite its apparent humility and self-abasement, such a creed can issue in reckless audacity: "presuming upon their profess'd predestinating Notions, and of every Man's End being predetermin'd and unalterably before-hand decreed, [the Moslems] would go unconcern'd into infected Places, and converse with infected Persons, by which Means they died at the Rate of Ten or Fifteen Thousand a Week" (11). What might seem the most pious possible response to the plague may therefore have "mischievous Consequences," for one's spiritual soundness as well as one's bodily health. H. F. is never drawn to the hypothesis that God has nothing to do with the plague: such "audacious Boldness," later ascribed to "a dreadful Set of Fellows" in London, is even worse than that of the Turks. But if he is in no danger of falling into atheism, he eventually adopts an attitude that is meant to seem equally free from religious fanaticism. "The best Method I can advise any Person to take in such a Case," he concludes, "especially, if he be one that makes Conscience of his Duty, and would be directed what to do in it . . . [is] that he should keep his Eye upon the particular Providences which occur . . . and look upon them complexly, as they regard one another, and as altogether regard the Question before him, and then I think, he may safely take them for Intimations from Heaven of what is his unquestion'd Duty to do in such a Case" (10). H. F. resolves his dilemma by recognizing that the operation of divine providence does not preclude human responsibility, and that far from encouraging supineness, heaven will direct and sustain the actions of those who carefully observe and interpret the visible manifestations of its will.[18]

For our purposes, the doctrinal content of this proposition matters less than its tone, and the manner in which it is reached. It is noteworthy that this "advice" or "Direction" extends only to the decision-making process, not to the substance of the eventual choice: the narrator suggests a "Method" for discovering one's duty rather than laying down the duty itself. In other words, this is an extremely undogmatic sort of prescription, that leaves open the question of going or staying. Moreover, it prepares us to endorse H. F.'s own decision to stay, and yet to grant the justice of his view that most people would do better to flee. More will be said about this paradox after a further point is made about the effect of assigning distinct dramatic roles to the narrator and his brother in the debate between them. H. F.'s initial deliberations on God's role in the plague evince his confirmed religiosity, but his resolution to stay is challenged—first "quite confuted," later "quite turn'd," still later "chang'd . . . again" (9, 11, 12)— by the arguments of the brother. It is he who has observed the dire effect of "predestinating Notions" among Mohammed-

---

[18] Defoe elaborates this thesis elsewhere in his writings: see esp. "On Listening to the Voice of Providence," *Serious Reflections*, in *Romances and Narratives*, III, 190-91. Cf. also my *Defoe and Spiritual Autobiography* (Princeton, 1965), pp. 188-91, and J. Paul Hunter, *The Reluctant Pilgrim* (Baltimore, 1966), pp. 51 f.

ans, and labels the behavior of all such people "ridiculous,"
"foolhardy," and presumptuous. "Tho' a very Religious Man
himself," this brother is a man of the world; he is not a devil's
advocate like Amy in *Roxana*, or the Colchester rake and
Mother Midnight in *Moll Flanders*, yet he repeatedly dis-
lodges H. F. from his convictions, if never from his house in
the City. In the process, the narrator's grounds for staying are
clarified: not explicitly defended, but allowed to develop a
cumulative urgency. His irresoluteness does not ultimately let
him yield to his brother's advice (as is so often the case in
Roxana and *Moll Flanders*), but enables him in some sense
to incorporate his brother's opposed point of view into his
own. At the end of the scene—his decision to stay in London
confirmed by a providentially found Biblical text—H. F. declares that "from that Moment I resolv'd that I would stay
in the Town, and casting my self entirely upon the Goodness
and Protection of the Almighty, would not seek any other
Shelter whatever; and that as my Times were in his Hands,
he was able to keep me in a Time of the Infection as in a
Time of Health; and if he did not think fit to deliver me,
still I was in his Hands, and it was meet he should do with
me as should seem good to him" (13). Taken in isolation,
these lines might suggest a relapse into the Islamic inertia discredited earlier by the merchant brother, but they follow pages
of troubled wavering, in which H. F. has been "greatly op-
press'd in [his] Mind" and has struggled "to resolve . . . what
was [his] Duty to do" (12). By taking into account the arguments for fleeing, as well as the "strong Impressions," the
"visible Call," and the "Intimations" by which Providence
seems to be directing him to stay, he counters any inclination
the reader might otherwise have to regard his decision as impulsive or rash. His brother's contrary arguments and his own
prolonged misgivings help to prevent his final resolution from
seeming blindly superstitious. H. F. can assert himself so

strongly because he has so fully felt and acknowledged the other side of the case.[14]

It is important to note that the brother's arguments are never refuted, and invariably sway the narrator for a time. Although not finally acted upon, they are assimilated into H. F.'s total vision: like most things said and done by secondary characters in Defoe's novels, they can be regarded as expressing or projecting one side of the hero's own nature or outlook. Thus we are not startled to find the narrator asserting one hundred pages later, "I am much for Peoples flying away and emptying such a Town as this, upon the first Appearance of a like Visitation," and that "all People who have any possible Retreat, should make use of it in Time, and begone," or still later that "it is my opinion, and I must leave it as a Prescription, (*viz.*) *that the best Physick against the Plague is to run away from it.* I know People encourage themselves, by saying, God is able to keep us in the midst of Danger, and able to overtake us when we think our selves out of Danger; and

[14] By the same token, the narrator's subsequent failures of nerve (pp. 76, 177, and *passim*), do not belie but help to evince his basic firmness of character. He illustrates Defoe's belief that a thoughtful courage, restrained by a sense of one's weaknesses and sustained by an alert faith in God's providence, is better able to withstand prolonged trials than a more unhesitating, heroic kind of courage. H. F. is not unflinchingly brave in the face of danger, since his spirit flags time and again; not unflinchingly gallant in his duty, since he shrinks from being an examiner of houses partly on selfish grounds; and not unflinchingly steadfast in his convictions, since he regularly modifies his boldest assertions. Yet he is unflinching in his curiosity and his candor, and because his most characteristic role within the narrative is to inquire and deliberate, his very waverings seem signs of strength rather than weakness. He is rather severe towards the "Boldness" which some men owe to "their Ignorance, and despising the Hand of their Maker, which is a criminal kind of Desperation, and not a true Courage"; and towards the "precipitant Courage" which he castigates as "unwary Conduct," "imprudent rash Conduct," and "rash and foolish Conduct" (pp. 238, 225-27).

this kept Thousands in the Town, whose Carcasses went into the great Pits by Cart Loads; and who, if they had fled from the Danger, had, I believe, been safe from the Disaster; at least 'tis probable they had been safe."[15] Here he adopts the very words which his brother had used to dissuade him from staying in London. But no real inconsistency is involved, since H. F. had never challenged the soundness of his brother's maxim about running away. What he had denied was its applicability to his own situation: the special circumstances of his case had excepted him from the general rule, valid as he acknowledges it to be. Defoe's fiction contains innumerable variations on this fundamental encounter between the exception and the rule; his heroes and heroines constantly justify— or seek to extenuate—nonobservance of ordinary laws by appealing to their extraordinary circumstances.

In his decision to stay in London, the narrator obeys a conscience attuned to and sanctioned by "Intimations from Heaven," rather than precepts founded on prudence and experience. The rival claims of duty and expediency are both recognized, and the triumph of duty is engaging partly because the merchant brother's voice of worldly wisdom is allowed its full force. Late in the book H. F. defends one of his opinions with the remark, "let the Atheistic part of Mankind call my Saying this what they please, it is no Enthusiasm" (246): he is constantly at pains to steer a course of judicious piety, untainted by atheism on the one hand or enthusiasm on the other. This object is clear in his discussion of how the plague is communicated. Convinced that it is spread by "Infection," he supports this theory partly by representing it as a reasonable middle course, which neither ascribes everything to the direct hand of God, nor lays all to the exclusive operation of natural causes. His first enunciation of the contagion

[15] Pp. 121, 197-98; note also the progressive muting of the emphatic "Prescription" in the second sentence.

theory is very emphatic, but immediately gives way to uncertainties; speaking of the fatal progress of the plague within families that were shut up together, he says: "This put it out of Question to me, that the Calamity was spread by Infection, that is to say, by some certain Steams, or Fumes, which the Physicians call *Effluvia*, by the Breath, or by the Sweat, or by the Stench of the Sores of the Sick Persons, or some other way, perhaps, beyond even the Reach of the Physicians themselves" (74). It should be noted that these conflicting hypotheses do not really weaken the force of the initial assertion, since only the mechanism of infection is called in question, not the fact of infection: by introducing a more tentative and doubtful note, these hypotheses modify the assured tone of the main proposition without abating its substance. "I shall give some Instances," the narrator continues, "that cannot but convince those who seriously consider it; and I cannot but with some Wonder, find some People, now the Contagion is over, talk of its being an immediate Stroke from Heaven, without the Agency of Means, . . . which I look upon with Contempt, as the Effect of manifest Ignorance and Enthusiasm; likewise the Opinion of others, who talk of infection being carried on by the Air only, . . . a Discourse full of learned Simplicity, and manifested to be so by universal Experience."[16] H. F. is equally wary of the zeal of the ignorant and the unbelief of the medically learned.

His discussion of meteorological portents show a similar caution. He begins by ridiculing the superstitious awe in which the comet was held by "the old Women, and the Phlegmatic Hypocondriac Part of the other Sex, who I could almost call *old Women* too" (19). But because he is intent on dissociating

---

[16] P. 75; for the background of the controversy between contagionists and miasmatists, which Defoe enters as a contagionist both here and in *Due Preparations for the Plague*, see Landa, Introduction, pp. xxvi-xxix.

himself from enthusiasts and atheists alike, he lays aside irony for a more guarded statement of his position. After recounting the fears and "fancies" which the comet gave rise to in the popular mind, the narrator says

"I must confess, [I] had so much of the common Notion of such Things in my Head, that I was apt to look upon them, as the Forerunners and Warnings of Gods Judgments. . . . But I cou'd not at the same Time carry these Things to the heighth that others did, knowing, too that natural Causes are assign'd by the Astronomers for such Things . . . so that they cannot be so perfectly call'd the Fore-runners, or Fore-tellers, much less the procurers of such Events, as Pestilence, War, Fire, and the like. But let my Thoughts, and the Thoughts of the Philosophers be, or have been what they will, these Things had a more than ordinary Influence upon the Minds of the common People."[17]

[17] P. 20; in *Mist's Weekly Journal*, Defoe's discussion of meteors attempts a similar reconciliation of religion and rationality: "though I am no more for terrifying ignorant People than they ought to be, or for crying out of Miracles and Judgments, threatning Plagues and Scourges, upon the Appearance of Things in the Air, however uncommon; yet . . . I am not for taking all supernatural Agency away, and taking, as it were, the Power out of God's Hand. . . . this would be an Extreme as irreligious as the other is said to be pernicious. . . . Let us keep the middle way . . . and neither esteem such things altogether miraculous and supernatural, nor yet entirely take them out of the Hand of him that governs Nature, as if he had nothing at all to do with them" (*A Collection of Miscellany Letters, Selected out of Mist's Weekly Journal*, Vol. 1 [1722], 101, 103). Elsewhere, Defoe's views on meteorology vary according to his rhetorical objective at the moment. In *The Compleat English Gentleman* (1729), he offers a completely rational account of comets, in the course of recommending scientific study as a part of genteel education (ed. Karl D. Bülbring [1890], p. 154). In light of such marked differences of emphasis, one can safely conclude only that H. F.'s moderate position on comets is appropriate to the general outlook which this book seeks to advance.

In such passages the narrator's own attitude is too ambivalent to permit sustained irony. Irony may provisionally establish his distance from an extreme view, but since the position he himself adopts is usually at some judicious midpoint between what he has satirized and the opposite extreme, he sooner or later abandons irony for equivocation.

Elsewhere in the book he finds it more difficult to keep from "lessening the Awe of the Judgments of God . . . which ought always to be on our Minds on such Occasions as these," and at the same time to avoid "putting it upon Supernaturals and Miracle" (193, 194). For instance, he inquires at length whether the plague was an instrument of divine vengeance on human sins, and specifically whether malefactors were noticeably singled out as victims. To both questions his answer is strongly affirmative—but just as strongly hedged; his qualifications have a crucial effect on the tone of his judgments, in that they lend an air of modest reasonableness to a position that would otherwise smack of zealous presumption. This is most noteworthy in the episode involving the carousers at the *"Pye-Tavern,"* men given to "Revelling and roaring extravagences" in the very midst of the plague (64). One night in the presence of the narrator they taunt a neighbor who has been brought to the tavern to recover from the shock of seeing the rest of his family pitched from a "Dead-Cart" into the "dreadful Gulph" of a mass grave. Besides jeering at the man's despondency, they add "some very profane, and even blasphemous Expressions" (64). H. F. comes away convinced that "the Hand of that Judgment which had visited the whole City" will "glorify his Vengeance upon them" (66), and sure enough within a few days "they were every one of them carried into the great Pit" themselves (66-67). This outline makes the narrator sound complacently priggish, and suggests a baldly exemplary story. But the bulk of the episode is so different in spirit that H. F.'s attitude, as well as the sequence of crime and punishment that he recounts, seems reasonable and just rather than arbitrary and oppressive.

For one thing, he engages himself in the action: he commiserates with his bereaved neighbor, and "gently reprov'd" the "hardened creatures" for abusing the poor man and persisting in "their Atheistical profane Mirth" at such a season. They respond by shifting their contempt to him, "making a Jest of my calling the Plague the Hand of God, mocking, and even laughing at the word Judgment, as if the Providence of God had no Concern in the inflicting such a desolating Stroke; and [maintaining] that the People calling upon God, as they saw the Carts carrying away the dead Bodies was all enthusiastick, absurd, and impertinent." In his first account of the incident he says that "I was indeed astonished at the Impudence of the Men, tho' not at all discomposed at their Treatment of me" (65); later, however, he reflects that "I had indeed, been in some Passion, at first, with them" (69). The reason for this inconsistency becomes clear only gradually. His passion, he explains, "was really raised, not by any Affront they had offered me personally, but by the Horror their blaspheming Tongues fill'd me with; however, I was doubtful in my Thoughts, whether the Resentment I retain'd was not all upon my own private Account, for they had given me a great deal of ill Language too." Filled with these misgivings he retires for an evening of charitable prayer and self-examination: "By this I not only did my Duty . . . to pray for those who dispitefully used me, but I fully try'd my own Heart . . . that it was not fill'd with any Spirit of Resentment. . . . I humbly recommend the Method to all those that would know, or be certain, how to distinguish between their real Zeal for the Honour of God, and the Effects of their private Passions and Resentment." Such remarks are psychologically realistic—but also rhetorically effective, for they help to combat the anticipated objection that the theory of plague-as-punishment is both presumptuous and uncharitable. H. F. faithfully records the worst that others can say of him, as well as the reproaches of his own conscience, and his modest candor disarms us. The fact that he has "fully try'd [his] own Heart" and has weighed everything "seriously, and with the utmost Earnestness" scarcely proves, of course, that his judgment is correct, but it does further suggest the humane sobriety of H. F. and of the "Method" of judging that he professes.

Other passages defend by different means the wrath-of-God theory against imputations of arbitrariness and self-righteousness. The following sentence, for instance, unfolds in a characteristically undogmatic manner:

> I went Home indeed, griev'd and afflicted in my Mind, at the Abominable Wickedness of those Men not doubting, however, that they would be made dreadful Examples of God's Justice; for I look'd upon this dismal Time to be a particular Season of Divine Vengeance, and that God would, on this Occasion, single out the proper Objects, of his Displeasure, in a more especial and remarkable Manner, than at another Time; and that, tho' I did believe that many good People would, and did, fall in the common Calamity, and that it was no certain Rule to judge of the eternal State of any one, by their being distinguish'd in such a Time of general Destruction, neither one Way or other; yet I say, it could not but seem reasonable to believe, that God would not think fit to spare by his Mercy such open declared Enemies (68).

The sentence continues for nearly a dozen more lines, but this sample adequately conveys its substance—and, more significantly, its structure and tone. A note of certainty, struck initially with such phrases as "indeed" and "not doubting," is progressively qualified and eventually replaced by the tentativeness of "it could not but seem reasonable to believe."[18] On the one hand, H. F. expresses his conviction that these "desperate Wretches" will be speedily struck down, thus supporting his general thesis about God's punitive intent in this "Day of Visitation." On the other hand, he acknowledges that the innocent suffer along with the guilty, and that no just inferences about their damnation can be drawn from the death of plague victims. But such considerations do not cause him to abandon his opinion; rather, they lead to a more guarded restatement of it. This is a frequent function of negative evidence in the *Journal*: it does not change the narrator's mind, but serves to keep firm contentions from seeming harsh or precipitate. The sequence is cumulative rather than dialectical, so that without tempering the substance of his opinions, the inclusion of an opposing fact or theory often moderates their tone. Only in a rhetorical sense is it true to say that all relevant data have been taken into account; yet this is the impression that H. F.'s deliberations generally convey, and it is an important source of his persuasiveness.

[18] In his polemical tracts on political questions, Defoe seizes on such phrases as signs of weakness in the positions of his adversaries: "He could have no other Foundation to begin upon," he says of one author, "and therefore is obliged to fly to the unhappy Shift of begging the Question throughout the Whole Work, which, to that Purpose, we find filled up with the Phrases necessary to such a Way of Arguing, *viz. It may be concluded, it may be supposed, it is Reasonable to believe, it is not therefore unlikely, it is probable*, and the like Figures of Speech, which in Rhetorick are always taken to signify something uncertain, and to argue from which is therefore called begging the Question" (*Not*[tingh]*am Politicks Examined* [1713], p. 6; according to John Robert Moore, this pamphlet was "apparently written in great haste and in anger" [*A Checklist of the Writings of Daniel Defoe* (Bloomington, 1960), p. 101]). The *Journal* is "filled up with" these phrases, but they serve to suggest the narrator's moderation, and the complexity of the problems posed by the plague, rather than seeming an "unhappy Shift" used to insinuate unfounded arguments.

The question which recurs most frequently in the *Journal*, and which illustrates most clearly Defoe's concern to interpret as well as recreate the past, is whether shutting up houses in time of plague is a sound policy. This broad topic has various aspects. Does a quarantine of victims effectually prevent the spread of the plague? What are the effects of confining the healthy together with those already stricken? Are there practicable and equitable ways of carrying out such a policy? In the course of the book the narrator repeatedly weighs the actual or supposed benefits of the quarantine policy against its demonstrable shortcomings, and his opposition becomes increasingly clear and emphatic. His first mention of shutting up houses grants that "it was with good Success; for in several Streets, where the Plague broke out, upon strict guarding the Houses that were infected . . . the Plague ceased in those Streets" (37). There is a similar air of open-mindedness about the statement that "there was an absolute Necessity for it, that must be confess'd, unless some other Measures had been timely enter'd upon, and it was too late for that" (164). Such remarks are frequent, but they scarcely add up to an endorsement of the quarantine policy; on the contrary, they are concessions which H. F. can afford to make precisely because of the abundance and strength of his anti-quarantine evidence. The bulk of the narrative demonstrates that the Lord Mayor's orders for the "Sequestration of the Sick" were widely thwarted and evaded; that when they were put into practice, they produced various hardships without achieving the effects desired; and that whatever good they might have done was vastly outweighed by the suffering and harm they caused. Nevertheless the narrator recognizes all the arguments in favor of the quarantine: he thus diversifies what might have become wearisome reiterations of his position, and shows how candid and deliberate his own attitude is.[19]

[19] The traditional arguments for and against this policy, which had

71

Journal of the Plague Year

One plausible defense of shutting up houses is that injurious as it may have been to individual families, it promoted the welfare of the public at large. This argument is introduced several times, but always in a context that neutralizes it. The first suggestion that "it was a publick Good that justified the private Mischief" occurs in the middle of a paragraph that begins, "It is true, that the locking up the Doors of Peoples Houses . . . looked very hard and cruel; and many People perished in these miserable Confinements, which 'tis reasonable to believe, would not have been distemper'd if they had had Liberty" (47-48). For several pages H. F. goes on to recount the stratagems and the violence used by desperate families to escape "these miserable Confinements." Here the argument that public good outweighs personal hardship is not directly countered, but simply submerged in a mass of evidence as to the extent and severity of the "private Mischief" caused by shutting up houses. One hundred pages later the argument is restated, but so as to be weakened by its very formulation as well as muted by its surroundings. Shutting up houses, H. F. reflects, "was authoriz'd by a Law, it had the publick Good in view, as the End chiefly aim'd at, and all the private Injuries that were done by the putting it in Execution, must be put to the account of the publick Benefit" (158). This apparent vindication of the quarantine policy is undercut by the suggestion that whatever law it was "authoriz'd by," and whatever beneficial end it "chiefly aim'd at," only private injuries were actually "done by the putting it in Execution." "It is doubtful to this day," the narrator continues, "whether in the whole it contributed any thing to the stop of the Infection, and indeed, I cannot say it did; for . . ." Although the tone remains cautious and moderate, the paradox that public benefits justified

been "common practice in England from 1518" and was "perhaps the most extensively discussed of all preventive measures," are surveyed by Landa, p. 267.

72

private mischiefs is further undermined: what were the vaunted public benefits?

Moreover, by the time a house was known to be infected, its occupants would all be either "stone dead" or "run away for Fear of being shut up," so that there was no point in declaring such a house infected and shutting it up. "This might be sufficient," H. F. declares, "to convince any reasonable Person, that as it was not in the Power of the Magistrates, or any human Methods or Policy, to prevent the spreading of the Infection; so that this way of shutting up of Houses was perfectly insufficient for that End. Indeed it seemed to have no manner of publick Good in it, equal or proportionable to the grievous Burthen that it was to the particular Families, that were so shut up; and as far as I was employed by the publick [as an examiner of houses] in directing that Severity, I frequently found occasion to see, that it was incapable of answering the End" (166). What with the opening and closing appeals to "any reasonable Person" and to his own actual experience, and the assertions first and last that shutting up houses was "perfectly insufficient" and "incapable of answering" its end, this passage roundly damns the quarantine policy. Yet between these absolute repudiations comes a comparative judgment, more guardedly introduced ("seemed") and itself carefully qualified, apparently for precision's sake ("equal or proportionable"): without in the least modifying the substance of the neighboring negations, this proposition somewhat tempers their magisterial finality.

Similar patterns of inflection are found throughout the book. Whenever the narrator's judgments verge on the peremptory, something is added to restore a more tentative atmosphere. Usually these retreats from certainty do not raise doubts but allay them, since they suggest a horror of exaggeration, a determination to see that all is "set down with Moderation, and rather within Compass than beyond it." At the first sign of hyperbole there is an immediate "at least I have great Reason to believe so" (78), or "at least, that ever I cou'd hear of" (21). Any proposition that is at all sweeping—"the Danger of immediate Death to ourselves, took away all Bowels of Love, all Concern for one another"—will be followed with some such abatement as, "I speak in general, for there were many Instances of immovable Affection, Pity, and Duty in many, and some that came to my Knowledge; that is to say, by here-say. For I shall not take upon me to vouch the Truth of the Particulars" (115). Although such reservations may appear to be a sign of uncertainty, they are frequently used in the *Journal* to reinforce rather than weaken assured contentions.[20]

At other times, conflicting evidence is introduced to dramatize the limitations of reason: however diligently pursued, certainty about the plague is finally unattainable.[21] Numerous

[20] "No dead Bodies lay unburied or uncovered," H. F. asserts, "and if one walk'd from one end of the City to another, no Funeral or sign of it was to be seen in the Day-time." But in "some Accounts which others have published since," he continues, "they say, that the Dead lay unburied, which *I am assured was utterly false*; AT LEAST, IF it had been any where so, *it must ha' been* in Houses where the Living were gone from the Dead . . . and where no Notice was given to the Officers: All which amounts to *nothing at all in the Case at Hand; for this I am positive in*, having myself been employ'd a little in the Direction of that part. . . . I say, *I am sure* that there were no dead Bodies remain'd unburied; THAT IS TO SAY, none that the proper Officers knew of; . . . *for it is most certain*, they were buried as soon as they were found" (pp. 180-81). This is probably the most positive utterance in the *Journal*, and the decisiveness of the phrases I have italicized is finally increased, not lessened, by those in small capitals.

[21] The following sentence, in which the problem of "coming at the Knowledge of the true state of any Family" is waived rather than settled, represents a characteristic impasse: "Seeing then that we cou'd come at the certainty of Things by no Method but that of Enquiry of the Neighbours, or of the Family, and on that we cou'd not justly depend, it was not possible, but that the incertainty of this Matter wou'd remain as above" (p. 167).

passages set up learned debates only to suggest their futility. On the subject of street bonfires, "some of the Physicians insisted that they were not only no Benefit, but injurious to the Health of People: This they made a loud Clamour about. . . . On the other hand, others of the same Faculty . . . oppos'd them. . . . I cannot give a full Account of their Arguments on both Sides, only this I remember, that they cavil'd very much with one another; some were for . . . Others were for . . . and others were for neither one or other. Upon the whole, the Lord Mayor ordered no more Fires, and especially on this Account, namely, that the Plague was so fierce that they saw evidently it defied all Means . . . nothing answer'd, the Infection rag'd" (172-73). Irony at the expense of physicians is probably not Defoe's object here, except insofar as they "made a loud Clamour" and "cavil'd"; his larger point is that the human intellect cannot decipher, let alone check, the workings of the plague.

In many such passages, paradoxes are not resolved but allowed to stand as mementos of human fallibility. How, for instance, is one to recognize infected persons before the obvious (and fatal) external symptoms appear? "My Friend Doctor *Heath*," H. F. reports, "was of Opinion, that it might be known by the smell of their Breath; but then," he goes on, "who durst Smell to that Breath for his Information?" "I have heard, it was the opinion of others," he continues, "that it might be distinguish'd by the Party's breathing upon a piece of Glass," which under a microscope would reveal "strange monstrous and frightful Shapes, such as Dragons, Snakes, Serpents, and Devils, horrible to behold." Again the narrator balks: "But this I very much question the Truth of, and we had no Microscopes at that Time, as I remember, to make the Experiment with." The next hypothesis he seems to find more attractive: "It was the opinion also of another learned Man, that the Breath of such a Person would poison, and instantly kill a Bird," or that it would cause the bird to lay rotten eggs. "But those are Opinions which I never found supported by any Experiments, or heard of others that had seen it; so I leave them as I find them, only with this Remark; namely, that I think the Probabilities are very strong for them." As a final hypothesis, he notes that "Some have proposed that such Persons should breathe hard upon warm Water, and that they would leave an unusual Scum upon it." At this point one expects H. F. to adjudicate between the rival theories, or perhaps to advance one of his own, more firmly supported by experiments. He foils such expectations: "But from the whole I found, that the Nature of this Contagion was such, that it was impossible to discover it at all, or to prevent its spreading from one to another by any human Skill" (203). The narrator leads us into a quandary, from which he never quite rescues us. He assembles conflicting facts and theories partly to do justice as a historian to the actual theses advanced by earlier authorities, but in part he deploys them as Donne had used the artifices of rhetoric, "to trouble the understanding, to displace, and discompose and disorder the judgment."[22] They testify to the terrible power and inscrutability of the plague—and, correspondingly, to man's weakness; but what

[22] Sermon lxxi, quoted in Martin Price, *Swift's Rhetorical Art* (New Haven, 1953), p. 16. Although Schonhorn's stress on "the steady, moderate, and tolerant mind behind the journalistic presentation" seems to me justified, I question his contention that "Everything has been seen in the best possible light," so as to allay popular anxiety in face of a new outbreak of the plague ("Defoe's *Journal*: Topography and Intention," pp. 398, 396). H. F. wishes he "could but tell this Part, in such moving Accents as should alarm the very Soul of the Reader," he seeks to "make the hardest Heart move," he asks "What can be said to represent the Misery of these Times, more lively to the Reader, or to give him a more perfect Idea of a complicated Distress?" (pp. 104, 119, 177). The reader is often addressed as if he were the lethargic, complacent elder brother in *Due Preparations*: only by being startled into a sense of his danger and frailty can he be brought to a proper reliance on the reason and faith which he does (or should) possess.

keeps fatalistic gloom from taking over such scenes is H. F.'s confidence that although "human Skill" can neither comprehend nor control the plague, divine providence rules all. It is this confidence that makes the *Journal*'s most somber negations simultaneous affirmations; and it is perhaps this confidence that imparts a quality of classical tragedy to H. F.'s chronicle of death and desolation.

At certain points, however, the marshalling of various hypotheses prepares a kind of Gordian knot which the narrator's own opinion eventually cuts through, and the persuasiveness of his position is heightened by the exhaustive and impartial hearing which he allows others. It is said, for instance, that "there was a seeming propensity, or a wicked Inclination in those that were Infected to infect others." H. F. reports that "There have been great Debates among our Physicians, as to the Reason of this," and three different explanations are given. Again we are perplexed—"Who can decide when doctors disagree?"—but this time the narrator decisively cuts the knot: "But I choose to give this grave Debate a quite different turn, and answer it or resolve it all by saying, *That I do not grant the Fact*. On the contrary, I say, that the Thing is not really so" (153-54). The "seeming propensity" which elicited such "grave Debate" is dismissed as a fiction, contrived "to justify, or at least excuse" the "Severities" of country people towards fleeing Londoners. Another problem is resolved in similar fashion near the end of the book. None appear to have died of the plague between December 1664 and April 1665, and "the question seems to lie thus: Where lay the seeds of the infection all this while?" After summarizing the theories of "the Doctors" and "the Learned," H. F. continues, "But there is another way of solving all this Difficulty, which I think my own Remembrance of the thing will supply; and that is, the Fact [that none died between December and April] is not granted" (204-05).

77

In such passages, the narrator's characterization and the structure of his account work together to foster confidence in his views. First, Defoe makes H. F. becomingly deferential towards the authorities.[23] Then he shows that "the Learned" are in hopeless disagreement among themselves.[24] Next he indicates that their opposed hypotheses often seek to elucidate nonfacts, or rest on ingenious speculation rather than experiment; and perhaps most tellingly, he emphasizes that the plague "defied all Means" (172) and resisted "any human Skill" (203), that "all the Remedies . . . were found fruitless" (170-71), and that the physicians themselves "fell in the common Calamity" (36). The narrator, in contrast, has no special expertise; he is therefore more reliant on personal observation, and more disinterested, than those professionally committed to one or another theory of the plague.[25] H. F.'s

[23] "I am not of the Number of the Physic-Haters, or Physic-Despisers; on the contrary, I have often mentioned the regard I had to the Dictates of my particular Friend Dr. *Heath*" (p. 239). "The Contagion [*not* H. F.] despised all Medicine" (p. 245). The narrator's occasional irony is more often directed against the Court (pp. 15-16, 234), the astrologers and fortune-tellers (pp. 21, 24-27), the quacks (pp. 29-35), and—most slyly of all—the Anglican ministers who fled (pp. 235-36), than against the physicians, who are represented as skillful, brave, and diligent, but powerless to "stop God's Judgments, or prevent a Distemper eminently armed from Heaven, from executing the Errand it was sent about" (p. 36).

[24] In addition to the cavilling and clamor over bonfires cited earlier, cf. the dispute over indoor fires (pp. 219-20). A number of passages also point out the instability of learned judgments: for instance, "I know that some, even of our Physicians, thought, for a time, that . . . but they found Reason to alter their Opinion afterward" (p. 168).

[25] Whatever steps were to be taken in 1722, the narrator could have no personal stake in them: it is probably in order to stress this disinterestedness that Defoe inserts the note, apropos of the Moorfields cemetery, that "The Author of this Journal, lyes buried in that very Ground" (p. 233).
On the question of disinterestedness, it seems to me that what James Sutherland says of Defoe's early polemical tracts is also true of the *Journal*: "Their effectiveness was due in great part to the innocent

piety enables him to perceive certain truths which the physicians overlook because of their predominantly secular point of view; at the same time, his familiarity with the theories of Dr. Heath and "others of the same Faculty," his untiring investigations, and his rational turn of mind prevent him from falling into "an officious canting of religious things, preaching a Sermon instead of writing a History" (247).

The foregoing pages have suggested that the *Journal* is largely organized around topics rather than events, and that "*Remarkable Occurrences*" are adduced not only for their own sake, or for the sake of historical truth, but also to illustrate or justify H. F.'s answers to questions mooted by the plague. It has also been suggested, however, that these answers tend to be unprescriptive in spirit, and that the narrator does not propose his own actions (such as staying in London or venturing into the streets) as a pattern to be imitated. Are these two positions reconcilable? If Defoe had been as intent on rhetorical persuasion as on historical narration, would he not have set forth systematically the most proper measures to be adopted in case of a new visitation? In *Due Preparations for the Plague*, his recommendations are clear and emphatic;[26]

---

way in which Defoe habitually discussed the most controversial topics of the day. Here, he seems to say, are the facts; and here, after due consideration of them, are the thoughts that have occurred to me. I have no axe to grind in this matter; I am merely letting you know what is bound to happen if we do this, and what must inevitably follow if we do that. Take it or leave it, but please understand that I am perfectly unbiased. Yet the innocence is only in Defoe's manner" (*Defoe*, 2nd edn. [1950,] p. 66).

[26] Not only are "*the properest Measures to prevent*" the plague set forth more programmatically, but the narrator's prevailing air is conclusive and assured rather than tentative and guarded. Cf. the dismissive tone toward those who doubt that the plague is "what we call catching or contagious: However, to avoid cavilling, or making this work, which is written with a better design, a scene of debate, I leave them to their own notions, and those that please to believe them may

could so experienced a projector and polemicist have failed
to be equally explicit here, if persuasion had been an object?
In my opinion, the resolution of this difficulty lies in the
nature of what this book recommends, which is more a way
of confronting experience than a specific course of action.
"Usefulness is, or ought to be the Principal Aim of Historians,"
Defoe says in the *Review*; but such usefulnes may extend beyond charting "a programme for civil reform."[27] Although
various expedients are examined in detail, Defoe's conclusions
are generally negative, as the discussion of shutting up houses
has indicated; once the plague starts, no scheme yet devised
is capable of stopping it. We might conclude from this that
Defoe's aim is indeed polemic, but that he simply wants to
persuade readers of the necessity of the government's embargo
on Mediterranean shipping: the plague must be prevented
from reaching England at all costs, since no effectual steps
can be taken after the plague has broken out. But this seems
an unduly limited view of what the book proffers for our
assent. More fundamentally and pervasively, the *Journal* advocates a frame of mind which can be brought to bear on
perplexities of all kinds. It is an attitude at once rational and
religious, but what matters is not so much the ingredients
themselves, both of which turn up sooner or later in nearly
all of Defoe's heroes and heroines, as the manner in which
they are combined. Elsewhere, even when both allegiances
are genuine and fully developed, they tend to appear consecu-
tively: worldly common sense alternates with otherworldly
zeal, and only the securely prosperous or the utterly terrified
can remit their calculating prudence for resigned piety. The

---

venture their lives upon the faith of it, if they think fit; but I believe
few will" (*Romances and Narratives*, xv, 81).

[27] *Review*, fac. ed. Arthur W. Secord, 22 vols. (N.Y., 1938), I (Aug.
1, 1704), 186; the latter phrase is Schonhorn's, "Defoe's *Journal*:
Topography and Intention," p. 397.

Journal of the Plague Year

Journal of the Plague Year presents a narrator whose constant task is to reconcile and combine these seemingly opposed outlooks; whose characteristic manner of going about it is to juxtapose and mediate between the claims of reason and faith; and whose posture thus comes to seem a model of sustained moderation, at once deliberate and devout. With a different sort of narrator, the *Journal* might have remained a vivid and powerful horror story, and although I have dwelt less than previous critics on this side of Defoe's achievement, there is no question that the agonies and terrors of his plague-stricken city are grimly fascinating. What I have chosen to stress, however, is that the book as Defoe wrote it also fascinates us by making the calamity problematic—"men reckon what it did and meant"—and by providing as interpreter a character who not only wins our sympathy, as even Defoe's most scapegrace heroes and heroines manage to do, but commands our respect as well. Here, uniquely, Defoe creates a hero whose own vision of the world is complex and carefully qualified, but toward whom our response is unequivocal.

Colonel Jack

IN *A Journal of the Plague Year*, the juxtaposition of piety and rationality leads to a meaningful synthesis of the two, for we are shown in the person of the narrator that these seemingly opposed ideals are in fact complementary. *Colonel Jack* contains many such paradoxes, but they are not resolved. For the first quarter of the story Defoe succeeds in making a ragged pickpocket the object of sympathetic understanding: crucial to this process is a casuistical distinction between what the hero does and is. But this achievement is not sustained, and Colonel Jack's character becomes more equivocal and elusive without growing more profound. His entire history is faithful to Defoe's sense of life as infinitely diverse and problematic; yet there is a difference between being preoccupied with complexity and attaining full mastery of it, and in this book Defoe's gift for perceiving incongruity seems to me to have exceeded his ability to control and interpret it.

Defoe says in an early work that "Contraries may Illustrate but Contraries never incorporate";[1] in *Colonel Jack* patterns of contrariety define and animate but fail to harmonize different systems of value. This technique can also be described as casuistical. Casuistry is not a higher ethical code than those singled out for notice by former commentators, but a medium in which competing standards are played off against each other. In other spheres as well, contrast provides a local structure; as a consequence, many episodes are inclusive rather than conclusive, and static rather than progressive. A long-range

---

[1] *The Lay-Man's Sermon upon the Great Storm* (1704), p. 21.

progression from rags to riches and gentility affects our expectations about the hero's eventual fate, yet other interests dominate much of the narrative, and at any given moment we
may be more intent on immediate moral, social, or psychological problems. What gives *Colonel Jack* its characteristic tex-
ture is the way these problems are stated: Defoe shifts attention from overt acts to their contexts, and brings out conflicting strands in the narrator's circumstances, motives, and reflections. Not that the novel is organized entirely in this way; its
very title page warns us that a succession of outward events
is to loom large in the fabric of this "*History.*" More significant, however, is the way the "Life of Wonders" promised in
the subtitle is actually handled in the text, for what Defoe
gives us is not a mere chronicle of adventure, and the posing
of questions and alternative responses saves *Colonel Jack* from
the bustling fatuity of its title page précis.

A yoking together of opposites permeates the whole story,
not merely its cases of conscience, and this tendency is reflected in a prose style rich in figures of balance. One is often
struck by the elaborate formality of sentences and entire paragraphs. The hero's gentleman-convict slave-tutor exclaims,
"Here I live miserable, but honest; suffer wrong, but do no
wrong; my Body is punish'd, but my Conscience is not
loaded"; and he goes on to explain "the delightful Sorrow"
of his repentance—which "makes Smiles sit on [his] Face,
while Tears run from [his] Eyes"—with a series of contrasts
between his former and present situations.[2] Considered as a

---

[2] "Before I Revell'd in fulness, and here, I struggl'd with hard fare;
then I wallow'd in Sloth and Voluptuous Ease; here, I labour'd till
Nature sometimes was just sinking under the Load; . . . there I had
a Hell in my Soul, was fill'd with Horror and Confusion, was a daily
Terror to my self, and always expected a miserable End; Whereas
here, I had a bless'd Calm of Soul, an Emblem, and fore-runner of
Heaven: . . . [such thoughts] made my most weary Hours Pleasant
to me, my Labour light, and my Heart Chearful." (*Colonel Jack*, ed.

fragment of dialogue between servant and master, the passage is unrealistic; the vocabulary is highly abstract, and although the length and the internal structure of individual phrases are in keeping with ordinary speech, the insistent antitheses, parallels, and oxymorons are not. Yet the very qualities that render it implausible as conversation are appropriate to a tallying of complicated accounts. For this ledger does not simply balance a good present against an evil past: rather, physical hardship and moral well-being "here" stand in paradoxical relation to each other, and (jointly) to the corresponding paradox of physical ease and moral disease "there." A failure according to standards of narrative realism, the slave-tutor's speech succeeds in defining and evaluating behavior through contrasts and equations. What is uncharacteristic about the passage is not its lack of verisimilitude, but the fact that the paradox is resolved: the joys of repentance prove "sufficient to Sweeten the bitterest Sorrow, and make any Man be thankful for *Virginia,* or a worse Place, if that can be" (167). Qualified as it is, this degree of conclusiveness is rare in *Colonel Jack.* But when it is found—and in this respect the slave-tutor's speech is no exception—conclusiveness tends to give way, in a larger perspective, to yet more inclusive paradoxes which are *not* resolved. The slave-tutor weighs austere religiosity against prosperous mischief, and finds the scales tipped toward the former. In the preface and the last three pages the editor and the narrator make similar points. But I do not think these passages give the work a predominantly religious orientation, or establish the superiority of divine to secular considerations, for the book as a whole does not really choose. Worldly and otherworldly values alike are affirmed: *Colonel Jack* comprehends both, but without ultimately ranking or reconciling them.

Samuel Holt Monk, Oxford English Novels [1965], pp. 162, 166-67; all further references are to this edition).

Colonel Jack

Many antitheses have to do only marginally with moral problems. "Nothing can be finer," Hazlitt once observed, "than the whole of the feeling conveyed in the commencement of this novel, about wealth and finery from the immediate contrast of privation and poverty."[3] Hazlitt's appreciation is just, for it is "the immediate contrast" that gives each of the opposed states its meaning and emotional force. A number of analogous contrasts, not primarily moral in nature, organize and enliven other parts of the story. In the psychological sphere, dominance is set against submission, anxiety against security; geographically, the book plays off wandering exile against fixed abode; socially, it sets delinquency over against respectability. Certain traits of mind and character are contrasted: an equally vivid presentation of their antonyms enables "tractability," "gratitude," and "courage" to become significant motifs.

Several of these concepts have definite moral overtones, and in their narrative contexts all raise questions of value that are in some sense ethical. It should therefore be made clear that extremely varied forms of morality emerge in the course of the novel. By isolating single strands in its complex value system, past critics have shed valuable light on some of its major themes, but have tended to obscure the full range of competing norms which Defoe has worked into *Colonel Jack*. According to one study, "mercantile morality" is the main criterion by which the hero is to be judged, especially in the latter part of the book.[4] The thesis of another study by the same

[3] "On the Want of Money," from *The Monthly Magazine* of January 1827, in *The Complete Works of William Hazlitt*, ed. P. P. Howe, 21 vols. (London and Toronto, 1930-34), XVII, 181.

[4] See Maximillian E. Novak, *Economics and the Fiction of Daniel Defoe* (Berkeley and Los Angeles, 1961), pp. 125-26: "He is carried away from the path of mercantile morality. . . . in violating the rules of mercantile morality he has committed a far worse crime than any of his petty thefts. . . . Jack's avarice leads him to commit a breach of trade morality."

critic is that "the answer to the problem of morality in Defoe's
fiction may be found in his allegiance to the laws of nature;
it is by this standard that almost all of Defoe's characters must
be judged"; and in various passages of *Colonel Jack*, it is
suggested, Defoe invites us to assess the hero according to
natural law.[5] A third study locates the evaluative standards of
the book not in Defoe's economic or philosophical convictions
but in his social ideals; this essay stresses the affinities between
Colonel Jack and Defoe's *Compleat English Gentleman*, and
suggests that Defoe's conceptions of "honor" and "gentility"
provide crucial norms.[6] Another standard, which has received
little critical attention, is that of divine law: Colonel Jack
comes to feel that he "was brought into this miserable Condition of a Slave by some strange directing Power, as a Punishment for the Wickedness of [his] younger Years" (119);
by despoiling the possessors of "ill gotten Goods" and reward-
ing honest industry, Providence and the author collaborate in
*"Discouraging every thing that is Evil, and encouraging every
thing that is vertuous and good."*[7] The working of retributive
justice is not quite uniform—it operates less rigorously and
more intermittently towards the hero than towards the other
characters—yet *Colonel Jack* takes into account divine law
along with the ethical criteria discussed by previous critics.
Still another relevant standard is positive law, for Defoe makes
the hero and many of his associates run afoul of English (and

[5] Maximillian E. Novak, *Defoe and the Nature of Man* (Oxford,
1963), p. 2 and *passim*.

[6] William H. McBurney, *"Colonel Jacque*: Defoe's Definition of the
Complete English Gentleman," *SEL*, II (1962), 321-26. Cf. also Michael
Shinagel, *Daniel Defoe and Middle-Class Gentility* (Cambridge, Mass.,
1968), pp. 161-67 and *passim*.

[7] See Monk, Introduction, p. xvi; Preface, p. 2; the scene in which
a ship bringing Colonel Jack a cargo purchased from the proceeds of
thievery sinks near Cape Charles, pp. 154, 157; the earlier scene in
which a swollen Scottish stream "wetted and spoil'd [Captain Jack's]
stolen Goods," p. 99.

occasionally French) matrimonial and criminal statutes. Each of these codes of conduct plays a part in *Colonel Jack*, and credit must be given to past studies which have called attention to the presence of several of them; what I wish to question is the dominant role previously assigned to one or another. Rather than offering a consistent hierarchy of values, with mercantile morality or natural law or divine law or genteel honor at its summit, *Colonel Jack* pits these codes against each other, dramatically but inconclusively.

Diverse moral standards are brought to bear on the characters' behavior, and these standards tend to be juxtaposed but not reconciled. To elucidate these points it will be helpful to examine specific instances of unresolved conflicts of value. We may begin by inquiring whether there is any real dialectic between honor and religion in *Colonel Jack*, and whether any synthesis of the two can be said to emerge;[8] in other words, whether Defoe has created a hero who is at once a Christian and a gentleman. That contemporary writers were interested in synthesizing "The Christian Hero" is well documented in Professor Blanchard's introduction to the work of that title by Richard Steele.[9] That Defoe himself believed such a synthesis possible, and attempted to create characters who exemplify it, is evident in several of his other works. The exiled Russian grandee whom Robinson Crusoe meets in Siberia illustrates Defoe's belief that nobility of rank, mind, and mien

[8] The difficulty of harmonizing them had been forcibly expressed a few years earlier by Bernard Mandeville: "The only thing of weight that can be said against modern Honour is, that it is directly opposite to Religion. The one bids you bear Injuries with Patience, the other tells you if you don't resent them, you are not fit to live. . . . Religion is built on Humility, and Honour upon Pride: How to reconcile them must be left to wiser Heads than mine" (*The Fable of the Bees*, ed. F. B. Kaye, 2 vols. [Oxford, 1957], I, 221-22).
[9] *The Christian Hero* (1701), ed. Rae Blanchard (Oxford, 1932), pp. ix-xxix.

Colonel Jack

ought to be reinforced, not weakened, by Christian principles.[10] And elsewhere Defoe maintains that "it was so far from being true, that Religion was not suited to the Life of a Gentleman, that it was certain a Man could not truly be a Gentleman without it."[11] Nothing could be plainer, yet it is equally plain that Colonel Jack embodies no such synthesis. He manages at different times to be a Christian and a gentleman, but one or the other is always in abeyance. In Virginia his religiosity thrives but he looks upon himself "as one Buried alive, in a remote Part of the World," he can "receive no Satisfaction" from his new life, and he is still tormented by "the old Reproach" that "this was not yet, the Life of a Gentleman" (172). At the end of the book there is a renewed burst of piety, but this occurs only after the hero is disabled from participation in the world of honor: from the perspective of Campechean "Exile," when his "way [is] hedg'd up,"[12] he deems his twenty-four years as a gentleman "a Life of levity, and profligate Wickedness" (308). On occasion the dictates of honor and religion happen to coincide;[13] more often each ethos goes its own way, and Colonel Jack oscillates between them. Not only is there no union of religion and honor, but since neither is treated as an ultimate point of moral reference, neither can be appealed to for authoritative judgments on the other.

This is noteworthy in the case of duelling. The custom had

[10] See *Farther Adventures*, in *Romances and Narratives of Daniel Defoe*, ed. George A. Aitken, 16 vols. (1895), II, 300-02, 307-08.

[11] *Religious Courtship*, 2nd edn. (1729), p. 56; cf. *The Compleat English Gentleman*, ed. Karl D. Bülbring (1890), p. 242 and *passim*.

[12] Pp. 307-09; cf. Hosea 2:6, where God's judgment on the idolatry of his people is to hedge up their way with thorns.

[13] Swearing is wicked as well as ungentlemanly (pp. 60-61); a man who rebels against a prince who has already forgiven him a capital offense is held to deserve "no Pardon after it, either from God or Man," since such an act is both "a forfeiture of his Vertue, and an irreparable Breach of his Honour" (p. 277).

been sharply reproved by earlier casuists,[14] and imaginative writers were to inveigh against it for more than a century after Defoe's death.[15] In divine and secular writings alike, two objections constantly reappear: one, that duelling reflects a "Christless code that must have life for a blow"; the other, that "the innocent person is exposed to equal danger with the criminal, and hath been oftentimes oppressed."[16] The first line of thought rejects all attempts at retaliation as unchristian; the second stigmatizes duelling as a risky means to an end tacitly recognized as legitimate. Defoe evidently regarded

[14] See Joseph Hall, *Resolutions and Decisions of Divers Practical Cases of Conscience*, in *Works*, ed. Philip Wynter, 10 vols. (Oxford, 1863), VII, 298 f.; Jeremy Taylor, *Ductor Dubitantium*, ed. Alexander Taylor, in *Whole Works*, ed. Reginald Heber, rev. Charles P. Eden, 10 vols. (1852), X, 139. Cf. also "The Casuistry of Duelling," in *The Uncollected Writings of Thomas De Quincey*, ed. James Hogg, 2 vols. (1892), II, 65-112.

[15] For earlier fictional attacks on duelling, see Arthur J. Tieje, "The Expressed Aim of the Long Prose Fiction from 1579 to 1740," *JEGP*, XI (1912), 415, n. 25. Among journalistic criticisms, see those in the *Tatler*, No. 253 (Nov. 21, 1710), ed. George A. Aitken, 4 vols. (1899), IV, 285; No. 25 (June 7, 1709), I, 207-09. Professor Shinagel suggests that the production of Steele's *Conscious Lovers* in the fall of 1722 made the question of duelling especially topical at the time *Colonel Jack* was written (*Daniel Defoe and Middle-Class Gentility*, pp. 174-75). Also contributing to current interest in the problem may have been the fact that in March 1720, Owen Buckingham, M.P. for Reading, had been killed in a duel by "his intimate Friend" William Aldworth, "being both elevated with Wine"; a *"Bill for preventing the impious Practice of Duelling"* was immediately introduced and eventually passed in the House of Commons, but "was laid by in the House of Peers" in May (Abel Boyer, *The Political State of Great Britain*, XIX [1720], 316-17, 530-31).

[16] Tennyson, *Maud*, II, i, 1, lines 26-27; Taylor, *Ductor Dubitantium*, in *Whole Works*, X, 139. Cf. Steele's contention that "the most pernicious circumstance in this case is, that the man who suffers the injury must put himself upon the same foot of danger with him that gave it, before he can have his just revenge; so that the punishment is altogether accidental, and may fall as well upon the innocent as the guilty" (*Tatler*, No. 253).

duelling as the most bizarre feature of the code of honor, and his other writings more often ridicule its absurdity than lament its sinfulness.[17] In this book, Colonel Jack eventually fights duels, but remains convinced that "there was no Reason in the thing, that after any Man should have found the way into my Bed, I, who am injur'd should go, and stake my Life upon an equal Hazard against the Men who have abus'd me."[18] The appeal is not from "Gentleman's Law" (201) to divine law, but to ordinary prudence.

Here one might inquire whether prudence itself is not the ultimate test of conduct in *Colonel Jack*. In my opinion prudential considerations are decisive at various points in the story, but they no more provide a consistent or conclusive standard of judgment than the other evaluative norms already mentioned. The hero's circumspection and cunning are frequently noted.[19] Like Moll Flanders and Roxana, he is more candid towards us than toward anyone he encounters in the tale,[20] and his discreet reserve sometimes leads, like theirs, to

---

[17] "Or suppose the Adulterer wore a Sword; what then? Why I must fight him, must I? And that's another good Tale; that because he has debauched my Wife, I must lay an Even Wager who shall Die for it, he or I?" (*Applebee's Journal*, Aug. 15, 1724, reprinted in William Lee, *Daniel Defoe: His Life and Recently Discovered Writings*, 3 vols. [1869], III, 293). But there is less levity in the discussion of a case of conscience involving duelling in the *Review* (fac. ed. Arthur W. Secord, 22 vols. [N.Y., 1938], I [Dec. 30, 1704], 359); cf. also the Appendix to this volume of the *Review*, in which Defoe reprints and recommends Louis XIV's edict against duelling.

[18] P. 228; cf. also p. 242.

[19] As a young thief he is "Wary and Dextrous," p. 7; on the trip to Scotland Captain Jack calls him "a wary Politick Gentleman," p. 91, and he is too "wary" to join Captain Jack in "desperate Attempts," p. 102; he is twice "too cunning" for his Virginia master, pp. 132, 148; he is "too many" for his errant first wife, p. 207.

[20] Instead of exchanging confessions with his slave-tutor, he does not, "as is usual in such Cases, enter into any Confidence with him on my *own* Story. . . . it was no Business of mine to expose myself;

disingenuousness.[21] Often prudence sanctions actions desirable on other grounds as well: the brutal treatment of slaves is held to be "not only wrong, as it is barbarous and cruel; but it is wrong too, as it is the worst way of Managing, and of having your Business done," and thus "wrong, in Respect of Interest"; "Humanity" and "Prudence" equally sanction the "gentler Methods" which Colonel Jack introduces.[22] At other times prudence enters into the hero's longing for security and stability. As a boy he asks a fellow pickpocket, "If we get a great

so I kept that Part [i.e., his own criminal past] close" (pp. 167-68; cf. p. 41, "I had Money indeed in my Pocket, but I let no Body know it"). After abandoning his second wife he resolves to settle "somewhere in *England*, where I might know every Body, and no Body know me" (p. 233).

[21] After the return of a merchant's letter case, the men who interrogate Colonel Jack are "surpriz'd at the Innocence of [his] Talk," and Jack represents himself to us as having "no manner of thoughts about the Good or Evil of what I was embark'd in"; yet when asked by one man what sort of people he lives among, "I told him they were . . . very wicked Boys, Thieves and Pick-Pockets, *said I*, such as stole this Letter Case, a sad Pack, I can't abide 'em" (pp. 40, 60, 39). Later, when asked by his Virginia master what had so visibly affected him when a young pickpocket was being religiously harangued, and whether there was any similarity between their cases, Colonel Jack blandly replies, "Indeed Sir, I have been a wicked idle Boy, and was left Desolate in the World; but that Boy is a Thief, and condemn'd to be hang'd, I never was before a Court of Justice in my Life" (pp. 123-24).

[22] Pp. 145, 144, 150. Earlier, Colonel Jack had found it "a sad thing indeed to take a Man's Bills away for so much Money, and not have any Advantage by it neither," so he made a policy of not "destroying their Bills, and Papers, which were things that would do them a great deal of hurt, and do me no good" (pp. 29, 55). Here the hero's "strange kind of uninstructed Conscience" is drolly reinforced by an alert calculation of self-interest; through such reasoning he becomes a precocious Jonathan Wild, but I do not believe any irony is intended. Later in life Colonel Jack boasts that his Italian military campaign gained him "the Reputation of a good Officer," but also "somewhat that [he] lik'd much better, and that was a good deal of Money" (p. 209).

deal of Money, shan't we leave this Trade off, and sit down, and be Safe and Quiet?" And at the height of his prosperity he says, "Now was my time to have sat still contented with what I had got," and adds, "my prudent Wife gave it as her Opinion, that I should sit down satisfy'd."[23]

But the sway of prudence over the hero is not uncontested. For one thing, he can never "sit down satisfy'd": he has "an unquenchable Thirst . . . after seeing something that was doing in the World," "a wandring kind of Taste" which no sense of well-being can restrain (172, 233). Such passages place prudence in opposition to restless ambition. Two years earlier Defoe had maintained that man's discontent with his state is "the Essence and Beginning of Crime; and if I may be allowed such an Expression, is the Original of Original Sin"; yet in the same essay he had recognized that man's progress springs from the same questionable source.[24] His other writings fre-

---

[23] Pp. 67, 296. As a man he declares that "a settled family Life was the thing I Lov'd," and he twice idealizes "a comfortable Retreat" (pp. 234, 263, 307). Elsewhere Defoe maintains that it is an essential point of prudence for a man "to know *when he is well*," and regards English merchants as wiser than those on the Continent in that "they know when they have enough; for they retire to their estates, and enjoy the fruits of their labours," and in short "become gentlemen." See *The Compleat English Tradesman*, 2 vols. (1727), II, 55; *The Voyage of Don Manoel Gonzales*, in *A Collection of Voyages and Travels*, ed. Thomas Osborne, 2 vols. (1745), I, 149. On the question of how much of the latter work is Defoe's, see John Robert Moore, *A Checklist of the Writings of Daniel Defoe* (Bloomington, 1960), No. 517, p. 229.

[24] See *The Commentator*, No. XL (May 20, 1720), where Defoe says, "Being discontented with our present Condition, sets all our Thoughts to work to mend it. This sets the Wheels of Industry and Application a-going; all the Springs of our Faculties are wound up, the whole Machine, call'd Man, is put in Motion, for the great End of transposing the Situation of his Affairs, and altering the Circumstances"; and one of his personae declares, "I hate a Man with no Ambition; Nature dictates to Life, that it should be progressive and increasing; and Improvement is a Study of the greatest Minds, and the greatest Men upon Earth."

quently exploit this paradox. Robinson Crusoe repeatedly undertakes imprudent ventures, for he has "a great mind to be upon the wing" and "rambling thoughts" similar to Colonel Jack's.[25] His reenactments of Adam's fall are culpable, and are duly punished, yet his restless strivings are understandable and appealing, and in the long run they are rewarded. Only if we recognize the paradox of his fortunate fall can we savor Crusoe's story fully: we must perceive that what he calls his "original sin" is in some sense wrong, yet feel at the same time that it calls into play his most admirable traits. In Defoe's other novels, such as *Moll Flanders* and *Roxana*, this paradox is less patent but no less significant; an "unquenchable Thirst," whether for gentility, money, or sheer experience, prevents each hero and heroine from acquiescing in his Providentially ordained lot, and drives him to commit actions which—criminal or sinful as they may be—are nevertheless compelling as displays of determination, energy, and resourcefulness. A foolish vice, responsible for all human misery beginning with the loss of paradise, discontent is also a necessary virtue, responsible for bringing out man's full resources, and for whatever he has achieved since the Fall.

In *Colonel Jack* this paradox is clearly present. At various points the hero's path towards gentility may be smoothed by his prudent words and actions, yet the consuming ambition of a nameless, penniless orphan to become a gentleman is fundamentally imprudent, as is his insatiable longing to see, do, or become something more, especially after he has attained security and respectability. All the same, this very imprudence is probably his greatest source of vitality, nor are we simply invited to deplore it, as we would be if prudence were the highest ideal of the novel. We are shown that prudence is desira-

---

[25] See *Robinson Crusoe*, in *Romances and Narratives*, I, 340, 2; cf. also his "restless desire of seeing the world" in *Farther Adventures*, in *Romances and Narratives*, II, 213.

ble; we are also shown that imprudence, faulty as it may be from the standpoint of "mercantile morality," and bordering as it does in Colonel Jack's case on the sins of pride and avarice, is nevertheless in its way a good thing too. To be able to "sit down satisfy'd" is important for Christians and tradesmen, and Colonel Jack is something of both, but it is fatal to the hero of a novel.

Prudence, then, is not the ultimate norm of conduct in this book, but rather one value placed in juxtaposition with various others. Often in the ascendant, it wins no lasting triumph. It is never decisively repudiated, either, although at times its utility is called in question, by assertions such as "Man, a short sighted Creature, sees so little before him, that he can neither anticipate his Joys, nor prevent his Disasters, be they at ever so little Distance from him."[26] The value of prudence is constantly explored, and the interplay between prudence and imprudence allows both themes to emerge with clarity and vigor, yet the book as a whole cannot be said to enforce, as any kind of "moral," the cardinal virtue of prudence. Whatever socio-economic doctrines Colonel Jack's quest for gentility may be thought to illustrate, it is no more an exemplum of prudence than Crusoe's obsession with rambling, or Moll's similar yearning to become a gentlewoman; nevertheless it is by this radical imprudence that each first captures and continues to hold our interest.[27] On the way toward the fulfillment of their romantic

[26] P. 292; cf. p. 263. It might be objected that such passages do not question the inherent value of prudence, merely its human attainability; but in practice I suspect this comes to the same thing. Ecclesiastes' argument against taking thought for the morrow (that it is fruitless) is no less cogent than Christ's (that it is needless).

[27] Novak contends that "If any economic moral can be drawn from Crusoe's narrative, it is a conservative warning that Englishmen . . . should mind their callings and stick to the sure road of trade" (*Economics and the Fiction of Daniel Defoe*, p. 48). The "economic moral" of the book seems more equivocal: although this prudent course is indeed commended, and departures from it are labeled sinful as well

dreams, all three display great prudence—at times; yet does their prudence, in the final analysis, have very much to do with their wishes coming true? Rather, has not Defoe's stress on prudence served to camouflage this very element of fantasy, by implying that prudence, the most down-to-earth of virtues, has enabled his characters to "earn" their good fortunes?[28]

It was suggested earlier that the book unfolds as a series of unresolved paradoxes, and that these permeate the entire narrative, not merely its cases of conscience. Here it may be useful to demonstrate further that patterns of contrariety organize the presentation of character and action even when moral questions are not chiefly at issue. One instance is noted by Professor Monk: "Defoe artfully introduces us to Jack, placed between the brutal and naturally criminal Captain . . . and the gay and careless Major, a criminal through mere thought-

---

as rash, its desirability is belied by the story itself. How many readers finish *Robinson Crusoe* convinced that the hero ought to have stayed in York, or that he should at least have "remained in Brazil to cultivate his garden" (*ibid.*, p. 46)?

[28] In an earlier study I criticized Ian Watt's assertion, apropos of *Robinson Crusoe*, that "If we draw a moral, it can only be that for all the ailments of man and his society, Defoe confidently prescribes the therapy of work." My general objection was that Crusoe's extraordinary "triumph," as Watt rightly calls it, owes as much to the providential beneficence of God as to the untiring labors of the hero. I might now modify the argument as follows: Defoe proffers *both* an economic and a religious "explanation" of Crusoe's success, but this success cannot fully be accounted for in any such terms, and one function of such explanations may be to provide a rationale for what we might otherwise balk at as fantasy. (See *"Robinson Crusoe* as a Myth," in *Eighteenth-Century English Literature: Modern Essays in Criticism*, ed. James L. Clifford [N.Y., 1959], pp. 165, 167, and *passim*, and my *Defoe and Spiritual Autobiography* [Princeton, 1965], pp. 185-97). In short, I would suggest that the emphasis on industry (as on prudence) probably reflects Defoe's genuine conviction of its value, but is also to be seen, at least in part, as a tribute that romance pays to reality.

lessness."[29] No less effective, in my opinion, are the paradoxes within Colonel Jack's own nature and experience.[30] The contrast between wealth and poverty which impressed Hazlitt has a number of variants, all of which tend towards the paradoxical. Of his early days as "a dirty Glass-Bottle House Boy" Colonel Jack says, "I wanted nothing, who wanted every thing" (40); when he gets his first few pounds he declares, "now as I was full of Wealth, behold! I was full of Care" (23). Beyond a certain point, which as Defoe recognized is hard to define, ambition becomes avarice:[31] if we are to sympathize with young Colonel Jack, his cunning, grasping side must be neutralized. He is therefore presented as an ingenu, so far from being mercenary that he does not know "how to tell Money" or the value of it (36). Many similar touches induce us to share the response of a gentleman who rewards him for returning a letter case: "Poor Child! *says he,* Thou knowest little of the World, indeed" (*ibid.*). The paradox of carefree

[29] Introduction, p. xv.

[30] Indeed, the ostensibly external contrasts may be most meaningful when interpreted as in some sense internal to the hero—as projections onto others of traits which the hero cannot afford to acknowledge in himself, but which his actions nevertheless indicate that he possesses. This function of secondary characters is more pronounced in *Moll Flanders* and *Roxana,* but it is worth asking whether Colonel Jack, The Reluctant Footpad, is as utterly unlike his youthful associates as he seeks to suggest. An aggressiveness which is muted by being assigned to Captain Jack and Will in the early episodes emerges rather baldly when the hero later comes to deal with women and with rivals for their affection.

[31] "There is . . . little visible Difference between the lawful Applications of Industry and Business, and the unlawful Desires after exorbitant Wealth. . . . Every Man's Business in the World, is to increase and improve his Fortune; And getting Money is so general a Duty, that it seems to be one of the Ends of Life; how then shall we distinguish the Vertue from that Extreme? And where are the Bounds between the Duty and the Crime? The Confines of Virtue reach to the Frontiers of Vice, and where this ends that begins" (*The Commentator,* No. XLVI [June 10, 1720]).

poverty vs. anxious wealth contributes to the same effect: not only does this unspoilt naif not seek wealth, but he finds it burdensome when it is thrust upon him, and protests that he was happier without it. We are therefore kept from being disturbed by the passages quoted earlier, in connection with the question of prudence, which suggest that even at this stage of his career Jack is also shrewdly acquisitive.

If the hero is both ingenuous and rather knowing as a child, we can accept only in a qualified way the view of the book as a proto-*Bildungsroman*.[32] Neither the character nor the experience of the hero is cumulative in the way that such a term would seem to require. This is most obvious with respect to Colonel Jack's outward status, but it is true of his moral and intellectual attainments as well. Socially and economically, he undoubtedly advances: alluding to Job, the editor describes the hero's "latter End" as "better than his Beginning."[33] But the process is not incremental. "Seeing my Life has been such a Checquer Work of Nature . . ." are the narrator's first words, and he frequently remarks on the "long Series of Changes, and Turns, which have appear'd in the narrow Compass of one private mean Person's Life" (3, 307). His career is marked by a series of windfalls and losses, not steady gains; and although allusions to Job imply a logic of riches-as-divine-reward (just as certain passages already discussed imply a logic of riches prudently earned), this rationale for the hero's ultimate prosperity is borne out only fitfully by the text itself.

It is possible, of course, for the outward action of a *Bildungsroman* to be a "Series of Changes, and Turns," and to reflect

[32] See Monk, Introduction, p. xvi.

[33] P. 2; the prodigal son is mentioned in the preceding phrase, but the quotation is from Job 42:12, which is echoed again at p. 118, where the hero says "My Part was harder at the Beginning, tho' better at the latter End" than Captain Jack's.

a "Checquer Work of Nature," so long as the hero himself undergoes some kind of development amidst these vicissitudes. Professor Monk maintains that "as he moves through the varied scenes of his adventurous life," Colonel Jack acquires "a knowledge of himself and of the world and his relation to it";[34] but considering the number and variety of the hero's adventures, the remarkable thing is not how much but how little he learns. His marital imbroglios reveal a curious imperviousness to experience, and there is a somewhat obsessive quality in most of Colonel Jack's human relations, for he seems compelled to reenact endlessly certain basic ordeals rather than mastering them. I have already mentioned, as one of the book's organizing contrasts, the fact that the hero alternates between extremes of dominance and submission. In his dealings with other people, Colonel Jack's role tends repeatedly to be that of ideally cherished and ideally grateful child (towards the London merchant, the Virginia master, and King George, all of whom are referred to as father figures); of cruelly betrayed child (towards his Scottish employer, the Newcastle "spirit" Gilliman, and especially his wives); or of benignly forgiving and protective parent (towards Mouchat and his penitent wife). If he matures, it is never, in my opinion, to the point of treating others on terms of equality; he is forever the aggrieved orphan, showing either what a splendid son he would have made if his parents had not abandoned him, or what a splendid parent he would have made if he had been in their situation. My concern here, however, is not to determine the psychological substructure of the novel, but merely to suggest that for a *Bildungsroman* this tale involves little developing or maturing.[35]

[34] See Monk, Introduction, p. xvi.

[35] Admittedly, there is learning and growth in some areas. When Colonel Jack fights bravely at the battle of Cremona, he says "I NOW had the satisfaction of knowing, and that for the first time too, that

For purposes of the present study a crucial question is whether Colonel Jack achieves moral growth. I find little evidence that he does. It may be, as the preface claims, that *"a strange Rectitude of Principles remain[s] with him"* despite the corrupting influences of his early environment; but whether he ever manages *"to improve the generous Principles he had in him"* is doubtful.[36] Early episodes, it is true, deal with the hero's emerging moral consciousness, and trace a coherent process in distinct stages. Briefly, his initial innocence gives way to crimes committed from ignorance, and his ignorance renders him excusable on grounds that he is not yet a responsible moral agent. But once he is able to realize the nature and consequences of his acts, he becomes responsible for them morally, as he had been all along legally, and the scenes with Dame Smith of Kentish Town bring him to a full sense of "WHAT a Villain" he has been. The problem is that he gains this awareness a quarter of the way through the book, and subsequent scenes add nothing to it. Colonel Jack's conscience remains active, but after his eighteenth year its development ceases, and since there is neither consistent growth nor decline, the hero's moral evolution fails to pro-

---

I was not that cowardly low spirited Wretch, that I was, when the Fellow Bullied me in my Lodgings. . . . but Men never know themselves till they are tried, and Courage is acquir'd by time, and Experience of things" (p. 208). I take such a passage to be in the true spirit of a *Bildungsroman*, yet the idea that through testing one gains new powers or self-knowledge is not sustained elsewhere in the story.

[36] P. 1. One could just as plausibly maintain that Colonel Jack comes into the world trailing clouds of natural gentility, and that his efforts to recover the true meaning and substance of his birthright are increasingly wide of the mark as he becomes more and more of a gentleman in worldly terms. Shinagel more cautiously suggests that the latter part of the book is to be seen as a series of negative exempla, a "dropping off" from the "ascending action" of the first part (*Daniel Defoe and Middle-Class Gentility*, pp. 172-73). Certain episodes can be interpreted in this way, but I do not think the book supports for long any theory of the hero's waning (*or* waxing) stature.

vide a thematic structure for the book as a whole. The absence of such a structure suggests that *Colonel Jack* is different in kind from the *Bildungsroman*, not an early but faulty experiment in that genre.

Even if the book as a whole does not exhibit one kind of progression sometimes ascribed to it, there is an element of gradual unfolding within individual episodes: the lost-and-found adventure with the hollow tree could be cited as a memorable instance of sequential plotting (24-26). Nevertheless, the internal action of a scene usually involves peripety rather than continuity. Such reversals establish or reinforce the patterns of contrast fundamental to *Colonel Jack*: thus the hollow-tree scene juxtaposes extreme experiences of possession and loss, and the resulting emotions of elation and despair. Many similar episodes, spanning a good deal of time and space and containing various dramatic events, create a dominant impression of static contrast: the narrative moves forward, but does so partly to permit an essential standing still— that is, to allow paradoxes of all kinds to be developed and explored. Defoe describes at some length the voyage which the hero and Captain Jack are forced to make to Virginia: the main focus of attention is the captain of the ship, about whose character one is never quite sure.[37] There is no need to summarize the debates over the captain's ethics in carrying the men to Virginia against their will; the point is that these

[37] Colonel Jack's final reference to him as "our Captain, or *Kidnapper, call him as you will*" (p. 117) certainly suggests that he is as guilty as "that Kidnapping Rogue *Gilliman*" who had originally betrayed them (p. 111); it is hardly to the captain's credit that he "wanted to be Fingering very much" Colonel Jack's bill for £94 (p. 117); and even Captain Jack waxes eloquent in his indictment of the ship-captain as a "Confederate in this Villainy" (p. 113). Yet there is at least as much evidence that the captain genuinely sympathizes with the unfortunate men, and that he would have returned them to British soil "if the Weather had not really hindered it" (pp. 112-14).

debates are the heart of the episode, and are never conclusively resolved. The captain remains an enigmatic figure. It is perhaps typical of Defoe that the puzzle is not owing to any vagueness or paucity of evidence, but to its very clarity and abundance: each detail seems so unequivocal that the incoherence of the total picture is all the more unsettling. Also typical is the fact that the narrative furnishes no criteria for distinguishing valid from invalid evidence. Each fragment of testimony makes a small but ineradicable impression: the captain's total character comprises his own actions and protestations and the depositions of others in the story, shifting and contradictory as these all are. The more we learn the less certain we become; the captain cannot be numbered unequivocally among the hero's protectors or betrayers, for he combines both roles. The kidnapping of young people for service in the American colonies was a serious social problem in the late seventeenth century, and Defoe may simply have chosen this as a historically plausible way of getting his hero to the New World.[38] But whatever narrative or topical purposes the episode may have been intended to serve, it raises more questions than it answers, and despite the many weeks and miles it traverses, its probing of the captain's contradictory nature is essentially static.

More commonly the hero's own career poses such problems,

[38] For extensive background on this subject see Cheesman A. Herrick, *White Servitude in Pennsylvania* (Philadelphia, 1926), pp. 144-46; cf. also M. Dorothy George, *London Life in the XVIIIth Century* (N.Y., 1925), p. 363, n. 98. Despite various attempts to curb the practices of "spirits" and "crimps," clandestine transportation continued in the eighteenth century; that Defoe's object was to call attention to this evil would be a credible inference, were it not for the equivocal light in which the captain is presented. Besides, it eventually appears that however reluctantly a poor man may arrive in America, and by whatever dubious means he may be fetched there, he will probably do better in the plantations than in England if he is willing to be diligent and honest.

many of which echo traditional cases of conscience. In the course of his four marriages, Colonel Jack encounters some of the same "Cases Matrimonial" which had been raised by correspondents of John Dunton's Athenian Society and Defoe's Scandal Club, and which also confront Moll Flanders and Roxana. Does the adultery of one spouse release the other from conjugal vows? On what terms (if at all) is one obliged to receive again a spouse guilty of desertion or adultery? Is the justice done by marrying a woman one has debauched greater than the imprudence? Apart from legal obligations, how far is one obliged in conscience to maintain a spouse from whom one is separated? Are such separations justifiable in themselves? The casuistical background of such questions is to be sketched in the next two chapters; here it is sufficient to note that Colonel Jack's matrimonial entanglements, bizarre as they may be, often reflect issues discussed at length elsewhere by Defoe and reputable writers of the preceding century.[39]

The matrimonial episodes raise frequent problems of moral obligation, involving the dictates of natural law, divine law, the law of England, and expediency. But the most striking

---

[39] One of the hero's moral perplexities connected with marriage should perhaps be mentioned here, since nothing quite like it arises in *Moll Flanders* or *Roxana*: namely, the question of punishing the man who had debauched his third wife and her maid. Believing that such a man "deserv'd no fair Play for his Life," Colonel Jack resolves to ambush and shoot him some dark night, but then recoils from the idea: "It shock'd my Temper too, as well as Principle, and I could not be a Murderer." Neither "Temper" nor "Principle," however, prevents him from challenging the man to a duel; when the coward refuses, Jack canes him "as severely as I was able, and as long as I could hold it, for want of Breath" (pp. 242-43). By disavowing murder, the hero apparently seeks to tone down the intemperateness of his retaliation, and to associate revenge itself with "Principle." Robinson Crusoe's somewhat similar conflict over killing the savages—an impulse he eventually rejects as murder rather than legitimate self-defense—is one of the best-canvassed and best-resolved cases of conscience in Defoe's fiction; see *Romances and Narratives*, I, 186-92.

contrast in these scenes is on a more elementary plane, ethically and psychologically: namely that between feminine chastity and fidelity on the one hand, and wantonness and betrayal on the other. Colonel Jack's account of his first wife juxtaposes "the Mask of her Gravity, and good Conduct" with "what really she was, a wild untam'd Colt, perfectly loose, and careless" (193). We are shown that the modest reserve of this "Camelion" belies her "natural Disposition" (190), and this paradoxical image of woman recurs with little variation in the story of subsequent marriages.[40] The third wife remains "virtuous, modest, chaste, sober" for six years, but takes to drink during a spell of illness, loses "her Beauty, her Shape, her Manners, and at last her Virtue," and becomes "a Beast" given over to "Hellish Excess" (240-41). As is also true of the gentleman whom Moll Flanders meets in Bartholomew Fair, a complete metamorphosis takes place, and in both passages Defoe is evidently fascinated by the way "Drink, like the Devil, when it gets hold of any one, tho' but a little, it goes on by little and little to their Destruction." But despite his interest in the "Power of Intemperance" as the agent of change, and in the way that it takes "Possession" by degrees, the crux of the episode is not the process itself but the paradox that it sets up between contrary aspects of the same person. At all events, the story of Colonel Jack's successive mismatches is partially casuistical both in its subject matter and its mode of balancing alternatives, but less is made of the hero's moral perplexities than of the divided and inconsistent natures of his wives.[41]

[40] Even the fourth marriage, sound enough while it lasts, is cankered in retrospect by Colonel Jack's discovery, after his wife's early death, that "after all the Blushing, and Backwardness of Mrs. *Moggy* at first, Mrs. *Moggy* had, it seems, made a Slip in her younger days" (p. 249).

[41] The only marriage to prove completely successful is the final one —Colonel Jack's remarriage to his original wife. Their reunion seems

Episodes not only center as much on questions as events, but tend to explore rather than simply propounding theories. It is true that the preface and some of Colonel Jack's own reflections are quite tendentious, but bald affirmations are transformed into moot questions by contrary assertions or by implicit negations in the text itself. The preface mentions as one *"useful and instructive"* argument of the book, *"how much publick Schools, and Charities might be improv'd to prevent the Destruction of so many unhappy Children, as, in this Town, are every Year Bred up for the Gallows"* (1). We know from his other writings, such as *Charity Still a Christian Virtue* (1719), that Defoe had long been a staunch advocate of the contemporary charity school movement. Furthermore, we see that early schooling might have enabled Captain Jack and Will to avoid the gallows. But the evidence regarding Colonel Jack himself is ambiguous. A charity school education might have deflected him from crime, but since its main object was to inculcate in young paupers a prudent, pious acquiescence in the humble but useful station assigned them by Providence,[42] we are forced by the book as a whole to wonder

---

to establish his dominance through forgiveness of her past prodigality, yet some of their eventual happiness is owing to a virtual reversal of these roles, as the hero gives himself "chearfully up to her Management" (p. 271). It may be equally significant that in describing this idyllic match Colonel Jack repeatedly praises his wife's "Fidelity" (pp. 268, 270), and that sex no longer seems to be an issue, for his previous "Fate in Wives" (p. 249) had involved the constant association of sex and betrayal. But the psychological implications of his matrimonial vicissitudes cannot be pursued here, beyond noting that Colonel Jack, like Defoe's other heroes, escapes or outlives a dilemma over sex rather than resolving it.

[42] Instructors were urged to take "all proper measures to inure the children to labour and industry," lest "the advantages they received from a pious education should incline them to put too great a value upon themselves"; young paupers were to be taught to accept those "servile offices which are necessary in all communities and for which the wise Governor of the World had by his Providence designed them"

whether Colonel Jack was not fortunate to escape it. The senior Crusoe's preachment on accepting one's divinely ordained social rank wins our intellectual assent, but we are nevertheless glad that his son disregards it. Charity schools have a similarly equivocal value in *Colonel Jack*: we feel that however desirable they may be for the ordinary breed of young beggars and pickpockets, it is just as well that Colonel Jack never attended one, to be cowed into lifelong servility.

Similar ambiguities attend most theories about the nature of man or specific social institutions that have been extrapolated from *Colonel Jack*. Does the book reflect a "new optimism about human nature?" Is its hero "Defoe's Émile?"[43] Responsible critics have felt that there are grounds for thinking so, but the evidence is contradictory and inconclusive. Captain Jack is as lurid a specimen of natural depravity as any Defoe novel has to offer, and even if one rejects the notion that he embodies qualities which the hero possesses but cannot acknowledge, Captain Jack's very presence in the tale would seem to rule out man's inborn goodness as an implicit thesis of the book. Moreover, Colonel Jack's youthful inno-

---

(S.P.C.K. Circular Letters of 1712 and 1719, quoted in M. G. Jones, *The Charity School Movement* [Cambridge, 1938], p. 92; cf. also M. Dorothy George, *London Life in the XVIIIth Century* [N.Y., 1925], p. 221; Dorothy Marshall, *English People in the Eighteenth Century* [N.Y., 1956], p. 152; Jacob Viner, "Man's Economic Status," in *Man Versus Society in Eighteenth-Century Britain*, ed. James L. Clifford [Cambridge, 1968], pp. 33-35; and my *Defoe and Spiritual Autobiography*, pp. 128-30). It should be added, however, that Defoe was subsequently to defend charity schools against attacks by John Trenchard and Bernard Mandeville, who claimed that the ranks of the laboring poor would be thinned if its youth were trained for better things, by arguing that England would be enriched if the offspring of its servant class were to learn more productive occupations, and that fresh servants could be recruited from abroad (*Applebee's Journal*, July 13, 1724; Lee, III, 157-59).

[43] See Monk, Introduction, p. xv; Novak, *Defoe and the Nature of Man*, p. 75.

cence (such as it is) may owe less to Defoe's philosophical convictions than to his dramatic sense. Setting out to win the reader's sympathy for a young criminal, he distinguishes the "poor unhappy tractable Dog" (6) from his reprehensible deeds. His crimes are shown to be unavoidable (the necessary consequences of poverty); the responsibility of others (he is "made a Thief involuntarily" by the devil and older boys [17, 19]); and without grave consequences to victims (merchants are lucky to have their pockets picked by Colonel Jack, since for a negligible fee they recover their valuables—which other rogues would destroy—and receive useful lectures on carelessness into the bargain [54]). Most importantly, Defoe emphasizes the hero's childish ignorance of good and evil, and the absence of "Evil in [his] Intentions" (40, 19, and *passim*). Similar casuistical strategies are employed in the early episodes of *Moll Flanders* and *Roxana*, and with the same object—that of emotionally involving the respectable reader in the fate of a character whose social position and overt actions might otherwise seem altogether alien and contemptible. In the case of *Colonel Jack*, these devices do not seem to me to warrant the inference that Defoe had temporarily grown more optimistic about human nature in general, for their effect depends partly on the fact that the hero is exceptional. Our ordinary assumptions about juvenile delinquents are not simply invalidated—Captain Jack, Will, etc. tend to confirm them—but shown to be inadequate and potentially unjust in special cases. Needless to say, all of Defoe's heroes and heroines are special cases. What strikes me as humane in Defoe's conception of human nature is that he imagines and forces us to see special cases where we should not have expected to find them; in place of alien types we discover kindred individuals.

Does "optimism" account for Defoe's responsiveness to the special case? I think not. Nor does Defoe's attitude seem to me one of pessimism tempered by charity, which might have led him (as I believe it led Samuel Johnson) to treat sympatheti- cally the effects of poverty, ignorance, and fear on individual conduct. Both optimism and pessimism imply that the ob- server, having surveyed mankind from China to Peru, has made up his mind about the nature of man. As Professor Novak has shown, this abstraction fascinated Defoe; in the novels, however, Defoe treats generalizations about human nature—and the moral imperatives inferrable from them, which constitute natural law—as hypotheses, not as self-evi- dent first principles from which one can deduce what indi- vidual human beings are or ought to be. In his imaginative writings Defoe can thus use theories about innate, universal, and timeless features of human nature without committing himself as to their validity; he can let flawed but engaging characters tell their own stories, and record not only the multi- fariousness of human motives and actions, but the diversity of norms by which they can be judged. There is a tentative, conditional quality about even the most assured moral pro- nouncements in his fiction; however categorically they are expressed, they may be modified or contradicted by the next turn of the action. From the standpoint of "Augustan Human- ism," Defoe's attitude is apt to seem vacillating and confused rather than broad-minded or flexible—indeed apt to seem ac- tively immoral for failing to acknowledge absolute and immu- table moral truths, for refusing to brand certain deeds as un- equivocally evil, and thus for conniving at sin and crime. Be- hind several of these objections lies the assumption that "value and justice are aspects of a reality called good and evil and rest upon some foundation other than custom":[44] but if one regards this humanist creed as a *mere* assumption, a statement of belief

[44] Joseph Wood Krutch, *Human Nature and the Human Condition* (New York, 1959), p. 170, quoted in Paul Fussell, *The Rhetorical World of Augustan Humanism* (Oxford, 1965), p. 10.

rather than of fact, criticisms of Defoe based upon it lose some of their force.

Still, this is hardly enough to vindicate Defoe as a moralist, for one can be troubled by confusion and vacillation without sharing the beliefs of "Augustan Humanism." Several lines of defense are possible. Most popular in recent years has been the argument that it is not Defoe but his characters who are muddled: Defoe manipulates their self-contradictions with deliberate irony, and is in consistent, clear-sighted control of the moral wobbling and obtuseness he portrays. My reasons for questioning this view will be indicated in subsequent chapters; here it is sufficient to note that although *Colonel Jack* has not yet (to my knowledge) been interpreted as an ironic work, it contains most of the features that have lately been cited as proof of Defoe's ironic intent in *Moll Flanders*. A second line of argument would dismiss the charge as irrelevant to Defoe's intentions and achievements, which are seen as those of the realist rather than the moralist: on this view, Defoe is interested in moral questions only insofar as they might naturally arise in the minds of the characters he has created; what he wishes to show is how things would look to a given person under given circumstances, not how they look to him. Like the ironic interpretation, this reading would stress Defoe's artistic detachment and control; unlike the ironic interpretation, it would find mimetic accuracy a sufficient justification for the fictional presentation of moral problems. Like the ironic interpretation, this reading would dissociate Defoe from the attitudes and values ascribed to his characters; unlike the ironic interpretation, it would hold that Defoe was a master of moral subject matter in spite of (or perhaps because of) his lack of moral purpose.[45] This view, too, I would question. It sets up

[45] This reading is suggested by a paper on *Moll Flanders* delivered at a recent eighteenth-century conference in Los Angeles by my colleague Ralph Rader; but so brief a summary may do an injustice to

what may be a false dichotomy between realistic and moral purposes, and confines unduly the very concept of moral purpose by equating it with moral advocacy. Without attempting to refute the hypothesis that Defoe is a realist rather than a moralist, I would therefore suggest that it concedes too much, insofar as it implicitly accepts the view of a moralist as one who moralizes, points or teaches morals. It may be as seriously moral an undertaking to explore as to expound values, to examine processes of choosing as to recommend certain choices.

A third line of argument may, like the preceding one, strike some readers as a concession or evasion rather than a defense of Defoe's stature as a moralist. It is that whether one calls Defoe's moral attitude flexible or vacillating, broad-minded or confused, one can admire his refusal to impose uniformities or certainties which he was not convinced of. On this view, an honestly recorded dilemma may entitle a work to moral interest. Nor is this necessarily to prize paradox and ambiguity for their own sakes; it is simply to hold that there may be significance in raising questions as well as in proposing answers, and that to have perceived and faithfully reported difficulties may deserve little less respect than to have solved them. On these grounds one can regard *Colonel Jack* as a more ambitious if less satisfying work than *A Journal of the Plague Year*. In neither work do good and evil characteristically collide: the contending forces tend rather to be rival goods, or values which are both equivocal, or alternatives which are each undesirable. In the *Journal* the basic conflict is between two ideals, piety and rationality; their opposition is more constantly kept in view and more succesfully resolved than similar conflicts in *Colonel Jack*, yet the latter work brings into play a greater range of competing values. H. F. the saddler is a more consistent, more exemplary, and no less credible char-

---

the substance, as it certainly does to the subtlety, of Professor Rader's provocative argument.

acter than Colonel Jack, but a somewhat narrower one. The problem of value pursued in the *Journal* gives that book a more sustained moral intensity; in *Colonel Jack* such problems are less developed but more diverse. Action, characterization, and norms of conduct are all less coherent in *Colonel Jack* than in the *Journal*, yet *Colonel Jack* has an integrity of its own as an expression of various tensions—social and psychological as well as moral—which in this book Defoe saw but failed to settle. This view of *Colonel Jack* suggests some of its limitations as a case history of extensive but unresolved groping for meaningful values. But it also points to one of the strengths of the book, which is that Defoe has represented this process without attenuating it in the interest of one or another socio-economic, philosophical, or ethical thesis.

Moll Flanders

OUR HUMAN sympathies must sometimes be at odds with our moral judgments: this principle resonates through the writings of Defoe. In the *Review*, he points out that "the Scripture bids us not despise . . . a Thief, who steals to satisfie his Hunger; not that the Man is less a Thief, but despise him not, you that know not what Hunger is."[1] In another gloss on Proverbs 6:30 two decades later, Defoe says "the very Text itself speaks, tho' not in favour of the Crime, yet in great Compassion and Pity for the Criminal Men."[2] Robinson Crusoe develops the same argument: I do not pretend, he says, "that these circumstances render my failing, or any man's else, the less a sin, but they make the reason why we that have fallen should rather be pitied than reproached by those who think they stand, because, when the same assaults are made upon the chastity of their honour, it may be every jot as likely to be prostituted as their neighbour's."[3] In the same vein, Roxana stresses the role of poverty in inducing her to become her landlord's mistress, but is careful to add, "not that I plead this as a Justification of my Conduct, but that it may move the Pity, even of those that abhor the Crime."[4] Throughout

[1] *Review*, fac. ed. Arthur W. Secord, 22 vols. (N.Y., 1938), v (Feb. 8, 1709), 543-44; cf. *Serious Reflections*, in *Romances and Narratives of Daniel Defoe*, ed. George A. Aitken, 16 vols. (1895), III, 35.

[2] *The Compleat English Tradesman*, 2 vols. (1727), II, 193; cf. also *The Just Complaint of the Poor Weavers* (1719), p. 5.

[3] *Serious Reflections*, in *Romances and Narratives*, III, 55.

[4] *Roxana*, ed. Jane Jack, Oxford English Novels (1964), p. 39. Cf. *Mercurius Politicus* for Jan. 1717, in which Defoe, personating a Whig who has contributed to the relief of Jacobite prisoners in Lancaster

Moll Flanders it is assumed that the respectable reader abhors crime and despises thieves, and that (as one critic has said of Moll herself) he "struggles with no confusion as to what is right and what is wrong," but accepts "a classical moralism which drew a sharp line between goodness and badness."[5] Much of the book seeks to support this "classical moralism," not to subvert it; from the preface onwards, we are invited to abhor Moll's crimes, but urged not to despise the criminal herself. We are asked to distinguish between act and agent—between what Moll does and what she essentially is: without minimizing her culpability, the narrative seeks to deflect our severity from the doer to the deed, and to retain sympathy for the erring heroine.

This kind of appeal to the reader is most overt when she is about to commit her first theft, and plays an important part elsewhere in the book as well. But it is not the only pattern in which sympathy and judgment are related. At times, Moll's story tends to subvert "classical moralism," and casts doubt on the legitimacy of rigid distinctions between "goodness and badness." With this object, considerable emphasis is put on the principle that circumstances alter cases. William Perkins, the Puritan father of English casuistry, had asserted a century earlier that "the circumstances of time, place, person, and manner of doing, doe serue to enlarge or extenuate the sinne committed,"[6] and Defoe frequently reiterates this concept. "Few things in nature are simply unlawful and dishonest,"

Castle, is told by a friend, *"but they are our Enemies,* and I am sure you abhor them." "So I do," he replies, "I abhor their crime, but I pity their persons" (in William Lee, *Daniel Defoe: His Life and Recently Discovered Writings,* 3 vols. [1869], II, 4).

[5] Carl Van Doren, Introduction to *Moll Flanders* (N.Y., 1923), pp. xii, xiii. All citations of *Moll Flanders* in the text refer to the World's Classics edition, ed. Herbert Davis, with an Introduction by Bonamy Dobrée (1961)—the only modern reprint based on the first edition.

[6] *The Whole Treatise of the Cases of Conscience, Distingvished into Three Bookes* (1617), p. 10.

he observes in one work, "but . . . all crime is made so by the addition and concurrence of circumstances"; "Circumstances, Time, and Place alter things very much," he says in another; elsewhere, that "as Sin is Circumstantiated, those Accounts are sinful under one Government, which are not so under another"; and that "what may be simply Lawful, may be unlawful *Circumstantially*."[7] Moll never explicitly maintains that her extraordinary situation alters the sinful or criminal character of an action, but she often adduces circumstances that serve to palliate if not justify what she has just done or is about to do. In the process, the notion that an act is inherently right or wrong is at least called in question; moral judgment, it is suggested, must take into account the total context of a given act, and the context often works to Moll's advantage.

These are two of Moll's ways of gaining and holding our sympathy: she distinguishes her essential self from her admittedly reprehensible doings, but also lessens the stigma usually attached to specific acts. Other qualities contribute to the same effect, of course. Moll's independence and vitality are captivating;[8] the candor, directness, and very persistence of her speaking voice are disarming;[9] and her siding penitently with the reader against her former waywardness can

[7] *The Compleat English Tradesman*, I, 241; cf. I, 97-98, "there are very few things in the world that are simply evil, but things are made circumstantially evil when they are not so in themselves"; *Little Review* (July 4, 1705), pp. 35, 36; *A Letter to Mr. How* [1701], in *A True Collection of the Writings of the Author of the True Born English-man* (1703), p. 336.

[8] See especially Ian Watt, *The Rise of the Novel* (1957), p. 132 and *passim*. A number of Robert Langbaum's remarks about Browning and Tennyson are highly relevant to this aspect of *Moll Flanders*: see "The Dramatic Monologue: Sympathy versus Judgment," in *The Poetry of Experience* (N.Y., 1963), pp. 75-108.

[9] On these points see Sheldon Sacks, *Fiction and the Shape of Belief* (Berkeley and Los Angeles, 1964), pp. 267-70, and Martin Price's remark quoted in n. 60 below.

113

also be insinuating. I mention various ways in which Moll gains sympathy, partly to make clear that casuistry is not being proposed as her sole means of keeping our affection, and partly to indicate my grounds for not regarding the book as consistently ironic. Those who find the heroine an object of continual irony imply that we are always coolly judging her, and never emotionally involved in what she says or does. My objection to this is not that we never judge her, but that we are not allowed to do so with any such rigor, or from any such comfortable distance, as we might ordinarily adopt in the face of "all the progression of crime which she ran through in three-score years."[10] Sympathy keeps breaking in, and our ironic detachment—along with Defoe's—is tempered by imaginative identification.

The first important episode in Moll's story is her seduction by the elder brother in the Colchester family, which she does not, at the time, regard as a case of conscience at all. On the contrary, she admits that "I gave myself up to a readiness of being ruined without the least concern" (30). So far is she from weighing her situation morally that she does not even think practically; the brother is more deliberate, but Moll reflects that "he made more circumlocution than, if he had known my thoughts, he had occasion for" (31). Her opinion of the preliminaries to her seduction is that "Nothing was ever so stupid on both sides" (30), and when she says, "I had not one thought of my own safety or of my virtue about me" (26), her point is not that she forfeits both, but that she does so without a thought. By stressing the folly that precedes the act, and by blaming herself for this folly, she seeks to deflect the reader's judgment from a question of fornication to one of

[10] Preface, pp. 3-4. The debate over irony is surveyed admirably by Ian Watt in "The Recent Critical Fortunes of *Moll Flanders*," *Eighteenth-Century Studies*, 1 (1967), 109-26.

stupidity, and to soften his verdict by forestalling it herself.
The preface claims that this episode has "many happy turns
given it to expose the crime, and . . . the foolish, thoughtless,
and abhorred conduct of both the parties" (5). Without denying that Moll's behavior is criminal and abhorrent, Defoe
emphasizes that it is foolish and thoughtless, and thus enables
her to retain sympathy that she would forfeit if her action had
been more calculated.

With the same object, all initiative is ascribed to the man,
and much is made of Moll's passivity. As she will do on later
occasions, she represents herself as carried along by her circumstances (here, the precarious dependence of her role in
the Colchester family); by external inducements well adapted
to her situation (here, a great deal of gold); and by the persuasiveness and cunning of others (here, a man full of flattery
and stratagems, who knows "as well how to catch a woman
in his net as a partridge when he went a-setting"). Moreover,
"Knowing nothing of the wickedness of the times," Moll is
told an "abundance of . . . fine things, which [she], poor fool,
did not understand the drift of"; she acts "as if there was no
such thing as any kind of love but that which tended to matrimony" (28-29). These touches of the ingenue minimize further the element of deliberate choice on her part, so that she
seems to undergo mischief—to be deluded by the promises
and entrapped by the wiles of her seducer—rather than doing
mischief. Along with her passivity and her naïveté, Moll acknowledges her frailty; yet what appear to be confessions may
tend to raise her, not lower her, in our esteem. The episode
is punctuated by frequent admissions of vanity. But by mentioning that she had mastered French, the harpsichord, sing-
ing, dancing, and other genteel skills, and that she was "taken
for very handsome, or, if you please, for a great beauty" (22),
Moll indicates that her pride was neither groundless nor self-
generated. Other confessions of frailty have a similar effect.

She admits at one point that "I had no room, as well as no power, to have said no"; and, at the moment of her seduction, that "I could not say a word" (29, 33). She thus suggests that she was overwhelmed, not induced through inclination or interest to give her assent, and by presenting herself in this light—as frail rather than wanton—she further allays our severity. The foregoing details enforce a distinction between an act and its circumstances; in this case, between a seduction and various factors that complicate its moral status. These complicating factors tend in some degree to displace the actual deed as the object of our attention. Moreover, Moll herself is characterized less by what she does than by an array of motives and pressures that contribute to her seduction. A summary of her overt actions can only lead to the conclusion reached in the preface that they are criminal and abhorrent. Yet what Defoe gives us is anything but a summary of overt actions, and the transfer of emphasis is crucial to our sympathy for the heroine.

After her seduction, Moll's situation is entangled further by the younger brother, who seeks to marry her. "I resisted the proposal with obstinacy," she reports, "I laid before him the inequality of the match; the treatment I should meet with in the family; the ingratitude it would be to his good father and mother, who had taken me into their house upon such generous principles" (34-35). We might suppose that Moll's conscience is aroused, and that she has begun to weigh her conduct in the light of moral principles, but no such awakening has taken place. "I said everything to dissuade him from his design that I could imagine," Moll confesses, "except telling him the truth . . . but that I durst not think of mentioning. . . . I repented heartily my easiness with the eldest brother; not from any reflection of conscience, but from a view of the happiness I might have enjoyed, and had now made impossible; for though I had no great scruples of conscience . . .

to struggle with, yet I could not think of being a whore to one brother and a wife to the other" (35, 36). Moll's celebration of legitimate ideals serves to cloak the truth, her repentance of past "easiness" springs from a sense of lost opportunity, and her misgivings over the proposed marriage arise from squeamishness about what she evidently regards as incest. Her reticence towards the younger brother, however natural and blameless in itself,[11] leads not only to disguise and concealment, but to a kind of sophistry which exempts itself from the very sanctions it invokes.

What Moll undergoes, then, is not a crisis of conscience. When she says, "I was now in a very great strait, and really

[11] Cf. Moll's later remark that "I was not obliged to tell him that I was his brother's whore, though I had no other way to put him off" (p. 67). Jeremy Taylor had observed that "*Nemo tenetur infamare se*, is a rule universally admitted among the casuists, 'no man is bound to discover his own shame'" (*Ductor Dubitantium*, ed. Alexander Taylor, in *Whole Works*, ed. Reginald Heber, rev. Charles P. Eden, 10 vols. [1850], x, 113.) For a case resembling Moll's, and further discussion of the obligation of self-accusation, see the *Athenian Mercury*, IX, xxviii, 2. A young lady confesses that "*A certain lewd and infamous riffler of my Honour . . . has . . . been a little too busie where he had nothing to do: But I'd since the Good Fortune to enter Matrimony with a Person as far above me in Estate as Desert, and . . . manag'd all things so that he knew nothing of the Matter——However, I'm since that extreamly troubled for the Cheat I've put upon him, and the Injury I conceive I have done him. . . . Your Advice pray in this Condition?*" The Athenian Society replies, "We'll first give you the Opinion of a late Author, and then our own. . . . He tells your Ladyship, 'Your Sin when committed was against Heaven, not your *Honourable Lover*. . . . when he made his *Addresses*, you were not oblig'd to be your own *Accuser*, and . . . 'twas afterwards no part of yours to unveil the mistake'; and in all this still he is *right*, but here lyes the *Juggle*, Why did you *marry* him, which you ought not in strict *Virtue* and *Honour* to have done. . . . You ought to have been the *Wife* of your first Acquaintance, or else always to have liv'd *unmarry'd*, and are however as Cases are, tho not oblig'd, We think, to accuse your self to any upon *Earth*, yet to do it before *Heaven*, and endeavor to expiate your former long habitual *lewdness* with one, and *cheat* on the other, by a continued hearty *Penitency*."

knew not what to do" (37), her perplexity is essentially tacti-
cal, not ethical. She produces moral arguments for strategic
reasons, not because she regards them as relevant to her own
decisions, and as we shall find her doing on various other occasions, she endorses doctrines which she does not feel herself
bound by. It is easy enough to deplore her pharisaism, and to
condemn her failure to take personally the norms of conduct
she so persuasively advocates. Nevertheless she herself has acknowledged the existence of moral sanctions, and their hypothetical (if not practical) bearing on her behavior. The resulting impression is not one of hypocrisy—it is from her own
mouth, after all, that we learn how far short of her lofty
protestations her actions fall—but of disarming candor. However deceptive and evasive she may be toward the younger
brother, she seems engagingly open and confidential toward
us.

When Moll seeks her lover's advice about escaping the other
brother's importunate suit, her anxieties are still prudential
rather than moral, but they are cast in the form of a traditional case of conscience. The man counsels her to delay giving his brother a firm answer: Moll is startled, and tells him
"he knew very well that I had no consent to give; that he had
engaged himself to marry me, and that my consent was at
the same time engaged to him; that he had all along told me
I was his wife, and I looked upon myself as effectually so as
if the ceremony had passed" (41). And soon afterwards she
declares to him that "I was your wife intentionally, though
not in the eyes of the world. . . . it was as effectual a marriage
. . . as if we had been publicly wedded by the parson of the
parish" (45-46). Two long-debated problems underlie Moll's
reproaches to her seducer: what constitutes a valid marriage,
and more specifically, what formal ceremony (if any) is required? Moll echoes attitudes that Defoe had expressed two
decades earlier, in the "Advice from the Scandal Club," which

in turn are based largely on seventeenth-century casuistical discussions of matrimony.[12] In a *Supplement* to the *Review*, Defoe had pointed out to a querist that "Marriage being nothing but a Promise, the Ceremony is no Addition to the Contract, only a Thing exacted by the Law, to prevent Knaves doing what seems here to be attempted, and therefore the Society insist upon it, when the Promise was made, the Man and Woman were actually Marryed; and he can never go off from it, nor Marry any other Woman."[13] Here Moll uses

[12] See *A.M.*, VIII, iii, 1: the querist reports that "*Having for a long time pretended kindness to a Young Woman, and promis'd her Marriage if ever in a Capacity to maintain her, she thereupon yielded to my unlawful desires. Since this I'm sensible of my Crime . . . but am not yet in a capacity to live with her, tho' she's extreamly apprehensive that I'll forsake her, and I under Temptation of doing it.*" He is advised that "His first Duty is, to be sure he's truly sensible of his *Crime*, and troubled for it, and endeavour to make her *Partner* in his *Repentance*, as she has bin in the *Sin*. Then we think 'tis a plain case, that he ought to *marry* her." See *A.M.*, v, ii, 4: "A publick Marriage signifies no more before God than a private Contract . . . only here's the difference, the first gives a satisfaction to the World, and renders the party proper Subjects of the Law as to Estates, &c." Cf. also *A.M.*, XIII, vi, 6, and XI, xxiv, 3. Among the earlier casuists, see Joseph Hall, *Resolutions and Decisions of Divers Practical Cases of Conscience*, in *Works*, ed. Philip Wynter, 10 vols. (Oxford, 1863), VII, 393-95.

[13] *Review, Supplement*, 1 (Nov., 1704), 19-20; in another *Supplement*, the querist is "oblig'd by many Engagements" to a marriage which "forshews nothing but both our Ruins," and inquires whether "I may not leave her, and try my Fortune elsewhere." In reply, Defoe's Scandal Club declares that "his promises to the young Woman cannot be so broken as to marry another, he having engaged (as he says) to marry her; which the Society always allows to be a Marriage, and cannot prevail upon themselves yet to dispense with private Contracts on future Accidents; Promises of Marriage being things not to be trifled with on any Occasion whatsoever" (1 [Jan., 1705], 13). Four months earlier, Defoe had observed more cynically that "he that Lyes with a Woman on a promise of Matrimony, is a Knave if he does not perform his promise, and a Fool if he does" (*Review*, 1 [Sept. 5, 1704], 227; for further discussion of this topic see Spiro Peterson, "The Matrimonial Theme of Defoe's *Roxana*," *PMLA*, LXX [1955], 180-81 and *passim*).

similar doctrines to affect our attitude towards what she has already done, and what she is about to do. As she pleads with the elder brother, "I am really, and in the essence of the thing, your wife" (46), she makes it harder than ever for us to be severe toward her. We may not share her view that mutual consent constitutes the essence of marriage, yet we cannot deny her argument a degree of plausibility; we may recall that she was originally willing to accept her lover on any terms (or none at all), yet it now appears that she has somehow been abused. Similarly, to keep us from sympathizing with the duped younger brother at her expense, Moll suggests that she is the victim of a worse betrayal. She reminds her lover of "the long discourses you have had with me, and the many hours' pains you have taken to persuade me to believe myself an honest woman" (45). Such pleas do not alter her lover's determination to palm Moll off on his younger brother, nor do they quite persuade us that she is "an honest woman," yet they induce us to commiserate when we might otherwise condemn.

A further dimension of this episode is the elder brother's own verbal manoeuvering. Among the "abundance of fine things" with which he had wooed her, he had told Moll that "though he could not mention such a thing till he came to his estate, yet he was resolved to make me happy then, and himself too; that is to say, to marry me" (28-29). To avoid baldly repudiating a promise which he has no intention of keeping, he resorts to a ruse worthy of Moll herself. In reply to her reproaches, he calmly declares, "I did tell you I would marry you when I was come to my estate; but you see my father is a hale, healthy man, and may live these thirty years still, and not be older than several are round us in the town" (45). He thus acknowledges the force of the promise, but denies that the condition for fulfilling it has been met. Moll is in one sense the victim of this evasion, but in a more im-

120

portant sense its beneficiary. We forget that her compliance was not grounded on the promise of marriage, and are impressed rather by the cunning that her naïveté—or at worst her folly—had to contend with.

But this is only a faint sample of the sophistry which the elder brother goes on to display in persuading Moll to accept the younger brother. This is the first of several episodes in which she eventually does something that she originally finds abhorrent, and in which her shift in attitude—from revulsion through reluctance to resigned acquiescence—is brought about by the eloquence of her advisers. Or so she means us to feel. More striking instances of this process occur later in the book, but the debate with the elder brother over marrying the younger illustrates its main outlines. Moll's summaries of the discussion emphasize her antagonist's persuasive powers and her own constant (though diminishing) opposition.[14] Nor does she make the mistake of implying that any of the elder brother's arguments are sound. When he represents to her "in lively figures" the prospect of being "turned out to the wide world a mere cast-off whore," she does not suggest that this is a valid argument for marrying Robin, but merely that "all this terrified me to the last degree" (65). The elder brother's persuasion, she says, "at length prevailed with me to consent, though with so much reluctance, that it was easy to see I should go to church like a bear to the stake" (66): the entire scene asks who could be so heartless as to condemn the bear, which strikes out at the dogs only to defend itself. Although the overt sophistry is all ascribed to the elder brother,

[14] "He answered all my objections," she says, "and fortified his discourse with all the arguments that human wit and art could devise. . . . He answered all that I could object from affection, and from former engagements, with telling me the necessity that was before us of taking other measures now. . . . he wrought me up, in short, to a kind of hesitation in the matter. . . . Thus, in a word, I may say, he reasoned me out of my reason" (pp. 64-66).

the real sophist throughout the scene is Moll. One would not wish to reduce this man to a mere projection of the heroine, since he has an identity of his own—nameless and faceless, but no less substantial than that of any other supporting character in the book. Nevertheless one cannot help regarding him as a conveniently external prompter and apologist for Moll's behavior, and thus in some sense an embodiment of one side of her total personality. Like the devil and Mother Midnight later in the book, Moll's lover expresses notions which she cannot afford to acknowledge, let alone to advocate, but which she eventually acts upon all the same.

After the marriage, Moll says of her former lover that "I committed adultery and incest with him every day in my desires, which, without doubt, was as effectually criminal in the nature of the guilt as if I had actually done it."[15] She reiterates this principle at several other points in the book; for instance, she holds that to give up one's child to a hired nurse is "an intentional murder, whether the child lives or dies."[16] "*The Intention of Murther*," Defoe had maintained two decades earlier, "*is equally Criminal in the Eyes of God with the Act it self*";[17] and in *Roxana*, when Amy swears that she

[15] P. 68; in *An Essay on the History and Reality of Apparitions* (1727), a woman is told that by loving a married man "she had intentionally committed Whoredom with him"; "you wish'd you were a-bed with him, and you are as guilty by wishing to Sin, as if you had done it" (p. 195). The Scandal Club advises one would-be adulterer "to reflect what *Intentional* Guilt lies on your Thoughts in this Case," and another "to repent of the Sin of Adultery, since according to the known Text, *Matt.* 5.28. you have as much already committed it, as if you had actually lain together" (*Review, Supplement*, 1 [Jan., 1705], 7; 1 [Sept., 1704], 7). Cf. also *A.M.*, XIII, ix, 8.

[16] P. 201; cf. *Farther Adventures*, where Crusoe speaks of a "murderous intent, or to do justice to the crime, the intentional murder" (*Romances and Narratives*, II, 69).

[17] *A New Test of the Church of England's Loyalty* [1702], in *A True Collection*, p. 405; cf. *Review*, III (Aug. 20, 1706), 400: "the Murther is already committed, and your Guilt determin'd in the Intention."

will kill the heroine's troublesome daughter, Roxana exclaims, "Why you ought to be hang'd for what you have done already; for having resolv'd on it, is doing it, as to the Guilt of the Fact; you are a Murtherer already, as much as if you had done it already."[18]

The principle itself is not peculiar to casuistry. " 'Tis a Maxim in the Civil Law," a contemporary essayist points out, "and 'tis applicable in many Cases in the Common and Statute Laws of this Nation, and 'tis always so in the Law of God, that *Voluntas pro Facto reputatur*."[19] But Moll's way of using this proposition is casuistical. In proclaiming that she is guilty of adultery and incest, she puts the harshest possible construction on her attachment to her first lover. Yet it is doubtful whether our response is quite as harsh as hers. First of all there is the fact that Moll is her own accuser. However culpable her desires, it is she herself who acknowledges and deplores them: the narrator's values are thus aligned with those of the respectable reader against those of her former self. Moreover, by equating criminal desires with criminal acts, she matches even the most scrupulous reader in the rigor of his ethical standards; ostensibly an admission of frailty, Moll's remark is at the same time an assertion of moral equality. In short, Moll offers—and overtly seeks from her readers—a negative judgment of her criminal longings; nevertheless, her gesture of self-reproach may also involve an appeal to our fellow feeling.

---

[18] P. 273; Defoe makes a similar point in *Serious Reflections,* where he argues that "a vicious inclination removed from the object is still a vicious inclination, and contracts the same guilt as if the object were at hand; . . . it is true, separating the man from the object is the way to make any act impossible to be committed, yet . . . the guilt does not lie in the act only, but in the intention or desire to commit it" (*Romances and Narratives,* iii, 8). Cf. *Applebee's Journal* for March 11, 1721 (Lee, ii, 350), and *The Perjur'd Free Mason Detected* (1730), pp. 10, 22.

[19] Whitelock Bulstrode, *Essays upon the Following Subjects* (1724), p. 126.

Whatever our response to this particular confession, it is part of a larger strategy that clearly tends to her advantage. Here Moll maintains, seemingly against her own interest, that wicked desires are "as effectually criminal" as wicked deeds. If we accept this view, we are apt to acquiesce in a doctrine that is implicit in much of what she says of herself: namely that innocent desires are as effectually virtuous as innocent deeds. On this occasion she candidly concedes that her outward virtue belies her true guilt; many other episodes make the point that her outward guilt belies her true virtue. I have already noted the passage in which an "intentional" marriage is held to be as "effectual" as a public ceremony, and although the terminology elsewhere in the book is often less explicit, the role of motive or purpose remains crucial. "A Good Intention," says Addison, "joined to an Evil Action, extenuates its Malignity, and in some cases may take it wholly away";[20] it is towards this principle, so essential to Moll's pleas for sympathy, that even her confession of adulterous desires paradoxically points.

Moll describes her second spouse, a linen draper, as "this land-water thing called a gentleman-tradesman" (70), and soon after their marriage a case of conscience arises over what a wife should do when her husband's extravagances threaten family ruin. Or rather, Moll once again finds herself in a

[20] The *Spectator*, No. 213 (Nov. 3, 1711), ed. Donald F. Bond, 5 vols. (Oxford, 1965), II, 331. " 'Tis a kind of good Action to mean well, and the Intention ought to palliate the Failure," Defoe says in *Augusta Triumphans* (1728), p. 3; in *More Reformation* [1703], he says "If thou hast err'd, tho' with a good Intent,/ One merits Pity, t'other Punishment" (in *A Second Volume Of The Writings Of The Author Of The True-Born Englishman* [1705], p. 57). For "intention" used to aggravate rather than lighten a misdeed, cf. also *Conjugal Lewdness* (1727), where contraception is held to be as bad as abortion, since they "are equally wicked in their Intention, and it is the End of everything, that makes it Good or Evil" (p. 139).

plight that corresponds to a traditional case of conscience, but reacts in a manner which has little to do with conscience. When the man is finally arrested for debt, Moll says, "I had foreseen sometime that all was going to wreck, and had been taking care to reserve something if I could, though it was not much, for myself" (72). The Athenian Society, when asked whether such practices are justifiable, had maintained that "in some Cases such secret securing one parties separate interest, without giving the other any account, may be very just, ver-tuous, and prudent. . . . when either the Man or the Wife run on willfully and obstinately in an unavoidable Course of ruining themselves and their Families . . . all convenient ten-derness, Admonition and Counsel . . . ought to be made use of; which if to no purpose, the last Remedy is as reasonable as to lay things of value out of the way of Children and Fools."[21] Moll takes this doctrine so much for granted that she feels no need to defend her action; if "all [is] going to wreck," it is better to conduct salvage operations beforehand than afterwards.

Once the remaining goods have become the legal property of her husband's creditors, however, Moll cannot so easily escape the moral implications of salvaging them for herself.[22] Without denying that the act itself is culpable, she concen-trates on the question of responsibility for it. Her husband, she says, "would have me go home, and in the night take

[21] *A.M.*, v, ix, 2; cf. *A.M.*, ix, xiv, 9, and William Ames, *Conscience With The Power And Cases thereof* (1643), pp. 207, 259.

[22] In answer to a debtor's question "*Whether it be Lawful to run to* . . . priviledged *places* [such as the Mint] *for protection*," the Athenian Society points out that "there's difference between getting out of the way ones self, and carrying off Effects and Goods . . . which are none of our own. . . . One of the vilest sort of Knaveries, and in some Sence worse than *Publick Robbery* . . . Of t'other side, it must be own'd *every thing wou'd fain live*, and 'tis a *severe Tryal* of a mans *Honesty* to give that out of his *Hands*, which shou'd keep him from *Starving*" (*A.M.*, xii, xxiv, 2).

away everything I had in the house of any value, and secure it" (72). Any suspicion that Moll might have done the same thing on her own initiative is thus forestalled by labeling the act his suggestion. Moreover, Moll acknowledges the fact of the theft in such a way as to shift its onus to him: "He used me very handsomely and with good manners upon all occasions, even to the last, only spent all I had, and left me to rob the creditors for something to subsist on" (*ibid.*). Moll does not rob the creditors of her own volition, but is "left" to rob them by her husband: the parallel phrases "[he] spent all I had, and [he] left me to rob the creditors" again suggest that she is a mere tool, more victim than villain. Similarly, the final "for something to subsist on" introduces a further extenuation: Moll is prompted not only by her husband's counsel, but by her own necessity.

"My condition was very odd," Moll says at the end of this episode, "for . . . I was a widow bewitched; I had a husband and no husband, and I could not pretend to marry again, though I knew well enough my husband would never see England any more, if he lived fifty years. Thus, I say, I was limited from marriage, what offer soever might be made me; and I had not one friend to advise with in the condition I was in."[23] One noteworthy feature of this passage is the "husband and no husband" paradox, which will complicate Moll's subsequent marriages. She will also become involved more than once with men who have "a wife and no wife," so that the ambiguities of her own situation will be compounded by those of the people she moves among. Another point is her lack of "one friend to advise with": she must make her own way through the wilderness of matrimonial casuistry. Each of these factors probably makes us less critical of her subsequent

[23] P. 74; see Defoe's lengthy discussion of the similar case of a "Widower Bewitch'd" in the "Advice from the Scandal Club" (*Review*, II [April 24, 1705], 86-88).

matrimonial ventures than we would be if her status was altogether clear, or there was anyone trustworthy at hand to clar-
ify it for her.[24] Moll never denies that she remains married,
in the eyes of English law, to the gentleman-tradesman who
has absconded, but at opportune moments her odd husband-
and-no-husband condition allows her to overlook this incon-
venient fact. And she contrives to make us overlook it as well:
for instance, the next episode opens with the statement, "I
had made an acquaintance with a very sober, good sort of
a woman, who was a widow too, like me" (76). The final
three words, and others equally unobtrusive elsewhere, help
to make plausible Moll's widowhood, by dint of casual itera-
tion if not of legal argument; or at least they make us less
censorious than we would be if we found her deliberately
hypocritical about her marital status.[25]

In the episode that follows, Moll's own memoir comes to
a standstill as she tells of the courtship and marriage of her
next-door neighbor. Critics have noted that these pages touch
on a topic recurrent in Defoe's writings—the hazards and
hardships that marriage holds for women; nevertheless the
episode has been treated as a narrative digression, an extended

---

[24] Had she had access to the Athenian Society or Scandal Club, Moll
need not have felt so keenly the lack of a friend's advice, since those
learned bodies were familiar with her predicament. For an involved
query, the gist of which is *"whether is it not the same thing in the
sight of God (in this Womans case) as tho' her Husband were really
dead"*—so that the woman may proceed as if she were a widow—see
A.M., iii, xix, i.

[25] The reviewer of a recent book says that "its author can be excused
of dishonesty only on the grounds that before deceiving others he has
taken great pains to deceive himself"; and a recent commentator says
of Moll Flanders that "she deceives herself, but is unaware that she
is doing so." Moll's claims to widowhood would certainly be open to
one charge or the other, were it not for the fact that her position is
genuinely ambiguous. (P. B. Medawar, *The Art of the Soluble* [Lon-
don and N.Y., 1967], p. 71; Bonamy Dobrée, Introduction to *Moll
Flanders,* World's Classics, p. vi).

anecdote with little bearing on Moll's own character or actions. But the episode is built around a case of conscience which Moll is soon to face: namely, the question of whether it is legitimate to deceive a deceiver. Elsewhere Defoe was to cite "the old Latin Proverb, *Fallere fallentem non est fraus*, (which Men construe, or rather Render, by way of banter upon Satan) 'tis no Sin to cheat the *Devil*, which for all that, upon the whole I deny."[26] Here Defoe's answer to the question is negative, yet his heroine is about to respond with an implicit affirmative. He thus has a fresh opportunity to demonstrate the casuistical theorem that circumstances alter cases. To deceive a would-be deceiver is ordinarily a bad thing, but it may under special conditions become pardonable, if not commendable.

For Moll the actual question is whether, since "the men made no scruple to set themselves out as persons meriting a woman of fortune, when they had really no fortune of their own," it would be "just to deal with them in their own way" (89). Through the tale of her neighbor, Moll establishes that London marriages were "the consequences of politic schemes

[26] *Political History of the Devil* (1726), p. 353. On the question, "*Whether it be a Sin to deceive the Deceiver?*" see *A.M.*, ii, xx, 10, where it is pointed out that "although Circumstances may make an Action more or less sinful, yet they change not the nature of Sin; for Deceit is Deceit, though used to a Deceiver." On the other hand, the notorious Mary Carleton had appealed to her readers "whether, being prompted by such plain and public signs of a design upon me, to counterplot them I have done any more than what . . . a received principle of justice directs: 'to deceive the deceiver is no deceit' " (Francis Kirkman, *The Counterfeit Lady Unveiled* [1673], ed. Spiro Peterson [Garden City, 1951], p. 23). Similarly, "Tom a Bedlam" argues in *Applebee's Journal* that "*fallere fallentem non est fraus*; or, in English, 'Tis no Sin to Cheat the Devil' " (April 7, 1722; [Lee, ii, 508]); and in *Amusements Serious and Comical* (1700), Tom Brown (mistakenly) declares, "All our casuists agree that it is no more sin to cheat a Jew than to over-reach a Scot, or to put false dice upon a stock jobber" (ed. Arthur L. Hayward [1927], p. 200).

for forming interests, and carrying on business"; that "the men had such choice everywhere, that the case of the women was very unhappy"; and particularly that "the men made no scruple . . . to go a-fortune hunting . . . when they had really no fortune themselves to demand it, or merit to deserve it" (77, 78). These remarks echo Defoe's lamentations elsewhere over the crassness of contemporary match-making, and over the resulting indignity and injustice to women. Here, however, Moll's comments have the more immediate purpose of generating sympathy towards anything, however drastic, abused women may resort to in self-defense. She does not introduce these data to extenuate any action of her own: she presents them as casual reflections on the experience of her neighbor, and the air of disinterestedness not only helps to persuade us of their validity, but prevents us from suspecting that Moll is up to some anticipatory pleading in her own behalf.

Under Moll's guidance, "this young lady played her part so well, that . . . she made [her suitor's] obtaining her be to him the most difficult thing in the world" (84). "This she did," Moll goes on to say, ". . . by a just policy, turning the tables upon him, and playing back upon him his own game." The language of playing parts, turning tables, and playing games prevents our weighing this woman's actions too gravely, and makes us assent the more easily to the "justice" of her "policy." Part of Moll's task is to make such practices seem as innocuous as possible, which she achieves through metaphors of acting and gaming suggestive of Restoration comedy. Another part of her task, though, is to establish the parallel between her case and the other woman's: if we approve of her friend's table-turning, we are likely to condone her own version as well. These pages are therefore anything but a digression. They are an indispensable prelude to Moll's account of her matrimonial parleying with the Virginia planter in that they furnish prior justification for what she is about to do.

Moll also seeks to lessen her responsibility for this venture by portraying herself once more as a passive tool of others' cunning. "My intimate friend," she reports, "whom I had so faithfully served in her case with the captain . . . was as ready to serve me" (88). This woman proposes that she try to "deceive the deceiver"; left to herself, Moll suggests, she would never have thought of such a scheme, or managed to carry it out. "The captain's lady, in short, put this project into my head, and told me if I would be ruled by her I should certainly get a husband. . . . I told her . . . that I would give up myself wholly to her directions, and that I would have neither tongue to speak nor feet to step in that affair but as she should direct me, depending that she would extricate me out of every difficulty."[27] In fact, Moll needs no assistance

[27] When the middle-aged Moll uses makeup for the first time, she protests that "I had never yielded to the baseness of paint before" (p. 271). Bonamy Dobrée says of "yielded" that "the word is perfectly chosen" (Introduction, p. ix), and one must agree; yet it should be noted that this is one of Moll's favorite formulas for suggesting her passive or reluctant role in mischief of all kinds. Early in the book she declares to her seducer that "I have yielded to the importunities of my affection" (p. 46); later she assures the gentleman at Bath that their becoming lovers had been "all a surprise, and was owing to the accident of our having yielded too far to our mutual inclinations" (p. 138); and when she has become a hardened thief, and can no longer allege that poverty or the devil prompt her to continue her "horrid trade," she speaks of herself as "yielding to the importunities of my crime" (p. 239). If Fielding had written the book, one could speak confidently of "yielding" as an ironic motif, especially since other characters play on the word wittily: "They that yield when they're asked," Robin taunts his eldest sister in the Colchester household, "are one step before them that were never asked to yield, sister, and two steps before them that yield before they are asked" (p. 51). But with Defoe, as Dobrée observes elsewhere, "one never quite knows" ("Some Aspects of Defoe's Prose," in *Pope and His Contemporaries: Essays Presented to George Sherburn*, ed. James L. Clifford and Louis A. Landa [Oxford, 1949], p. 177).

whatever: after all, she had "faithfully served" the captain's lady in the first place by proposing (in Rochester's words) that she "revenge herself on her undoer, Man" (84). The passage makes sense only if we regard it as another piece of determined self-justification, and in any case the sense it makes is rhetorical rather than logical. The preceding episode sought to establish that it is legitimate for women to turn the tables on men. This passage, on the other hand, implies that the forthcoming attempt to turn the tables on man may be culpable, but that the fault is not Moll's but her friend's. The object is not consistency but comprehensiveness.[28]

Moll's ruse to obtain a husband involves deception, but its ethical status is complicated by two subordinate issues, each of which has a history of its own in the literature of casuistry. First, can one be guilty of lying without uttering a single untruth? And secondly, can one be guilty of lying through speaking literal truths? The two questions are closely related, and the traditional answers to both had been emphatically affirmative,[29] yet Moll speaks and acts on the assumption that each should be answered in the negative. The Virginia planter courts her "upon supposition . . . that I was very rich, though I never told him a word of it myself" (90); by avoiding overt misrepresentation, Moll feels that she escapes responsibility for the man's error. A bolder stroke is the exchange of verses, in

---

[28] Moll's tactics somewhat resemble those in the following story: "A. borrowed a copper kettle from B. and after he returned it was sued by B. because the kettle now had a big hole in it which made it unusable. His defense was: 'First, I never borrowed a kettle from B. at all; secondly, the kettle had a hole in it already when I got it from him; and thirdly, I gave him back the kettle undamaged'" (Sigmund Freud, *Jokes and their Relation to the Unconscious* [1905], in *Complete Psychological Works*, ed. James Strachey [1960], viii, 62).

[29] On these questions, see Taylor, *Ductor Dubitantium*, in *Whole Works*, x, 128-30, 106-10; Richard Baxter, *Christian Directory*, in *Practical Works*, ed. William Orme, 23 vols. (1830), iii, 512; and Appendix, below.

which she expresses literal truths with the intention of being disbelieved. In response to the man's "I scorn your gold, and yet I love," Moll writes "I'm poor: let's see how kind you'll prove,"[30] and concludes, "though I had jested with him (as he supposed it) so often about my poverty, yet, when he found it to be true, he had foreclosed all manner of objection, seeing, whether . . . I was in jest or in earnest, I had declared myself to be very poor . . . and though he might say afterwards he was cheated, yet he could never say that I cheated him" (92-93). What must be noted here is not simply that Moll's argument is specious, although generations of casuists had insisted that such reasoning sacrifices the spirit of truth to the letter, but that it is just plausible enough to prevent her husband, when he finally learns the facts, from being indignant toward her. "I have no reason to blame you," he assures Moll; "I may perhaps tell the captain [who officiously spread the rumor of her fortune] he has cheated me, but I can never say you have cheated me" (96). Such is "his affection to [Moll], and the goodness of his temper" (92) that he does not reproach her—yet he, after all, is the injured party. His benign response serves as a model for ours, and this seems to be the real point of these passages. Their object is not to gain our assent but our indulgence, and the husband's exemplary tol-

[30] Moll prefaces her final rhyme by saying, "I ventured all upon the last cast of poetry"; again the imagery of gambling allows her to sustain the excitement of the encounter, and yet to dispel its more somber implications with the pretence that it is all a civilized game. Robert Alter remarks that Moll's "variety of extralegal activities is not in the least a game for her; on the contrary, she envisages virtually everything she does as a very serious business" (*Rogue's Progress: Studies in the Picaresque Novel* [Cambridge, Mass., 1964], pp. 46-47). Broadly speaking this is so, and makes Moll's use of game-motifs to keep *us* from regarding her deception as "a very serious business" all the more noteworthy.

erance contributes to this effect as surely, if not as strikingly, as Moll's own ventures into verse and her accompanying rationalizations.

After Moll has taken such pains to offset the potential severity of our judgment, the following statement seems strangely at odds with the rest of her defense: "I often reflected on myself how doubly criminal it was to deceive such a man; but that necessity, which pressed me to a settlement suitable to my condition, was my authority for it" (92). Instead of denying the gravity of her deception, Moll here acknowledges it to the full; as on other occasions, her own sternness seems calculated to forestall ours.[31] At this point Moll wisely avoids dwelling on the "authority" of "necessity"; whatever its intrinsic validity, the plea of necessity will not bear close scrutiny in the present context. Yet the allusion to necessity plays its part, together with all the other lines of defense. Analyzed individually, none of Moll's arguments will exonerate her, and collectively they form a curious web of contradiction and inconsistency. To prevent our pausing to examine them singly *or* collectively, however, Moll presents her brief at a brisk pace. "It is well to expand the argument and insert things that it does not require at all," says Cicero, "for in the multitude of details the whereabouts of the fallacy is obscured"; and it is well, Moll might have added, to be quick about it, too.

[31] "He is extremely ready to own his errors," Clarissa says of Lovelace, "By this means, silencing by acknowledgment the objections he cannot answer; which may give him the praise of ingenuousness, when he can obtain no other; . . . He knows . . . that his own wild pranks cannot be concealed; and so owns just enough to palliate (because it teaches you not to be surprised at) any new one, that may come to your ears; and then, truly, he is, however faulty, a mighty ingenuous man; and by no means an *hypocrite*" (*Clarissa*, 9 vols. [Oxford, 1930], I, 295, II, 150). There is something of the same artful candor about Moll.

Moll's life becomes even more trying on the Virginia plantation than in London. She must act as vigorously and warily as ever, but does not feel called upon to spend so much ingenuity defending her action, because she is convinced of its justice. Again the basic situation grows out of a traditional case of conscience, and again the most interesting question is not where Defoe got his material, but what he makes of it. Moll discovers that her husband is actually her half-brother; what is she to do? The problem had already been considered by Jeremy Taylor and Joseph Hall: both take as their point of departure a Venetian case in which the husband was father as well as brother of his wife, but extend the discussion to all incestuous matches contracted in ignorance.[32] What had been an ethical dilemma for these earlier writers, however, is for Moll chiefly an emotional question. "I was not much touched with the crime of it," she says, "yet the action had something in it shocking to nature, and made my husband, as he thought himself, even nauseous to me" (103). Moll stresses the element of physical revulsion, and although she labels her status "open avowed incest and whoredom," she seems to find the immorality of the match only an incidental aggravation of its

[32] Taylor, *Ductor Dubitantium*, in *Whole Works*, ix, 149; Hall, *Resolutions and Decisions*, in *Works*, vii, 410-14; cf. *A.M.*, xvi, xx, 1; vi, xxvi, 3. The case seems to have been founded on popular tradition, but occurs as the 30th novel in *The Heptameron* of Margaret of Navarre. In this version, a "council of conscience" advises the guilty mother "never to reveal the secret to her children, who had not sinned, inasmuch as they had known nothing"—a decision endorsed by the English casuists. Horace Walpole heard the story of a lady "who, under uncommon agonies of mind, waited on Archbishop Tillotson, revealed her crime, and besought his counsel in what manner she should act. . . . The prelate charged her never to let her son or daughter know what had passed" (George Saintsbury, note to *The Heptameron*, 2 vols. [1903], ii, 40). The motif is also used in George Powell's *The Fatal Discovery* (1698): see Eric Rothstein, *Restoration Tragedy: Form and the Process of Change* (Madison, 1967), pp. 146, 156n.

enormity. Rather than make Moll grapple with the conventional arguments for and against dissolving such a marriage,
Defoe subjects her to a conflict in which her keenest impulses
are ranged against the demands of her external situation. Traces
of the traditional grounds of debate remain—Moll gives some
thought to the effect of the discovery on her husband and their
two children[33]—but the basic question is whether Moll can regain her peace of mind without causing "the ruin of the whole
family" (112). Defoe's art consists in first making it appear that
she cannot, then enabling her to do so. Seemingly opposed
claims are ultimately reconciled: such a procedure is analogous
to the resolution of a case of conscience, but between a horror
of incest on the one hand, and a horror of poverty and public
exposure on the other, Moll's conscience plays at best a minor
part in this episode.

Within a page of embarking from Virginia, the heroine
finds herself in Bath. Two decades earlier Defoe's Scandal
Club had considered a query that anticipates the scene at Bath
—"Whether the Woman that would permit a Man to set upon
her Bed, after she is in it, and the whole Family before that
time being gone to rest, would not, in all likelihood, admit
him in some time into the same," and thus whether "by the

[33] See pp. 106, 116-18. Moll also observes that "had the story never
been told me, all had been well; it had been no crime to have lain
with my husband, since as to his being my relation I had known
nothing of it" (p. 102). The same point had been made in earlier
discussions of the issue. Robert Donovan, however, finds Moll's remark
a "most suggestive" indication that "moral distinctions are not real,
since they exist only in our awareness of them," and argues that there
is "irony of a particularly devastating kind in Moll's innocent acknowledgment . . . that an immoral act is nullified if the perpetrator is
ignorant of its moral bearings. The agent's ignorance, in other words,
not only excuses him, it changes the nature of the act" (*The Shaping
Vision: Imagination in the English Novel from Defoe to Dickens*
[Ithaca, 1966], pp. 33, 44). The casuistical assumptions behind Moll's
remark may be questionable, but are less extreme than they become
in Professor Donovan's formulation.

frequent permission of the Man, the Virtue of the Woman might be seduced." "The Society," Defoe responds, "are by no means for allowing indecencies, and extraordinary freedoms between the Sexes, as what may be in their consequences Fatal to Vertue; nor do they believe, any one so secure of their Vertue, as to justifie their Leading it into Temptation; but on the other hand, they cannot suppose every Fredom to be Vitious. . . . in the present Case, they think the Censure Unjust, and too severe——But the persons may observe, how neer the brink of Crime they walk."[34] Thus Defoe had examined this question long before its incorporation in *Moll Flanders*; both the narrative situation and the ethical problems arising from it are sketched out in the *Review*.

In the present scene, Defoe greatly aggravates the circumstances of the case. The central question remains the same—whether "extraordinary freedoms" will prove "Fatal to Vertue." But what had been a euphemistic conclusion in the *Review*—"Whether the Woman that would permit a Man to set upon her Bed . . . would not . . . admit him in some time *into the same*"—is here taken literally as a point of departure: the Bath gentleman protests that "if he was naked in bed with [Moll], he would as sacredly preserve [her] virtue as he would defend it if [she] was assaulted by a ravisher" (132). Defoe thus puts the problem in its extremest form,[35] just as he poses other questions about human nature in extreme form by shipwrecking Robinson Crusoe on a desert island. He was to main-

[34] *Review, Supplement*, i (Nov. 1704), 20-21; cf. the Athenian Society's cynical response to the following query: "*A Married Lady meets another Womans Husband, stays frequently with him, some hours at a time, in secret, and permits all the Freedom and Liberty that Man and Wife are capable of, only the last* Favour *excepted, pretending to Conscience and Principles, because she does not go thro' stitch: Pray what do you think she means by Conscience and Principles under such a Practice?*" (*A.M.*, ix, xvii, 4; cf. also xvi, xix, i).

[35] The Jesuits had pushed this question to the same length: see Nicolas Perrault, *La Morale des Jesuites* (Mons, 1667), p. 20.

tain in another context that "It is true, Honour and Virtue may (speaking strictly) be said in some Cases to be preserved, though Decency is not so much, or equally regarded: But let all that plead the possibility of that Distinction *know*, that however possible it may be, it is . . . far from being probable (that where Decency is given up Honour should or can be preserved)."[36] This statement can serve as a gloss on the primary topic of the Bath episode—the hazards, as Moll puts it, of "venturing too near the brink of a command."[37] Its secondary topic is the factor that makes such trials of virtue rash: the power of "inclination" to overturn "moderation," "affection," "noble principle," and reason itself. Thus the Bath episode is concerned with the conditions that lead to misdeeds of all kinds. If there are good grounds for praying not to be led into temptation, there are still better grounds for not willfully seeking it out.

But to isolate such a motif as if it were a "moral" is to make the episode more schematic and tendentious than it actually is. It is true that at the time of writing, Moll reflects upon "the unhappy consequence of too great freedoms between persons stated as we were, upon the pretence of innocent intentions, love of friendship, and the like; for the flesh has generally so great a share in those friendships, that it is great odds but inclination prevails at last over the most solemn resolutions" (146). But her moralizing seldom exhausts the moral issues raised in the course of her story. Detachable from the narrative, her comminatory codas (as Watt calls them) are usu-

---

[36] *Conjugal Lewdness* (1727), p. 4.

[37] Bishop Hall reports that "it was wont to be worthy Mr. Perkins's expression to this purpose: 'Let those who must walk close to the brim of a steep precipice look well to their feet, and tread sure; and so they may come off perhaps as safely as those that are farther off; but if a man be to choose his way, let him so cast it as that he may not approach near the brink of danger'" (*Resolutions and Decisions,* in *Works,* vii, 386-87).

ally less subtle, let alone equivocal, than the events they so patly "improve." In this episode, various qualifying circumstances prevent us from drawing any simple moral. Those of the gentleman himself are relevant—or at all events Moll is intent on making them seem so. He had a wife, we are told, but "the lady was distempered in the head," and Moll once goes so far as to assert that "he had no wife, that is to say, she was as no wife to him" (126, 138). Whether such a predicament discharges one from marriage vows had been discussed by various casuists. There had been general agreement that it does not, and Defoe never endorses Moll's tacit assumption that it does, yet her bare mention of such circumstances tends to the Bath gentleman's advantage—and indirectly, of course, to her own—since it introduces the kind of complexity that can blunt the rigor of moral judgment without necessarily altering its substance.

The following scenes recount two further liaisons, with the banker's clerk and the highwayman. At several points the two episodes overlap, but it will be best to treat them separately, so as to bring out their distinct casuistical components. The banker's clerk initially describes himself as having "a wife, and no wife," like the Bath gentleman, but soon explains that his wife is unfaithful; what is more, "she is a whore not by necessity, which is the common bait of your sex, but by inclination, and for the sake of the vice."[38] For several pages, Moll and the clerk discuss ways of freeing him from his irksome bond. The major question is whether one can make a fresh contract conditional on the dissolution of an existing

[38] Moll's response to this news—"Well, I pitied him, and wished him well rid of her"—may typify her pharisaism, but rests on the casuistic principle that motivation rather than overt action is the proper basis of moral judgment: here and elsewhere, Moll distinguishes herself from others who do from "inclination" what she does only from "necessity."

marriage, and there are a number of subsidiary questions, each with a casuistical history of its own; whether it is sinful, for instance, to wish for the death of the wicked, and whether remarriage is permissible in cases of desertion.[39] A catalogue of the traditional cases of conscience which Defoe has adapted may suggest a more bookish procedure than he actually followed, or at any rate a more thorough and schematic approach to such questions than the text itself exhibits. What must be stressed is the word "adapted," for Defoe sometimes uses cases of conscience as he does other literary materials—rapidly, allusively, and in contexts very different from those in which he originally found them.

When the man asks, "What must a poor abused fellow do with a whore? What can I do to do myself justice upon her?" Moll replies, " 'Tis a case too nice for me to advise in"—the self-effacing preamble of a good casuist—"but it seems she has run away from you, so you are rid of her fairly." "I am not clear of her for all that," the man protests, "I would be rid of her so that I might marry again." "Well, sir," says Moll, "then you must divorce her." When the clerk laments, "That's very tedious and expensive," Moll's suggestion echoes several letters printed in the *Athenian Mercury*: "If you can get any woman you like to take your word, I suppose your wife would not dispute the liberty with you that she takes herself."[40] Fortunately for Moll, he understands her to advise an informal remarriage, not a bald turning of the tables on his errant wife, yet " 'twould be hard," he observes, "to bring an honest woman to do that." "It occurred to me presently," Moll ac-

---

[39] Contracts contingent on divorce from (or the death of) the superfluous spouse are frequently condemned in the *Athenian Mercury*: see VI, xxv, 6-8, and the questions submitted to the *Spectator's* "Love-Casuist," No. 614, Nov. 1, 1714 (V, 98). On the other questions, see *A.M.*, XVIII, i, 1 and the following note.

[40] P. 157; cf. *A.M.*, XVII, xxv, 7; XVIII, xi, 3. On this subject see also *Review*, II (Apr. 24, 1705), 86-88.

knowledges, " 'I would have taken your word with all my heart, if you had but asked me the question'; but that was to myself."[41]

In the course of this brief exchange Moll has shown that she knows what relief the law affords, and what steps it requires in cases of this sort, but that she can cheerfully exempt herself from its provisions. Throughout their subsequent dialogue, Moll continues to play a double role. Part of the time she answers the clerk's questions with the propriety of a Perkins or Baxter, without feeling that she need bind herself by the doctrines she expounds; and part of the time she evades answering his questions, but from motives very different from those she alleges to him. Up to the very time of their marriage, Moll's dealing with this man are marked by similar duplicity. While she is awaiting the birth of a child by her Lancashire husband, Moll receives a letter from the banker's clerk reporting the progress of his divorce, and "earnestly pressing [her] to return to London." In her answer, Moll reports, "I gave him joy of his deliverance, but raised some scruples at the lawfulness of his marrying again, and told him I supposed he would consider very seriously upon that point before he resolved on it, the consequence being too great for a man of his judgment to venture rashly upon a thing of that nature" (197). Again, scruples that are legitimate in themselves, or at any rate far from groundless, are raised quite unscrupulously, and lofty principles are invoked to further what Moll herself labels "a base design."[42]

[41] Pp. 157-58. One cannot overemphasize the psychological importance of the final words ("but that was to myself") and others like them throughout the book; for they are not to herself alone, but to us. Moll constantly confides to us thoughts and actions which she must conceal or disguise from husbands and lovers. By suggesting that she is more intimate with us than with anyone in her immediate milieu, she seeks to retain our sympathy in the very course of describing her baseness and duplicity towards others.

[42] In answer to the query *"Whether a Person Divorc'd by Law may lawfully Marry* another, *while those they were first marryed to*

The episode that delays Moll's marriage to the banker's clerk begins with the mutual deception of Moll and Lancashire Jemmy. Only afterwards, when she wishes to free herself from it, does Moll question the validity of a marriage contracted on such a basis. Prior to the marriage she does not view this as an ethical question at all, although the topic had been discussed by various casuists, and was raised more than once in the *Athenian Mercury*.[43] What Moll does treat as a case of conscience is the question of responsibility for the deception, and insists that "as I have had no hand in it, I desire I may be fairly acquitted of it, and that the blame may lie where it ought to lie, and nowhere else, for I wash my hands of every part of it" (168-69). Her defense rests entirely on assumptions which Defoe challenges elsewhere—that words alone deceive, and that there is no such thing as a tacit lie.[44] It is true that

---

are yet living?" the Athenian Society succinctly replies, "The best *Casuist* that ever was, resolves the Question in a few words, *5th.* of St. *Matth.* 32. *Whosoever shall Marry her that is Divorced, committeth Adultery;*——and that's enough to give the *importunate* Querist satisfaction, if he really either *wants* or *desires* it" (*A.M.*, I, iv, 2). The Church of England accordingly prescribes that "In all sentences pronounced for divorce and separation *a thoro et mensa . . .* the parties so separated shall live chastely and continently; neither shall they, during each other's life, contract matrimony with any other person" (*Constitutions and Canons Ecclesiastical . . . of the Church of England*, No. 107). On the other hand, the *Confession of Faith* of the Westminster Assembly of Divines (1643) finds it "lawful for the innocent party to sue out a divorce, and, after the divorce, to marry another, as if the offending party were dead" (Chap. XXIV, Par. V [Edinburgh, 1877], p. 104). Richard Baxter maintains that "They that are released by divorce upon the other's adultery &c. may marry again," as does Joseph Hall (*Christian Directory*, in *Practical Works*, IV, 167; *Resolutions and Decisions*, in *Works*, VII, 376-79). The Defoe-Farewell library contained a copy of Edm. Bunny, *Of Divorce for Adulterie, And Marrying Againe: that there is no sufficient warrant so to do* (Oxford, 1610); see *Librorum . . . Danielis De Foe, Gen. Catalogus* (1731), p. 50, item 157.

[43] See *A.M.*, III, iv, 7; IV, iii, 7; and n. 52 below.

[44] See Defoe's *Serious Reflections*, in *Romances and Narratives*, III, 48 f.; *The Compleat English Tradesman*, I, 241-48; and Appendix, below.

in her initial shock at discovering that she too has been taken in, Moll exclaims that "this has been a hellish juggle, for we are married here upon the foot of a double fraud" (171); but soon afterwards, when her husband asks how much money she really has, she prefaces her reply with the bland assurance that "I never willingly deceived him, and I never would" (173). Moll and a man of "true, gallant spirit," "of generous principles, good sense, and . . . abundance of good humor," have been put in a vexing predicament by the "baseness" of "the slut," "the creature," "this madam the procuress." Moll's pharisaism is certainly ironic; whether she is the object of conscious irony in this passage is more debatable.[45]

The latter part of this episode concerns Moll's difficulties over her child by the Lancashire husband. Early in her pregnancy she says, "I would have been glad to miscarry, but I could never be brought to entertain so much as a thought of . . . taking anything to make me miscarry; I abhorred, I say, so much as the thought of it" (186). Here is the subject matter of a traditional case of conscience,[46] but for Moll it is scarcely a case, since no real choice or conflict is involved, and it has little to do with conscience, since she rejects abortion (as she had rejected incest) on instinctive rather than ethical grounds. Defoe was acquainted with the traditional arguments concerning abortion, so that if he had chosen to have Moll rid herself of her burden in this way, he might have supplied her with a plausible defense. The abrupt manner in which

[45] I share Watt's doubts: see *The Rise of the Novel*, p. 125.

[46] See *A.M.*, v, Supplement, 12; viii, iv, 1; viii, xx, 6; xvi, xiii, 1; xvii, xxviii, 4. One of Bishop Hall's *Resolutions and Decisions* concerns abortion: see *Works*, vii, 300-03. Cf. also Thomas Wood, "Seventeenth-Century Moralists and the Marital Relationship," *Trivium*, 1 (1966), 78-80. In the *Review* and *Conjugal Lewdness* Defoe treats abortion as a full-fledged case of conscience; in both works he eventually condemns it as emphatically as Moll does here, but with elaborate reasoning and with appeals to various ethical sanctions; see *Review*, 1, *Supplement* (Jan. 1705), 14-15; *Conjugal Lewdness*, Chap. 5.

142

Moll repudiates the idea of abortion suggests, however, that Defoe's own abhorrence of it was so strong that he could not have made Moll a patroness of abortion without thinking of her as thoroughly depraved. He allows Roxana to confess that she "wou'd willingly have given ten Thousand Pounds of [her] Money, to have been rid of the Burthen [she] had in [her] Belly" (163), but for Moll he evidently wishes to retain more of the reader's sympathy, and abortion is quickly shunned. At all events, Defoe here introduces a traditional topic of casuistry without submitting it to casuistical treatment. An exploratory attitude is abandoned for a more decided and uncompromising one, and rational deliberation is bypassed, or at least overridden, by convictions of a very different order.[47]

Moll's dilemma over the child enters a new phase once it is born: the "brave boy" is as great an obstacle as ever to her marriage with the banker's clerk, since this man "would soon have discovered by the age of it that it was born, nay, and gotten too, since my parley with him." On the other hand, Moll declares that "it touched my heart so forcibly to think of parting entirely with the child, and . . . of having it murdered, or starved by neglect and ill-usage . . . that I could not think of it without horror." Her next sentence seems to rule out the chance of her adopting such a course: "I wish all those women who consent to the disposing their children out of the way, as it is called, for decency sake, would consider that 'tis only . . . a-killing their children with safety"

---

[47] Throughout Defoe's fiction, certain strong emotions—notably terror and loathing—act as signals that cool consideration is about to give way to deep-seated and not wholly conscious anxieties. Such scenes merit closer examination, and those in *Robinson Crusoe* appear to me particularly important. All that can be said of them here is that they do not seem to imply an abandonment of casuistry in favor of any particular ethical system, but lie in some sense beyond ethics. A valuable introduction to the problem is Benjamin Boyce's article, "The Question of Emotion in Defoe," *SP*, L (1953), 44-58.

(200). "All *those* women," Moll says, and once again we are alerted to the prospect that she will discover grounds for doing what she initially finds unthinkable, and for preserving a stance of virtuous indignation towards those who do the same thing under other circumstances. Christ had said, let those who are innocent throw the first stones, and Moll seems to infer that by throwing the first stones she establishes her innocence. Her anticipatory denunciations of the very misdeeds she is about to commit may not permanently banish a *tu quoque* from the reader's mind. But they serve to align her as narrator on the side of the respectable reader, and thus to distinguish her essential self from the sinner whose past she is recounting.

Moll proceeds to discuss the helplessness of young children. She reasons that "affection was placed by nature in the hearts of mothers to their children" to guarantee maternal care, without which most children would die; therefore to give children up to "those people who have none of that needful affection placed by nature in them, is to neglect them in the highest degree," and is merely "a contrived method for murder."[48] How, then, is she to avoid applying such arguments to her own case? At this point she reintroduces her "governess," the "old beldam" at the Sign of the Cradle whom she "had now learned to call mother." In the ensuing dialogue this scheming woman voices arguments much like those which Moll herself produces, elsewhere in the book, to justify what she knows to be dubious practices.[49] The effectiveness of this scene, however, depends

[48] Pp. 200-01; Moll echoes Crusoe's contention that "leaving life in a posture in which it must inevitably perish, is without question causing it to perish" (*Serious Reflections*, in *Romances and Narratives*, III, 20).

[49] The gist of her case (pp. 201-05) is that the nurses' professional reputation depends on the children's welfare, so that they have even stronger motives than maternal affection for taking good care of their charges. A character in another of Defoe's books observes that "I would

less on the ingenuity of the woman's arguments than on their being put in the mouth of someone other than Moll. In this way Moll's convictions can be presented as sincere, and if she eventually adopts a contrary course, she nevertheless seems less hard-hearted than if she had proposed such action all along.

Another case of conscience at the Sign of the Cradle concerns the validity of Moll's Lancashire marriage and the lawfulness of her marrying again. The scene is reminiscent of cases in the *Athenian Mercury* and the *Review*, with Moll as the perplexed querist and Mother Midnight as the respondent —although there are also important differences. The midwife has such "bewitching eloquence, and so great a power of persuasion, that there was no concealing anything from her," so Moll lays the case before her: "I told her the history of my Lancashire marriage, and how both of us had been disappointed; how we came together, and how we parted; how he absolutely discharged me, as far as lay in him, and gave me free liberty to marry again . . . that I thought I was free, but was dreadfully afraid to venture, for fear of the consequences that might follow in case of a discovery. Then I told her what a good offer I had. . . . She fell a-laughing at my scruples about marrying, and told me the other was no marriage, but a cheat on both sides; and that, as we were parted by mutual consent, the nature of the contract was destroyed, and the obligation was mutually discharged. She had arguments for this at the tip of her tongue; and, in short, reasoned me out of my reason; not but that it was too by the help of my own inclination" (199).

---

as soon trust a man whose interest binds him to be just to me as a man whose principle binds himself" (*Captain Singleton*, in *Romances and Narratives*, vi, 228); and in the *Whitehall Evening Post* for Dec. 30, 1718, "Meeting House" argues that " '*Tis safer to trust those whose Interest binds them to be honest,* than those *whose Principle binds them*" (Lee, ii, 86). Mother Midnight here makes skillful use of the same cynical doctrine.

From a casuistical standpoint the question here is whether
spouses have the right to "discharge" one another from matrimonial ties, and can grant one another liberty to marry again.
In defense of such rights it had long been urged, occasionally
even in reputable quarters, that marriage is a contract like any
other and can therefore be dissolved in the same way that it
was formed, by the mutual consent of the contracting parties.[50]
This argument is employed by Mother Midnight, but the analogy with ordinary contracts had been denied consistently by
earlier casuists. Divine and human law, they pointed out, contain special provisions governing matrimony, and private persons are thus sinful as well as criminal in usurping for themselves the power to dissolve existing marriages or permit further ones.[51] A second point in the midwife's argument is that

[50] One of the supposititious correspondents of *Applebee's Journal*
writes that "Mr. *Milton's* Arguments go a great way with me; for . . .
if my Wife and I,—by mere agreeing upon Terms,—came together and
married,—why may not my wife and I,—by the like mere agreeing upon
Terms,—separate again? For if mutual Consent be the Essence of the
Contract of Matrimony, why should not the dissolving that mutual
Consent dissolve likewise the Marriage, and disengage the Parties from
one another again?" These contentions are countered in another number: "I know they plead a learned and valuable Man as their Authority for dissolving the matrimonial Covenant, and for parting effectually,
both sides giving Consent; but neither will the Laws of God or Man
come into his Scheme, and all that can be said for so great a Man
. . . arguing for it, is, that he shew'd he had his Foibles, in the midst
of all his forcible Reasonings, and that . . . he had a bad Wife; nor
had his Wife the most agreeable Husband" (April 24, 1725 [Lee, III,
379-80]; Jan. 16, 1725 [Lee, III, 355-56]). Joseph Hall is probably
alluding to Milton's "too well penned pages" in *Resolutions and Decisions, Works*, VII, 371. Cf. also *The Counsellor's Plea for the Divorce
of Sir G. D. and Mrs. F.* (1715), pp. 7-9; and Locke's *Two Treatises
of Government*, II, 81, ed. Peter Laslett (Cambridge, 1967), p. 339.

[51] Among the casuists, see Robert Sanderson, *Works*, ed. William
Jacobson, 6 vols. (Oxford, 1854), V, 125-6; Richard Baxter, *Christian
Directory*, in *Practical Works*, IV, 159. Cf. *A.M.*, IV, ii, 6, and Defoe's
Conjugal Lewdness, p. 118: "No, no, I shall open no Doors to the
vitiated Wishes of the Times; where Men would have Marriage be a

Moll is now free to marry because "the other was no marriage,
but a cheat on both sides." That such deception invalidates
a marriage contract had also been denied by many seventeenth-
century casuists.[52] To argue, as Mother Midnight does, that "a
cheat on both sides" means "no marriage," is to flout not only
the prevailing laws of church and state, but the common judgment of casuists for a century past. The brief exchange between Moll and her governess thus parodies similar queries
and responses in Dunton's and Defoe's periodicals, for the
old lady does nothing but restate Moll's own case in more
plausible terms, rather than submitting it to the test of relevant sanctions. She "reasons [Moll] out of [her] reason," then,
in the sense that her specious arguments soothe Moll's conscience instead of arousing it. Moll's accusation makes it sound
as if the old woman is guilty of overcoming her wholesome

---

stated Contract; where as the Parties agreement made the Bargain, so
the same mutual Agreement might dissolve it." And Moll herself remarks of the Bath liaison that "I was all this while a married woman,
a wife to Mr. —— the linen-draper, who, though he had left me by
the necessity of his circumstances, had no power to discharge me from
the marriage contract that was between us, or to give me a legal
liberty to marry again" (p. 144).

[52] William Perkins maintains that "though the deceit be very of-
fensiue to the party deluded . . . yet it is not of force to breake the
contract: because the ability [i.e. wealth] of either, or both parties
belongs not to the essence of marriage" (*Workes*, 3 vols. [1616-18], II,
682). Jean La Placete summarizes other opinions in *The Christian
Casuist: Or, A Treatise of Conscience,* trans. Basil Kennett (1705),
p. 125. For somewhat more light-hearted discussions of this issue, see
Ben Jonson's *Epicoene, or the Silent Woman,* V, iii, and the *Spectator*,
No. 41 (April 17, 1711). The *Athenian Mercury* contains a number
of variations on this case. One man, whose wife turns out to have been
in debt at the time of marriage, asks whether he can lawfully leave
her, and is advised that "had the Woman only represented her Fortunes better than they really were, to get a good Husband, tho she
was therein imprudent and criminal, and ne'er the less so, because 'tis
so common a thing in the other sex, yet . . . it had been no reason
at all for parting with her, when once they had been together for
better for worse" (XIV, xxvi, 1).

convictions with pernicious doctrine and "bewitching eloquence," when in fact (as Moll herself goes on to admit) she
has merely reinforced with "reason" a decision that Moll had
already arrived at through her own "inclination."

In a case of conscience, various fears and desires within Moll,
various demands posed by her outward circumstances, and
various ethical norms converge, so that clear-cut choices on
her part (and clear-cut evaluations on ours) are often made
difficult. Once Moll plunges into her "depredations upon mankind," however, there is relatively little of this kind of complexity, and conflict tends to be mainly external, with Moll
on one side and society on the other. These scenes are not
without drama, but as Moll gradually hardens in crime her
actions become matters of habit, and the dramatic issue is no
longer what she will choose to do, or why, but whether she
will get away with it. Certain scenes resist such generalizations, for among the episodes of crime some, especially at the
outset, remain more in the casuistical mode than others. Indeed, the preliminaries to Moll's first theft are as elaborate
as any of her earlier attempts to palliate her misdeeds. Long
before there is any prospect of her becoming a thief, she begins erecting her defenses. "Now I seemed landed in a safe
harbour," she says of her marriage to the banker's clerk, "after
the stormy voyage of life past was at an end," and she tells
at length how she "wept over the remembrance of past follies,"
"abhorred the levity and extravagance of [her] former life,"
and settled with "the utmost tranquility" into the role of sober
matron. But she intersperses her account of this "uninter-
rupted course of ease and content" with a series of ominous
hints that her "stormy voyage" is not over. "Oh had this particular scene of life lasted," she exclaims, "and had I not fallen
into the poverty which is the sure bane of virtue, how happy
had I been" (217-18). At this point we do not know what pov-

erty will drive her to. But by being satisfied to live "in the ordinary way," without wanting to "make a figure, as the world calls it," she suggests that it will take drastic pressure to force her to relapse from her new "life of virtue and sobriety" back to the "loose ungoverned part [she] had acted before" (218, 217), and that if she subsequently does anything rash, it will be because fate has deprived her of "leisure to consider."

The death of her husband eventually plunges Moll into the straits she has gloomily anticipated. Nor does she rest her case solely on her financial plight: she also laments that she is left "perfectly friendless and helpless," and that "in this distress I had no assistant, no friend to comfort or advise me" (219). Her isolation not only aggravates her fears—"the utmost distress," she says, "seemed as if it was come, before it was really very near"—but deprives her of practical (not to speak of honest) means of coping with them, so that in the following passage "want of friends" is as crucial as "want of bread": "When I looked before me, my very heart would sink within me at the inevitable approach of misery and want. Oh let none read this part without seriously reflecting on the circumstances of a desolate state, and how they would grapple with mere want of friends and want of bread; it will certainly make them think not of sparing what they have only, but of looking up to heaven for support, and of the wise man's prayer, 'Give me not poverty, lest I steal.' Let them remember that a time of distress is a time of dreadful temptation, and all the strength to resist is taken away; poverty presses, the soul is made desperate by distress, and what can be done?" (220). This passage also echoes an earlier statement, made while Moll was still comfortably married, that "There are temptations which it is not in the power of human nature to resist, and few know what would be their case if driven to the same exigencies" (217). Her later appeal to the reader is still in the third person, but has become far more direct and impassioned. At no point in the book, in fact, is the reader more earnestly challenged to put himself in Moll's place, and it is only now that the full point of the foregoing prosperous-virtuous interlude becomes clear. Having first demonstrated that she could be as well behaved as the reader when she was as well off, and being about to concede that poverty forced her to crime, Moll in effect demands of the reader whether he supposes his virtue would be any more secure than hers under similar stress.[53]

Even now, Moll cannot hazard a bald recital of the facts of her first crime, but must find a way of acknowledging the deed without forfeiting the reader's esteem. This she does by raising to its highest pitch a device already used at the time of her first, third, and fifth marriages. She portrays herself as a passive instrument, manipulated by a will more powerful than her own, and asserts that her action was not only unpremeditated, but involuntary; she was a mere automaton, guided by irresistible forces outside herself.[54] Nor does she at once

[53] Another detail that deserves comment is the effectiveness of introducing the Biblical text "Give me not poverty, lest I steal" at this moment. Not only do Solomon's words seem to sanction the act Moll is about to commit, but they are the first specific indication of what the act will be. Moll's two earlier references to poverty, as "the sure bane of virtue" and "the worst of all snares" (pp. 217, 218), may point rather directly to the path Moll will take, but it is left to Solomon to spell out the inevitability of crime as a consequence of poverty, and thus to obviate any complacently moralistic answer to Moll's rhetorical question, "What can be done?" Defoe also quotes or alludes to Proverbs 9:30 in the *Review*, iii (Mar. 5, 1706), 110; *Robinson Crusoe*, in *Romances and Narratives*, i, 3; *Serious Reflections*, in *Romances and Narratives*, iii, 33; *Colonel Jack*, ed. Samuel Holt Monk, Oxford English Novels (1965), p. 163; *The Compleat English Tradesman*, ii, 193; *The Compleat English Gentleman*, pp. 102-03; other contemporary discussions of this theme are cited in my *Defoe and Spiritual Autobiography* (Princeton, 1965), p. 78 n.

[54] "I think I may truly say I was distracted and raving, when prompted by I know not what spirit, and, as it were, doing I did not know what or why, I dressed me . . . and went out. I am very sure

identify the devil as the culprit: by bringing in the devil only gradually she underlines the fact that at the time she "knew not"—the construction is repeated four times in two sentences —what she was doing, or what was causing her to do it. As the moment of the theft approaches, the role of the devil becomes more decisive. Moll sees a bundle on a stool in an apothecary's shop: "This was the bait; and the devil, who I said laid the snare, as readily prompted me as if he had spoke, for I remember, and shall never forget it, 'twas like a voice spoken to me over my shoulder, 'Take the bundle; be quick; do it this moment'" (221). As in her earlier self-portrait as a bear led to the stake, Moll is once again a helpless animal, this time the victim of "baits" and "snares" put cunningly and maliciously in her way. Conventional as they are, such images are appropriate to the air of bedeviled passivity she is trying to create.[55] After such a prelude the theft itself is the work of a moment, as indeed it must be if we are not to raise awkward questions; and to prevent them from arising once the deed is done, Moll immediately exclaims, "It is impossible to express the horror of my soul all the while I did it": then come two breathless paragraphs describing her escape, and our attention is diverted from the rights or wrongs of what she has done. An atmosphere of moral perplexity thus gives way to one of physical alarm. We are caught up in the pace and perils of her flight, and in wishing her good speed we move still fur-

---

I had no manner of design in my head when I went out; I neither knew nor considered where to go, or on what business; but as the devil carried me out and laid his bait for me, so he brought me, to be sure, to the place, for I knew not whither I was going or what I did" (pp. 220-21).

[55] It is also noteworthy that Moll never asserts the devil addressed her: it was *"as if* he had spoke," and " 'twas *like* a voice." Yet the instructions she goes on to quote are so terse and emphatic that we do her the favor of believing that it was the devil who spoke, without her actually saying so. We not only accept Moll's claim, but extend it farther than she herself does.

ther towards being her accomplices. Nor is the episode over once Moll safely reaches home. "I sat me down," she reports, "and cried most vehemently. . . . I went to my bed for that night, but slept little; the horror of the fact was upon my mind." The next day it occurs to her that the bundle may have belonged to someone as poor as herself, which "tormented me worse than all the rest, for three or four days' time" (222-23). Through these and similar details, Moll is at pains to show that the role of thief is still wholly alien and repugnant to her.

The entire scene rests on traditional discussions of the conditions under which theft is justifiable—discussions which were to be found, of course, in the philosophy and divinity of all periods. Earlier casuists, in other words, are by no means the sole authorities to have shaped Defoe's attitudes on so widely canvassed a topic. But whatever bodies of theory and doctrine influenced the substance of his views on theft, the manner in which they are introduced and manipulated throughout this episode can be described as casuistical. Once again, it is not a question of Moll treating her predicament as a case of conscience within the narrative. At no time before or after the crucial moment in Leadenhall Street does she explicitly weigh the pros and cons of snatching untended bundles from apothecaries' shops. On the other hand, she produces numerous defenses of her act, but with an air of unargumentative candor. Like the theft itself, they seem to arise casually and undesignedly, and to be thrust upon her rather than sought out. She apparently does no more than record her predicament, her state of mind, and some unexceptionable old saws on the connection between poverty and theft. The only "authority" she invokes is Solomon, but even he is cited almost inadvertently, not openly appealed to in her own behalf. Moll's procedure is thus casuistical both in method and tone, and although no single touch is enough to exonerate her, their cumulative effect is to dispose us in her favor. Without challenging the fact that a crime is a crime, she again demonstrates that circumstances alter cases, and that the agent cannot be equated with the act.

Moll's next adventure is introduced with some of the same casuistical paraphernalia. Despite her misgivings over the first theft, she has "an evil counsellor within," who is "continually prompting" her; "He tempted me again, by the same wicked impulse that had said 'Take that bundle,' to go out again and seek for what might happen" (223). By now, the twofold evasion is familiar. Temptations and impulses to mischief do not originate in Moll, but in her counsellors; and she herself is the first to label the counsellors "evil" and the impulses "wicked," so that she further dissociates herself from them, and aligns herself with the respectable reader by anticipating his severest judgment. As for the adventure itself, the robbery of a gold necklace from a child on its way home from dancing school, Moll's main line of defense is bold and successful. We are told at the outset that "the devil put a snare in my way of a dreadful nature indeed, and such a one as I have never had before or since" (223). This does not refer to robbing the child, which is easily accomplished, but to murdering it: "the devil put me upon killing the child in the dark alley, that it might not cry, but the very thought frighted me so that I was ready to drop down" (224). Our attention is shifted away from the robbery that was committed to a murder that was not; shunning a greater, hypothetical crime, Moll obscures the lesser, actual one.

Previous commentators have overlooked an interesting analogue to this scene in Defoe's *Political History of the Devil* (1726), in which a needy tradesman's deliberations over killing a child contrast sharply with Moll's immediate rejection of the idea.[56] The man's horror is eventually as decisive as Moll's fright, but his speculating beforehand that he "need do no more but twist the Neck of it a little, or crush it with his Knee," though appropriate in a passage designed to illustrate the devil's influence on dreams, introduces a note of cold-bloodedness that would have been fatal to the maternal self-image which Moll strives for throughout her version of the scene. Like the tradesman, she refers to the child as an "innocent creature," but she also calls it "the poor little lamb" and "the poor baby," which helps to make credible her claims that "I had a great many tender thoughts about me yet" (223, 225). Moreover, by chiding the mother for her "negligence" and "vanity," and by castigating the maid as a "careless jade"— to all of which we are bound to agree—Moll implies that her own concern for the child is greater than theirs.[57]

Nevertheless Moll's success here is at best partial and precarious. Her pretence to have given the parents a "just reproof for their negligence" and taught them to "take more care of it another time" is no more brazen or sanctimonious than various others, but it is too gratuitous and patent a piece of special pleading to be altogether effective. The point is not that it is special pleading, but that it is transparently so, and defeats itself by becoming obtrusive. By adopting the pose of public benefactor, Moll dissipates some of the force of her brilliant primary manoeuvre, which had been to divert us from the temptation she succumbed to by making much of the one

[56] Pp. 361-62. Alan D. McKillop has noted still another analogue in *An Essay on the History and Reality of Apparitions* (1727), pp. 207-09; in this version the negligence of the nurse and the vanity and ostentation of the child's parents are stressed, but the temptation to kill the child is omitted. See *The Early Masters of English Fiction* (Lawrence, 1956), p. 222, n. 39.

[57] On this passage, see James Sutherland's excellent Introduction to the Riverside *Moll Flanders* (Boston, 1957), p. xiv; *The Rise of the Novel*, p. 124; and Frank W. Chandler, *The Literature of Roguery*, 2 vols. (Boston, 1907), II, 291.

she resisted. Her biggest problem with rhetoric (as with shop-lifting) is not knowing when to stop.

This episode, Moll declares, "left no great concern upon me" (224), and in the scenes that follow, her rationalizations become steadily more perfunctory.[58] Only one further adventure, in fact, causes her any real qualms—her theft of the family plate from a burning house. "It is with horror that I tell what a treasure I found there," Moll says when she returns to her chamber and opens her bundle. (Most bedroom scenes in the latter part of the book are bundle-openings, and compared with the more familiar novelistic bedroom scene, these are narrated not only with as much zest, but with the same zest). After cataloguing the contents of this particular bundle, she declares that "This was the greatest and the worst prize that ever I was concerned in; for indeed, though . . . I was hardened now beyond the power of all reflection in other cases, yet it really touched me to the very soul when I looked into this treasure, to think of the poor disconsolate gentle-woman who had lost so much by the fire besides . . . I say, I confess the inhumanity of this action moved me very much,

[58] To disencumber himself, a pursued thief drops near Moll the bundle of silk and velvet which he has just stolen, and she naturally appropriates it. "This, indeed, I did with less disturbance than I had done formerly, for these things I did not steal, but they were stolen to my hand. . . . as I had only robbed the thief, I made no scruple at taking these goods, and being very glad of them too" (p. 226). In its emphasis on the fact that she has only robbed the robber, the scene oddly echoes her earlier essay at deceiving a deceiver. But to distract us from what is here little more than a verbal quibble, Moll lays great stress on what the "real" thieves had done, and thus implies by contrast how trifling her own role and its reward were. Moreover, the information that the mercer got back nearly all his goods is probably inserted in case we should object that he, and not the thief, is the victim of what she calls her "lucky adventure" (p. 225). The mercer and his assistants were "extremely well satisfied that they had recovered the booty and taken the thief"; since they are so content, who are we to complain?

and made me relent exceedingly, and tears stood in my eyes upon the subject; but with all my sense of its being cruel and inhuman, I could never find it in my heart to make any restitution" (238-39). Moll's very scruples indicate how hardened she has become, and how incapable of changing her course; she still knows right from wrong, but has lost the power to choose.[59] Yet her burst of sentiment may have the more immediate purpose of gaining sympathy for what might otherwise earn contempt: we are invited to deplore but not despise her sorry state. Whether her sentimentality has this effect on modern readers is nevertheless doubtful. Moll's compassion for victims is probably intended to elicit ours for her, but when she refers to little children as "poor lambs," our tendency by now is to suspect that there will soon be a fleecing.[60]

Moll has now reached the point at which, as she puts it, she "cast off all remorse and repentance," and in the midst of her recital of felonious triumphs, she remarks that "I could fill up this whole discourse with the variety of such adventures, which daily invention directed to, and which I managed with the utmost dexterity, and always with success" (277). We are given a good many of these adventures, in which dexterity and success are celebrated for their own sakes, as they are in the picaresque tradition. Before, Moll had distinguished her motives, reflections, and qualifying circumstances from her overt actions, but overt action now crowds out all else. Once more it is necessary to cite an exception. The episode

---

[59] See *Defoe and Spiritual Autobiography*, pp. 154-55.

[60] That Defoe does not intend any such irony is suggested by his making other sympathetic females speak of unfortunate children as "poor lambs": see *Roxana*, p. 21. On the passage just quoted, Martin Price perceptively comments that "Fielding was to make something beautifully ironic of this kind of mixture of motives. Defoe uses it differently; *candor disarms the moral judgment that irony would require*" (*To the Palace of Wisdom: Studies in Order and Energy from Dryden to Blake* [Garden City, 1964], p. 276; italics mine).

involving the baronet whom Moll meets in Bartholomew Fair is the longest in this part of the book, and harks back to the earlier narrative in more than its concern with sex; as in the scene at Bath, Moll's position is never really in doubt, and the drama centers instead on the man. The baronet's dilemma may have been suggested to Defoe by a case of conscience in the *Athenian Mercury*:

> I have long since continued in a very Vitious Course of Living, rendring my self incapable of resisting any Temptation, by first being guilty of Excessive Drinking, that inlett to all other Mischiefs. 'Tis my Misfortune to have Contracted too great a Familiarity with a Woman, who being sensible how much I despise her in my more sober and sedate Thoughts, endeavours chiefly to seduce me, in the midst of my Extravagance. . . . I can . . . easily perceive the Aversion I ought to have, and in what manner to treat her; but again she . . . diligently Uses all her Insinuating Charms and deluding Stratagems . . . which sometimes prove so Inviting, that the gaudy Baite tho' Treacherous and Destructive, becomes inevitably resistless, and Reason it self deprived of that Power which ought to withstand such damned Allurements. Thus I commit what is afterwards the Abhorrence of my Soul (xi, i, 9).

The man goes on *"humbly to entreat your Advice how I shall Disengage my self"*; the Athenian Society replies that there can be "no *Amendment* while you are *near* her," and advises him to "flye the *Fair Destroyer*, tho' 'twas to the Ends of the Earth." As in the Bath episode of *Moll Flanders*, the emphasis is on avoiding temptation by all possible means, rather than trying to withstand or overcome it; but the major temptation is assumed to be the *"Fair Destroyer."* In the Bartholomew Fair episode, the burden of responsibility is shifted from the "de-

luding Stratagems" and "damned Allurements" of the woman
—who after all is Moll herself—to the power of wine to make
men "worse than lunatic." What we are given, in effect, is
the *"Fair Destroyer's"* version of the story as well as the
man's, but its focus is on his ambiguous personality. For we
are given various views of him—his own, Moll's, her governess's, and that of a friend of his family—which not only
differ from each other, but shift individually as the scene
unfolds. They range from sympathy to extreme cynicism.[61]

If we ask which of these views is correct, the answer is that
they all are. Like the devil, wine is in some sense foreign to a
man, but once he comes under its spell he literally incorporates
its baneful nature.[62] Defoe was fascinated and appalled by the
resulting inconsistencies. Elsewhere in his writings he ascribes to wine the same quasi-Manichean powers, and in *The
Commentator* he presents a character who stands midway

[61] In a single paragraph we are told that "he is as civil a gentleman,
there is not a finer man, nor a soberer, graver, modester person in the
whole city," but also reminded that "your modest men in common
opinion are sometimes no better than other people, only they keep a
better character, or, if you please, are the better hypocrites" (pp. 264-
65). Moll calls him "a fop . . . blinded by his appetite," and finds
"nothing so absurd, so surfeiting, so ridiculous" as the spectacle he
makes of himself "heated by wine in his head, and a wicked gust in
his inclination." Yet she also refers to him as "a good sort of man in
himself: a gentleman that had no harm in his design; a man of sense,
and of a fine behaviour, a comely handsome person, a sober solid
countenance, a charming beautiful face, and everything that could be
agreeable" (pp. 260-61). Finally, the man himself, like his prototype
in the *Athenian Mercury*, "would often make just reflections . . . upon
the crime itself, and upon the particular circumstances of it with respect
to himself." ("He made the moral always himself," Moll assures us—
and had she in fact been content to leave the task to him, the episode
might have been more successful).

[62] Cf. *Colonel Jack*, p. 240: "Drink, like the Devil, when it gets hold
of any one, tho' but a little, it goes on by little and little to their
Destruction." Neither here nor in *Defoe and Spiritual Autobiography*
(pp. 153-54) have I dealt adequately with Defoe's conception of the
devil, a complex topic which deserves special study.

between the *Athenian Mercury* querist and the baronet in
Moll Flanders—"a Man of Temper and Gravity, of Sense and
good Humour, when himself; he was, by the Operation of
a little Wine, metamorphiz'd into a Mad-Man, a meer Fury;
qualified for any Mischief, and perhaps such as might be as
likely to ruin himself, as any of his Fellow-Creatures; just as
Fate presented Objects to his Distemper'd Fury, and to lye
unhappily in his Way: How such a Man . . . continually ex-
pos'd to the Hazard of being undone, should yet, by merciful
Providence be preserv'd so long . . . is a Subject that we may
Discourse upon again upon another Occasion."[63] The Bartholomew Fair episode furnished such an occasion, ill-chosen as it
may have been. Nevertheless, the limited success the episode
does achieve is owing to a retention and elaboration of the
paradox that the baronet is both admirable and absurd, modest and foppish, grave and foolish, sensible and mad.

The criminal phase of Moll's narrative culminates in her
seizure, her imprisonment in Newgate, her trial and conviction, and her eventual conversion. I have discussed these
scenes in detail elsewhere, and maintained that when Moll
ultimately repents, the significance of the process is emphasized not only by its contrast with the incomplete and ineffec-
tual versions that have preceded it, but also by its conformity
to a classic pattern of the soul's renewal.[64] I have suggested

[63] No. LVI (July 15, 1720); cf. *Colonel Jack*, p. 241: "O! The Power
of Intemperance! and how it Encroaches on the best Dispositions in
the World; how it comes upon us gradually and insensibly . . . changing the most Virtuous, regular, well instructed, and well inclin'd
Tempers, into worse than Brutal." See also *The Great Law of Subor-
dination consider'd* (1724), pp. 6, 64.

[64] See *Defoe and Spiritual Autobiography*, pp. 155-60. While Moll is
in Newgate, a traditional case of conscience is touched upon by the
Ordinary, who pesters her about "making a full discovery, and the
like, without which he told me God would never forgive me" (p. 320).
In Applebee's Journal for Dec. 29, 1722, Defoe says "It is a Question

that subsequent scenes in the New World (and the penulti-
mate sentence of the preface) call into question the complete-
ness of her moral regeneration, but not the genuineness of her
spiritual rebirth. Since the present study is concerned with
Defoe's treatment of moral rather than spiritual problems,[65]
it is appropriate to inquire whether the Virginia scenes present anything comparable in either form or substance to the
cases of conscience already examined.

One source of drama in these scenes is a fresh dilemma over
revealing or concealing awkward truths. Anxiety generated
by a guilty secret had dominated Moll's earlier experience in
Virginia, had nearly plunged her into a fatal consumption in
Colchester, and had given a somber undertone to her marriage with the banker's clerk. Her conversion, on the other
hand, had "unlocked the sluices of [her] passions" (332): con-
fessing her guilt to someone with the story, she had found

---

among Divines whether a Criminal can be a true Penitent, and may
expect God's Mercy, if he does not, when he confesses his Offence, add
to his Confession a full Discovery of all his Accomplices; so as that
to the utmost of his Power they may be brought to Justice. I am not
Casuist enough to decide this Cause, tho' in my Opinion, I incline to
the Negative, namely, that he cannot" (Lee, iii, 83). For an earlier
discussion, see Hall, *Resolutions and Decisions*, in *Works*, vii, 413.

[65] This distinction seems to me justified by Defoe's own tendency to
regard the realms of morality (man's relation to man) and spirituality
(the soul's relation to God) as distinct. I do not think he shares the
view of some modern readers that Moll's residual moral infirmities
must belie her alleged spiritual soundness. In so brief a note, there is
a danger of exaggerating and oversimplifying—in this instance, of
representing Defoe as an Antinomian. My point is that there *may* be
an intimate connection between the faith and the works of a Defoean
character, and hence between his spiritual and moral states, as in the
cases of Robinson Crusoe and H. F. the saddler; but that according to
Defoe's religious and ethical convictions, there is no *necessary* connection, let alone simple parity, between virtue and grace on the one
hand, or vice and reprobation on the other. It therefore seems legitimate to have dealt chiefly with spiritual questions in my former discussion of *Moll Flanders*, and to focus on moral questions here.

relief from anxiety. But as John Bunyan, Robinson Crusoe, and others in life and literature had discovered before her, anxiety is not banished once and for all by religious conversion. In prison, Moll had told Jemmy that by accepting transportation to Virginia they would be able to "live as new people in a new world, nobody having anything to say to us, or we to them," and that they would "look back on all our past disasters with infinite satisfaction" (350). Once she reaches Virginia, however, her cares revive: she cannot reveal herself to her former husband and son, because she has come as a transported convict with a new husband, nor can she "so much as think of breaking the secret of [her] former marriage to [her] husband" (373). As in the first Virginia scene, she finds herself trapped between threatening alternatives, and although she now has no incest taboo to struggle with, her dread of exposure proves to be almost as acute and disabling. Once again, her dilemma is more a psychological than a moral one. In the course of reflecting on the compulsion to disburden oneself of secrets, she does say that it works with particular vehemence "in the minds of those who are guilty of any atrocious villainy, such as secret murder" (374); and it is true that here as elsewhere, Defoe indicates "how necessary and inseperable a Companion, Fear is to Guilt."[66] Nevertheless Moll's comment on her earlier Virginia predicament—that "I had no great concern about it in point of conscience" (114)—applies equally to this new bout of anxiety. What troubles her is not a difficult moral choice in the present, but the danger of shameful revelations about her past.

For Moll, then, this is not really a case of conscience, yet it preserves something of the tone and formal structure of one. "Here was a perplexity," she says at the outset, "that I had not indeed skill to manage myself in, neither knew I what course to take. It lay heavy upon my mind night and day"

[66] *Colonel Jack*, p. 291; see p. 178 below.

(372). "Under the certain oppression of this weight upon my mind," she later declares, "I laboured in the case I have been naming" (376). Similar remarks throughout the scene convey the same air of protracted deliberation: Moll's mental state is emphasized, her action correspondingly played down. We may deplore her dissimulation, but her distress invites sympathy. Furthermore, Moll interrupts the account of her own crisis, first to "appeal to all human testimony" in support of her theory that a fundamental "necessity of nature" compels man to divulge secrets; then to ascribe the process to Providence, which uses "natural causes to produce . . . extraordinary effects"; next to give "several remarkable instances of this"; and finally to argue that her remarks have not been "an unnecessary digression" (374-75). Defoe often establishes the total context of an ethical problem by investing it with greater generality through abstractions, and with further concreteness through analogies. In this respect, too, the present scene is handled in a manner characteristic of a full-fledged case of conscience, even though conscience itself plays little part. Finally and perhaps most importantly, Moll's situation is set forth so as to suggest that the course she will choose is genuinely in doubt. To conceal her story is an almost insupportable "weight upon [her] spirits," but to disclose it to either son or husband will be disastrous. We may surmise skeptically that she will prefer concealment, and she herself hints as much midway in the episode ("let them say what they please of our sex not being able to keep a secret, my life is a plain conviction to me of the contrary" [374]). All the same, Defoe manages to keep the outcome of the episode in suspense by placing Moll in a dilemma that retains the mood and shape, if not the ethical substance, of a traditional case of conscience.

Moll's further dealings with both her son and husband continue to illustrate the kind of double vision which marks

Defoe's conception of her throughout the book. A tension
between the culpable and the engaging is sustained, in fact,
even when the heroine begins to experience the joys of family
reunion and capital gain that signalize a Defoean happy ending. The following passage occurs at the end of Moll's first
day with her son Humphry. She has already spoken with
faint contempt of her husband's ignorance of geography and
frontier estate-management, and in lines reminiscent of her
scorn for that "land-water thing called a gentleman-tradesman," she has remarked that "he was bred a gentleman, and
by consequence was not only unacquainted, but indolent"
(376-77). Here she more openly acknowledges that she finds
him a useless encumbrance. Elated by her son's kindness,
Moll concludes her account of their meeting, "thus I was as
if I had been in a new world, and began secretly now to wish
that I had not brought my Lancashire husband from England
at all." But as if abashed at her own callousness, she says at
once, "However, that wish was not hearty neither, for I loved
my Lancashire husband entirely, as indeed I had ever done
from the beginning; and he merited from me as much as it
was possible for a man to do; but that by the way" (386).

The sequence is curious but characteristic. Are the egotism
and treachery of Moll's secret wish nullified by her avowals of
constancy? Is the very existence of her wish somehow negated
by the assertion that it "was not hearty neither?" When Moll
contradicts herself, can her second, more emphatic proposition
ever quite cancel the first? It seems to me that her retractions
never fully "take back" whatever she has said or done; the
process is always additive, so that what appear to be clarifying
denials actually tend to make her position more ambiguous.
In examining the logically clashing elements of an earlier
episode, I suggested that the object was not consistency but
comprehensiveness. For all its brevity, the present passage
demonstrates the related principle that Moll's arguments reg-

ularly end *in*clusively, not *con*clusively. Both generous and selfish, both faithful and disloyal, her attitude towards this charming, good-for-nothing husband is deeply (and understandably) ambivalent; and the scene leaves us feeling no less ambivalent about her. We may recoil momentarily from her heartlessness, but so does she, with disarming humanity: once again, in a manner typical of the entire book, Defoe portrays Moll as both reprehensible and sympathetic.

Roxana

NOWHERE in Defoe's writings is the tension between sympathy and judgment more pronounced than in his last major work of fiction, *Roxana*. Martin Price has called attention to the "suppleness or elusiveness" of Defoe's characters, and to their "divided and inconsistent natures."[1] Roxana epitomizes these qualities. On the one hand, there are signs throughout the book, which become unmistakable towards the end, that Defoe regards his heroine as a damned soul. On the other hand, his imaginative oneness with her often seems virtually complete, and at such times we too may be drawn into a kind of complicity with her. Defoe revels vicariously in Roxana's opulence, and chronicles her triumphs with evident relish; yet a contrary impulse to disavow any such involvement is increasingly powerful as the book proceeds. Advocacy and reprobation, affection and loathing, amusement and horror—all are present. A contemporary caricature shows Satan playing leapfrog with Defoe,[2] and there is a sense in which Devil and Dissenter go leapfrogging through Roxana's narrative. Rather than balancing opposed attitudes, Defoe often engages himself unreservedly in his heroine's thoughts and actions, and then abruptly recoils. His periodic urge towards dissociation helps to explain some of the book's strange incongruities of diction: in this "unromantic romance," as Jane Jack shrewdly calls it, there is both more elevation and more bathos

[1] *To the Palace of Wisdom: Studies in Order and Energy from Dryden to Blake* (Garden City, 1964), p. 264; *PQ*, XLIII (1964), 353-54.
[2] Reproduced in James Sutherland, *Defoe*, 2nd edn. (1950), p. 118.

than in any of Defoe's other novels, and the bathetic lines express with striking literalness the down-to-earth, anti-romantic impulse that regularly (and brutally) trips up the heroine.[3] Other devices to be discussed later have the same effect; the point here is that on Defoe's part—and hence to some extent on ours—emotional involvement with Roxana and critical detachment from her occur successively, not simultaneously. Instead of sustaining a double vision that would make her appear at once sympathetic and reprehensible, much of the book oscillates between extremes of identification and repudiation, with the latter ultimately dominant.

At certain moments, however, a kind of double vision is in fact achieved. Sympathy and judgment remain in tension, but they come into play concurrently: fellow feeling and critical objectivity are brought to bear on the same action, rather than by turns dominating singly. This is particularly true early in the novel. When she is about to be seduced by her landlord, Roxana cites her poverty, her gratitude, her helpless isolation, and the "Rhetorick" of her maid Amy as factors that induce her to comply with the man's suit, yet she goes on to declare that she does not "plead this as a Justification of my Conduct, but that it may move the Pity, even of those that abhor the Crime."[4] Roxana frankly acknowledges that "in the Sence of the Laws, both of God and our Country," she and her landlord are "no more than two Adulterers, in

[3] *Roxana*, ed. Jane Jack, Oxford English Novels (1964), Introduction, p. 2; all quotations are from this edition. There is bathos in Roxana's departure from Holland with "all my Money in my Pocket, and a Bastard in my Belly" (p. 163); in the metaphor she uses to prove that it is preposterous for a woman to marry her lover (p. 152); and in her recurrent references to her body and Amy's as "this Carcass of mine," "her Carcass" (pp. 74, 215).

[4] P. 39. "Pity humane Frailty," she adds, "you that read of a Woman reduc'd in her Youth, and Prime, to the utmost Misery and Distress. . . . I say pity her if she was not able, after all these things, to make any more Resistance" (p. 42).

short, a Whore and a Rogue" (43); and elsewhere she *"makes frequent Excursions, in a just censuring and condemning her own Practice"* (2). It may be (as one critic has suggested) that her self-indictments "leave no doubt in the reader's mind of her complete culpability."[5] Yet there is something disarming about the blunt candor of Roxana's confessions, and they sometimes have the effect of increasing, not lessening, our sympathy for her. They do this by forcing us to distinguish between what Roxana is and what she does. We may "abhor the Crime," but no more so than the criminal herself, whose energetic strictures on her own conduct forestall ours, and align her values with our own. I shall have more to say about the heroine's frequent and strident self-reproaches; they do not all function alike, but some of them—especially in the opening episodes—evoke a response that is at once critical and sympathetic.

Rather than generalizing further about the impact that *Roxana* has upon us, it will be helpful to examine some of the significantly equivocal features of the heroine and her story. In the first place, there is the quality of the narrative itself: a style that simultaneously reveals and conceals. Roxana often knows what others in her story do not, and tells us, so that we know more than her husbands, lovers, children, and confidants. But sometimes she knows things that she will not tell us, and at others she appears (or pretends) not to know things that she would tell us if she could. As a consequence, someone is mystified nearly all the time: occasionally the heroine herself, more often the reader, and almost always the others in

---

[5] Maximillian E. Novak, "Crime and Punishment in Defoe's *Roxana*," *JEGP*, LXV (1966), 440. I have discussed these opening episodes at length in an essay entitled "Sympathy *v.* Judgment in Roxana's First Liaison," which is to appear in the forthcoming festschrift for Louis A. Landa (Oxford, 1970).

her tale. But whatever she withholds from us, Roxana hides far more from those closest to her within the story, and this is rather insinuating: without baldly addressing him as "*mon semblable, mon frère*," Roxana establishes a camaraderie in intrigue with the reader, and much of the narrative permits him to share Roxana's triumphs without forcing him to share her guilt.

Mystification thus generates a bond with the heroine as well as detachment from her. There are numerous scenes in which Roxana tells us the true state of things, but hoodwinks those she deals with in the story. The Dutch merchant is the man most befuddled by Roxana's elusiveness, yet we are its beneficiaries just as surely as he is its victim. Soon after their reunion in London, the Dutch merchant is in an "Extasie upon the Subject of his finding me out": "I cou'd easily have accounted for his not finding me," Roxana assures us, "if I had but set down the Detail for my real Retirement; but I gave it a new, and indeed, a truly hypocritical Turn" (225; "truly hypocritical" is the kind of oxymoron that often reinforces the equivocal character of Roxana's statements). "Poor Gentleman! thought I, you know little of me," Roxana says at one point: the effect of such scenes depends partly on the ingenuity with which Roxana dupes the "poor Gentleman," but more on the fact that we share secrets that are kept from him, even though she is as close to him as she can be to any man.[6]

The interview with Sir Robert Clayton shows a similar combination of reticence and openness. "Madam, says he, *I suppose your Honour has no children?* None, Sir *Robert*, said I, *but what are provided for*; so I left him in the dark, as much as I found him" (168). She has not left us in the dark, however, and it is a source of satisfaction to know that we

[6] P. 137; cf. also pp. 243, 249, and *passim*.

see farther into her doings than her most trusted counsellors. Again, she says of the belt or sash of her Turkish costume that "on both Ends where it join'd, or hooked, [it] was set with Diamonds for eight Inches either way, only they were not true Diamonds; but no-body knew that but myself" (174). But of course we know it, too, and like some of her graver confessions, this one disarms us by suggesting that we alone, of all her acquaintances, are fit to be confided in. When Roxana does her "Turkish" dance, "one Gentleman had the Folly to expose himself so much, as to say . . . that he had seen it danc'd at *Constantinople*; which was ridiculous enough" (176). But to whom does he expose himself? Only to Roxana—and to us; sharing the secret brings us closer to the heart of the action than the courtiers actually present.[7] Running through these scenes is a distinction which can also be expressed in dramatic terms: dialogue, one staple of Roxana's narrative, is punctuated with asides. Although the book often has an air of outspokenness, there is a great deal that Roxana holds back from others but communicates to us sotto voce.[8] Various exchanges exploit a tension between what is said aloud and what

---

[7] One pleasure here—that of turning the tables on one's social betters —would no doubt have been keener for the book's original public. Such passages suggest that *Roxana* may have afforded its middle-class readers a vicarious retaliation against aristocratic contempt and exclusion; in generic terms, such deflating passages contribute to the anti-romantic side of the book, and help to make it on balance more a satire than a celebration of genteel splendors.

[8] After her daughter has paid a long call, Roxana and the Quakeress have the following conversation: "I can't think, *says the* QUAKER, but she had some other Drift in that long Discourse; there's something else in her Head, *says she*, I am satisfy'd of that: *Thought I*, are you satisfy'd of it? I am sure I am the less satisfy'd for that; *at least*, 'tis but small Satisfaction to me, to hear you say so: What can this be? *says I*; and when will my Uneasinesses have an end? *But this was silent, and to myself, you may be sure*: But in Answer to my Friend the QUAKER, I return'd, by asking her a Question or two about it" (p. 292).

is only thought, but it is important to recognize that we are put in possession of both, and that in such scenes we participate more fully than any of Roxana's intimates.

At other moments, we too are excluded. Roxana is told things "not fit to repeat"; she "can go no farther in the Particulars of what pass'd at that time"; she acts "for particular Reasons" which are not disclosed; certain details she cannot "suffer [her]self to publish"; some "Part[s] of the Story will not bear telling" (64, 164, 207). The book is full of these teasing suppressions, but they are its lesser mysteries. Its greater mysteries involve the identity of characters. Ian Watt has called attention to the significance of the naming of characters in the early novel;[9] *Roxana* illustrates that the non-naming or pseudo-naming of characters can be equally important. We may recall that the book usually referred to as *Roxana* has for its actual title *The Fortunate Mistress or, a History of the Life and Vast Variety of Fortunes of Mademoiselle de Beleau, afterwards called the Countess de Wintelsheim in Germany Being the Person known by the Name of the Lady Roxana in the time of Charles II.* Within this title we find the same patterns of elusiveness that recur throughout the book: initial anonymity gives way to a proper name, but the certitude that a proper name affords is immediately denied us, since names change with each shift in place (the three names are associated with France, Germany, and England, respectively), or in period (*"afterwards . . . in the time of"*). Moreover, the title hints at an element of the capricious, or at least of the arbitrary, in the matter of names: the heroine was *"called"* the Countess de Wintelsheim—but was she? She was the person *"known by"* the name of Roxana—but was that her name? Names thus become untrustworthy guides to the heroine's identity: apart from the fallibility of those who gave her these

[9] *The Rise of the Novel* (1957), p. 18.

names, there would be something puzzling in the sheer multiplicity of names, since (good Lockeans that we are) we look for a one-to-one correspondence between names and persons, as well as between names and things. This is not to deny that there is anything revealing about the heroine's names, for they do have connotations appropriate to her roles—especially "Roxana."[10] But the fact that we must speak of names in the plural suggests that this book modifies the ordinary function of a proper name as "the verbal expression of the particular identity of each individual person."[11]

As several scholars have suggested, mystification about names is a convention of the romance and *chronique scandaleuse*; it fosters an illusion that these are all real people, whose true names could have been given if the narrator had dared to make free with the reputations of the great. This may be so, but does not quite account for the paradoxical effect that naming has upon readers of *Roxana*. This effect can perhaps be clarified by introducing another feature of the book which seems to me closely analogous: namely, the heroine's clothes. Roxana's Turkish costume, for instance, is revealing in various senses: it is "but one Degree off, from appearing in one's Shift" (247), its exotic splendor epitomizes the heroine's life in her "Apartments in the *Pall-mall*," and both the original frontispiece and Roxana's verbal descriptions bring it before our eyes with dramatic clarity. This costume thus seems a graphic and appropriate expression of Roxana's true self; at the same time, it is associated with artifice and deception, and leaves us finally in as much doubt as ever as to her real nature. Two decades earlier, Defoe had remarked that "Dis-

[10] See Paul Dottin, *Daniel De Foe et ses Romans* (Paris and London, 1924), p. 741; John Robert Moore, *Daniel Defoe: Citizen of the Modern World* (Chicago, 1958), pp. 249-50; Novak, "Crime and Punishment," pp. 460-62.

[11] *The Rise of the Novel*, p. 18.

guises are never used where nothing is to be concealed, and nothing is concealed, but what Shame, Fear, or Policy commands to be hid. A Genuine Cause carrys its Native Colours always outermost, is never shy of its Face, nor fond of being concealed."[12] From such moralistic passages one might infer that Defoe's attitude towards his heroine's disguises is one of utter execration, and there is little doubt that he disapproves intellectually, both of the Turkish habit and the later Quaker disguise, which is clearly adopted out of "Shame, Fear, [and] Policy." But it is no less certain that he is attracted imaginatively, and dresses his heroine "after the *Turkish* Mode" with considerable zest. Dottin observes that "L'habit turc de Roxana rivalise avec l'habit de peaux de Robinson: tous deux campent à nos yeux la silhouette du personnage et nous aident à en garder un impérissable souvenir."[13] Memorable as it is, it is *only* a silhouette, a shell within which Roxana continues to elude us. Her seeming self-disclosures fascinate us but keep us off "in a Corner," like her maidservant daughter on the gala evening (289); her varying names and costumes, each of which appears to tell so much about her, make it impossible to determine what her "Native Colours" actually are.

Many scenes in *Roxana*—particularly those set in "high life" —have this air of simultaneous revelation and concealment, forthrightness and duplicity, palpability and elusiveness; and whatever their literary antecedents, these qualities all tend to reinforce the effect of those materials and methods which can properly be called casuistical. To use a favorite term of Defoe's —which Johnson was to brand "a low, corrupt word" in his *Dictionary*—Roxana is "uncomeatable." Just when we begin to think we have seen through her, and especially when we are about to judge her, she says or does something that puts

[12] *Some Remarks on the First Chapter in Dr. Davenant's Essays* (1704), p. 2.
[13] *Daniel De Foe*, p. 740.

172

her out of our grasp, and forces us to qualify or abandon the confident pronouncement we were going to make. Only once is casuistry referred to by name, in the course of Roxana's Parisian liaison, but it frequently serves to modify our response to the heroine.

Roxana says of her affair with the prince that "the Devil had play'd a new Game with me, and prevail'd with me to satisfie myself with this Amour, as a lawful thing," on the grounds that the prince's courtship was irresistible, and that she herself was "perfectly single, and uningag'd to any other Man" (68). Having ascribed these arguments to the devil, she further devaluates them by adding, "It cannot be doubted but that I was the easier to perswade myself of the Truth of such a Doctrine as this, when it was so much for my Ease, and for the Repose of my Mind, to have it be so." Roxana thus implies that however deluded she was at the time, either by Satan's sophistry or her own, she is now acutely aware of the speciousness of the "Doctrine," and abhors it as much as we do. But the rhetoric of the passage is not quite this simple: hollow as they may be, the devil's arguments are just plausible enough to soften our potential rigor towards the heroine, and her own repudiation of them increases rather than cancels our tolerance. This strategy persists in what Roxana next says of casuistry: "Besides, I had no Casuists to resolve this Doubt; the same Devil that put this into my Head, bade me go to any of the *Romish* Clergy, and under the Pretence of Confession, state the Case exactly, and I should see they would either resolve it to be no Sin at all, or absolve me upon the easiest Pennance." Despite "a strong Inclination to try," she is kept from inquiring by religious scruples: "I could not be a Cheat in any thing that was esteem'd Sacred," she declares, "and could not act as if I was Popish, upon any Account whatsoever." The paragraph ends on this somewhat ludicrous note, but Roxana's surmise about what *"Romish"* casuists would

think of her case has interesting effects. The obvious suggestion is that such men are lax judges, willing to condone fla-
grant sins, and in league with the devil; yet when we hear
Roxana saying, "I could never bring myself to like having to
do with those Priests," we see that her object is not simply
to make us think badly of them, but to make us think well
of her for being unlike them and for refusing to meddle with
them. Roxana shifts our attention from the fornication actually
committed to a "cheat" which is contemplated but virtuously
eschewed: we may recall the parallel scene in which Moll
diverts us from her theft of a child's necklace by discussing the
emphatically resisted temptation to kill it.

Sharply as Roxana distinguishes herself from "those Priests"
(and from the devil), she by no means erases from our minds
their lenient view of her situation; their judgment in some
sense stays with us, discredited as it may be. Once a novelist
says something, he can never wholly negate it.[14] An impression
once made on us may be contradicted as vigorously and often
as the author pleases, without ever being quite effaced. Roxana's summary of the question further demonstrates this principle: "But, I say, I satisfy'd myself with the surprizing Occa-

---

[14] Illustrations of this principle are to be found throughout Defoe's
writings. One paragraph of the *Remarks on the Bill To Prevent Frauds
Committed by Bankrupts* (1706) imputes various base motives to the
enemies of the bill, in sentences that begin, "I am loth to suggest
. . . ," "I won't affirm . . . ," "Nor will I say . . . ," "*I won't say,*
(tho' I doubt 'tis too true) . . .*"; Defoe concludes, "*But this I will
say,* that unless these or such as these are the Reasons, 'tis a perfect
Mystery to the World, why these Gentlemen . . . should be against
this Bill" (p. 10). Here scurrilities are "unsaid" in advance; authorial
responsibility for them is lessened, but their effectiveness is not. Cf.
Applebee's Journal, Aug. 17, 1723: "I won't . . . by any means say
that the *Czar* of *Muscovy* is a Mimick,—that he makes a Water Theatre
of the *Baltick Sea,*—or that he makes War a Stage Play. Though I cannot forbear thinking of such Things as these, for my Life" (Lee, III,
171-72). For Defoe's use of a similar technique in his correspondence
with Harley, see Sutherland, *Defoe,* p. 151.

sion, that, as it was all irresistable, so it was all lawful; for that Heaven would not suffer us to be punish'd for that which it was not possible for us to avoid; and with these Absurdities I kept Conscience from giving me any considerable Disturbance in all this Matter" (69). The notion that what is genuinely and absolutely "irresistable" becomes "lawful" is surely not the absurdity here, as one scholar has suggested; if Roxana had used the shibboleth "necessity," this scholar might not have found her argument an "uncharacteristically romantic" piece of "affected sensibility."[15] No, the principle that Roxana invokes has a long and respectable ethical background. What is absurd is the pretence that it is germane to this particular case of conscience. Defoe observes elsewhere that "ill Men will always apply good Laws to the worst Use,"[16] and by doing so here, Roxana is guilty of the perverseness—the *corruptio optimi pessima*—for which casuists "of the *Romish* Clergy" were constantly attacked. It is not left to us, however, to see through the heroine's self-administered moral anaesthesia; the narrator passes so swift and severe a verdict on her former self that we are forestalled from doing so. On the other hand, before any of us, narrator or readers, have had time to label her reasonings absurd, various propositions tending to Roxana's advantage have been advanced; and although some of these propositions turn out to be false, and others to be true but irrelevant, the favorable impression that they make is never completely eradicated.

As a further example of the varied uses of casuistical material in *Roxana*, we may consider the heroine's eventual marriage to the Dutch merchant. "Still changing names, religion, climes,/ At length she turns a bride": this is the occasion for another of the periodic inventories which are Defoe's equiv-

[15] See Maximillian E. Novak, *Defoe and the Nature of Man* (Oxford, 1963), p. iii.
[16] *A Hint to the Blackwell-Hall Factors* (1705), p. 3.

alent of the endlessly varied couplings in pornography. But this particular inventory, "tho' it was chearful Work in the main" (259), arouses acute anxieties in the heroine: "I trembled every Joint of me, worse for ought I know, than ever *Belshazzer* did at the Hand-writing on the Wall." Her fears are generated by a case of conscience which had been debated by earlier casuists, and which Defoe had explored at other points in his writings. Roxana poses the problem in the following terms: "*Unhappy Wretch*, said I to myself, *shall my ill-got Wealth . . . be intermingled with the honest well-gotten Estate of this innocent Gentleman, to be a Moth and a Caterpillar among it, and bring the Judgments of Heaven upon him, and upon what he has, for my sake! Shall my Wickedness blast his Comforts! Shall I be Fire in his Flax!*" Her answer is energetically negative: "God forbid! *I'll keep them asunder, if it be possible.*" By managing to do so, Roxana says, "I, in some Measure, satisfied myself, that I should not bring my Husband under the Blast of a just Providence, for mingling my cursed ill-gotten Wealth with his honest Estate" (260). It is true that in the fifty pages that follow, the outward action is hardly affected by Roxana's decision to keep the two estates separate. But the emotional tone of her story is dominated by the apprehensions voiced here: from this point on, she lives in increasing dread of being punished for her misdeeds. This somber phase of the narrative is fittingly introduced by a traditional case of conscience, couched in ominous Biblical language.

Roxana's anxieties over mixing "*the Product of* prosperous Lust" with her husband's honestly earned money recapitulate a casuistical problem with which Defoe had long been familiar. In the *Athenian Mercury*, a man who has "very lately married a Wife of a considerable Fortune" is "credibly informed that it was got by very ill means," and reports that "I have ever since my Possession of this ill-gotten Wealth, been very uneasie, and have kept it by it self, not making use of it for fear of Poysoning that which was mine before"; he inquires *"Whether I may make Use of this Money without offence to God, or danger of Corrupting the rest?"* The Athenians suggest that "If you know any Person or Persons that have been wronged . . . you ought in Conscience to make reparation," and they advise him to be generally "as Charitable as your Circumstances will allow," but they assure him that "since you are free from the Guilt, you will also be free from the deserved Punishment."[17] A decade later, a similar case arises in Defoe's *Little Review*. A correspondent asks "If 'tis impossible for an Estate ill got, to Prosper in the hands of a Vertuous Person, that is innocent of the Villanies practis'd in the getting it?" Defoe's response is that "If all those Estates which have not been honestly got should be blasted, the Lord have Mercy upon our Rich Men," and he urges heirs to "endeavour to sanctifie an ill got Estate, by an honest Diligent Conduct."[18]

In light of these sensible resolutions of the case, how are we to regard Roxana's superstitious judgment on the present occasion? Had the Dutch merchant, who is innocent, decided to keep the two estates separate for fear of contaminating his own, we would be apt to find his behavior unreasonable; nevertheless it makes sense for Roxana, who is guilty, to dread the effect of joining them. We may recall Colonel Jack's remarks on the loss of a ship bringing him various goods pur-

[17] *Athenian Mercury*, XII, xi, 5.

[18] Fac. ed. Arthur W. Secord, 22 vols. (N.Y., 1938), II (July 13, 1705), 46-47. William Walters adopts a similar position towards the fortune which he and Captain Singleton have amassed by piracy. Since it cannot be restored to its true owners, Quaker William holds that "We ought to keep it carefully together, with a resolution to do what right with it we are able" (*Romances and Narratives*, VI, 304). The problem of restitution is also considered briefly in *Colonel Jack*, ed. Samuel Holt Monk, Oxford English Novels (1965), p. 87.

Roxana

chased from his earnings as a thief. In language very similar to Roxana's, he declares that "tho' it was a loss I could not but be glad, that those ill gotten Goods were gone, and that I had lost what I had stolen; for I look'd on it as none of mine, and that it would be fire in my Flax if I should mingle it with what I had now, which was come honestly by, and was as it were sent from Heaven, to lay the Foundation of my prosperity, which the other would be only as a Moth to consume."[19] The sense that both passages make is clearly psychological rather than logical. Elsewhere in his writings, Defoe repeatedly asserts "how necessary and inseperable a Companion, Fear is to Guilt."[20] This association is effectively introduced here by ascribing to the heroine a fear which the innocent can dismiss, but which understandably (if groundlessly) plagues the guilty.

[19] *Colonel Jack*, p. 157; cf. *The Whole Duty of Man* (1658), Sunday 14, par. 22, ed. William B. Hawkins (1842), p. 250.

[20] *Colonel Jack*, p. 291; cf. *A New Discovery of an Old Intreague* (1691): "And had his Guilt been less, so had his Fear" (in *A Second Volume*, p. 10); *Ye True-Born* Englishmen *proceed* [1701], p. 3: "For had your Guilt been less . . ./ So would have been your fear"; *The Mock Mourners* (1702), in *A True Collection*, p. 51: "*For where there's Guilt, there always will be Fear*"; (quoted again in *The Dyet of Poland* [1705], p. 25, and in *Serious Reflections*, in *Romances and Narratives*, iii, 69); *The Spanish Descent* (1702), p. 15: "His Constant Temper's all Serene and Clear;/ First, free from Guilt, and therefore free from Fear"; *Reformation of Manners* (1702), in *A True Collection*, p. 80: "Nothing but Guilt can be the Cause of Fear"; *The Storm. An Essay* (1704): "But Guilt will always be with Terror curst" (in *A Second Volume*, p. 96); *De Foe's Answer, To Dyer's Scandalous News Letter* [1707], p. 3: "I have no Guilt, and therefore no Fear"; *The Commentator*, No. liii (July 4, 1720): "Guilt makes all Men Cowards." The theme occurs in Defoe's earliest and latest works: see *Meditations*, ed. George H. Healey (Cummington, Mass., 1946), p. 21, and *An Effectual Scheme for the Immediate Preventing of Street Robberies* (1731), p. 34. The guilt feelings of Defoe's characters deserve closer psychological analysis than they have yet received, although there is a valuable general discussion of the omnipresence of anxiety by Benjamin Boyce, "The Question of Emotion in Defoe's Fiction," *SP*, l (1953), 44-58.

178

Roxana

I have spoken of several features of the book that keep us from detesting Roxana, as we might do if we were given no more than a stark chronicle of her actions. Even the trait which has disturbed readers most—the heroine's cold-bloodedness—has an equivocal, partly mitigating effect. Chandler, who found Roxana "almost without emotion," asserted that she "certainly wins no sympathy," and his charge that there is something "bloodless and unnatural" about "this somber story" has been echoed by most later commentators.[21] The usual comparison has been with Moll Flanders. Dottin found Roxana the worse of the two because she is more calculating; one can forgive her for a great deal, he says, "mais on ne peut lui pardonner le sang-froid qu'elle apporte dans ses intrigues, et on regrette l'impulsive Moll Flanders."[22] Yet Roxana's cold-bloodedness puts her at an emotional distance from us which is not wholly to her disadvantage: it is called forth by a social order which deserves little tenderness, for the values of society prove to be even less savory than the heroine's.

Roxana's cynicism about such topics as love and honor, for instance, frequently turns out to be directed against society's still more cynical corruptions of those concepts, so that even though her manner gains her little affection, it precludes facile condemnation. After assuring her in somewhat unromantic terms that he "did not come to make a Prize of me, or to pick my Pocket," the old English lord "then turn'd his Discourse to the Subject of Love; a Point so ridiculous to me, without the main thing, I mean the Money, that I had no Patience to hear him make so long a Story of it" (183). Whatever we think of Roxana's stress on money as "the main thing," we have to acknowledge that love is made ridiculous by this

[21] Frank W. Chandler, *The Literature of Roguery*, 2 vols. (Boston, 1907), II, 296.
[22] *Daniel De Foe*, pp. 742-43; cf. George A. Aitken's Introduction to *Roxana*, in *Romances and Narratives*, XII, x.

179

man's pretensions to it, and that her translation of lust into money is no more incongruous than his translation of lust into love.

The motif of honor is equally prominent in Roxana's dealing with this man, and has similar effects. Early in their negotiations she declares to him that "I knew how to be true to a Man of Honour, as I knew his Lordship to be." He replies that "the Bonds of Honour he knew I wou'd be ty'd by"; he scorns to expect "anything from me, but what he knew, as a Woman of Honour, I cou'd grant"; and he promises that "I shou'd find I was in the Hands of a Man of Honour" (184-85). She eventually becomes "sick of his Lordship," and has difficulty answering the question, *"Why I shou'd be a Whore now?"* Nevertheless the following consideration delays her break with him:

> It had for a-while been a little kind of Excuse to me, that I was engag'd with this wicked old Lord, and that I cou'd not, in Honour, forsake him; but how foolish and absurd did it look, to repeat the Word Honour on so vile an Occasion? As if a Woman shou'd prostitute her Honour in Point of Honour; horrid Inconsistency; Honour call'd upon me to detest the Crime and the Man too. . . . Honour, had it been consulted, wou'd have preserv'd me honest from the Beginning. . . . This however, shews us with what faint Excuses, and with what Trifles we pretend to satisfie ourselves, and suppress the Attempts of Conscience in the Pursuit of agreeable Crime, and in the possessing those Pleasures which we are loth to part with (201-02).

The object of irony is not a muddle on Roxana's part, since she herself exposes the "horrid Inconsistency" of appealing to honor in such circumstances. Her cynicism does not come off badly in such passages; what is made to appear vicious is the man and his society, who debase concepts like "honour" by blandly invoking them on vile occasions. The crucial difference is Roxana's clear-sightedness: she knows what is involved, and candidly tells us, whereas the self-styled "Man of Honour" seems "foolish and absurd" by failing to see through his own complacent rhetoric.

Throughout the book Roxana exclaims, in effect, "Look how wicked I am!" Hard on the heels of this declaration, however, there usually follows an unmistakable (if unspoken) caveat: "But *they* are even worse." This implicit proposition is at the heart of the book's irony—an irony that has society, not the heroine, as its primary object. It is precisely because this "Person of Honour" is "his Lordship," and represents the values that govern—or at least set the tone for—society at large, that his role as Roxana's foil in wickedness is so important. Bad as she may be, Roxana recognizes pretence when she sees it, including her own; in their thoughtless glibness, which corrupts language and morals alike, this "wicked old Lord" and the culture he represents seem far more malign. And they are particularly contemptible for undermining the very values on which they attempt to justify their existence: to act in this way is, as Roxana says in another unromantic passage, "to befoul one's-self, and live always in the Smell of it" (152). Roxana's personality may therefore be disquieting for more complicated reasons than those quoted earlier. It may indeed disturb us that (as John Robert Moore puts it) she has "a colder and harder and baser nature than the well-meaning Moll Flanders."[23] But we may also be disturbed to find society colder, harder, baser, and no more well-intentioned than Roxana herself.

Although various features of the story may prevent the reader from judging Roxana with rigorous detachment, and

[23] *Daniel Defoe: Citizen of the Modern World* (Chicago, 1958), p. 250.

induce him to identify imaginatively with her, Defoe also tries to distance the reader from his erring and unregenerate heroine. For one thing, he refuses to allow this "Amazonian" woman to belong fully to anyone, or to settle fully anywhere: her career is a repeated thwarting of the Forster injunction, "Only connect." Even when personal relationships are sustained for some time, and are cordial and cooperative rather than predatory, they are marred (and usually broken) by a reserve on Roxana's part. Although her impulse to "connect" is strong, it is overborne by gestures of guardedness and withdrawal, and her uprootedness finally puts us at an emotional distance as well. It might be objected that Roxana's detachment from others in the book only links her the more closely to us: was it not suggested earlier that her isolation tends to make the reader her confidant and accomplice? In answer, I would stress here the importance of physical as well as human environment, for the metaphor of "emotional *distance*" has a special appropriateness to Roxana. I have argued elsewhere that *Robinson Crusoe* uses wandering, fleeing, straying, and other images of anxious motion to indicate the hero's alienation from "the true center of his being."[24] Through a kind of allusive shorthand, Defoe associates geographical remoteness with spiritual malaise (Adam unparadised, the Prodigal "in a far country," etc.). Crusoe is "errant" at first in both body and soul; eventually, returning home and coming to rest indicate his achievement (however precarious or temporary) of spiritual soundness. The careers of all of Defoe's heroes and heroines can be charted spatially in the same way: centrifugal motion sooner or later gives way to centripetal motion, which culminates in motifs of return, reunion, and repose.

Or rather, the careers of all but two follow this pattern. At the end of *The King of Pirates*, Captain Avery is left languish-

[24] *Defoe and Spiritual Autobiography* (Princeton, 1965), p. 84.

ing in France, and no more explicit authorial judgment is required to make clear that he is ultimately outside the pale. Sometimes Defoe shows a certain affection and even respect for Avery, as he does for Roxana. But at other times he seems to recoil, and his final gesture is one of repudiation. By what amounts to a sentence of banishment, Defoe disengages the reader (and possibly himself) from the scapegrace hero.

The other exception is Roxana. One can easily imagine this book ending on a note of reunion and repose, but its actual denouement is the opposite. Having created the prospect, tantalizing to heroine and readers alike, of a reintegration of this pathetic family, Defoe proceeds to explode it by suggesting the murder of the eldest daughter, the dispersal of the other children, and Roxana's own departure for yet another exile. Various critics have found the closing paragraph abrupt and inconclusive, yet it is fully in keeping with the final fifth of the book. The "dreadful Course of Calamities" and the "Blast of Heaven" which Roxana refers to in her last sentence are "the very Reverse of [her] former Good Days" only in the sense that they destroy her "flourishing, and outwardly happy Circumstances." In a more basic sense they mark the culmination of a process that recurs throughout the book, and dominates the final sixty pages. Instead of the reconciliation scenes typical of a Defoean conclusion, there are fresh estrangements and rejections; instead of peace, new alarm and dejection. Finally, in terms of spatial imagery, Roxana again abandons "Beloved *England*," where she had earlier acknowledged "a longing Desire to be" (122). Like Captain Avery, she is expatriated from the ideal security of "home"—which is to say London, the assumed center of the author's and reader's universe. Her banishment across the channel thus expresses Defoe's final verdict on her, that "Between us and you there is a great gulf fixed."

Defoe's heroes and heroines are all quick-witted and articulate, and it is clear that their creator admired verbal resourcefulness as much as inventive energy in other spheres.[25] His characters seldom lack presence of mind, and whatever their other lapses, they are never at a loss for words. Defoe was able to appreciate an ingeniously contrived or deftly executed theft on aesthetic grounds;[26] casuistical dexterity evidently appealed to him in much the same way, quite apart from its moral status. Nevertheless, he frequently observes that articulateness can be abused. He says of one villainess that "she had the Tongue of a *Siren*; 'twas neatly hung, but hellishly employ'd," and of another, who draws "More nice Distinctions than *Ignatius* knows," that "to the Whore she joins the Jesuit."[27] In a third work he observes that "It is easy to entangle a cause by subtilty of Words, and by long Harangues; and when Men are resolv'd to impose artfully upon Mankind, they often make such Circumstances as may amuse and confound the Judgment."[28] And he sympathizes with a man resembling the Dutch merchant in *Roxana*, who complains of his wife, "with such Magick she dozes the Understanding, that I am not able

[25] Colonel Jack "had a natural Talent of Talking," and even as a child "could say as much to the Purpose as most People that had been taught no more than I" (p. 7); Roxana takes pride in "the Management of [her] Tongue" (p. 77); "Mother Midnight" in *Moll Flanders* is "a woman of a rare tongue," exceeded in "art and dexterity"— whether criminal or casuistical—only by Moll herself (ed. Herbert Davis, Introduction by Bonamy Dobrée, World's Classics [1961], p. 246); instances from *Robinson Crusoe, Captain Singleton*, and *Religious Courtship* are cited in the Appendix, below.

[26] See Sutherland, *Defoe*, pp. 247 f.

[27] *Religious Courtship*, 2nd edn. (1729), p. 314; *Reformation of Manners* (1702), in *A True Collection*, p. 82.

[28] *Applebee's Journal*, Dec. 6, 1721 (Lee, II, 462); cf. *An Enquiry Into the Case of Mr. Asgil's General Translation* (1704): "Men by nice Reasoning, may distinguish themselves into, and out of . . . any Opinion" (p. 10). Cf. also *A Letter to Mr. How* (1701), in *A True Collection*, pp. 328, 331-32.

to make my Passions appear Rational, or to reconcile my Resentments to my Senses. If I enter into Arguments with her, tho' I have the most evident Claim of Reason on my Side, she baffles me in a Moment, and I am as stupid as a Brute. ... in a Word, I am talked out of my Reason, my Understanding, and my Argument all at once."[29] Furthermore, Defoe holds at various times that sophistry merely aggravates the faults or errors which it is designed to lessen or defend. In *Jure Divino* he analyzes the rhetorical strategy of Genesis 3:12, "The woman whom thou gavest to be with me": " 'Tis spoken as a kind of a Retort," Defoe says, "as if [Adam] should reflect upon his Maker, for putting such a Snare in his Way, lodging such a Syren in his Bosom, that had betray'd him. ... Thus he pleads Guilty, but extenuates the Crime, throws it off upon his Wife, and tacitely upon his Maker." These remarks indicate that Defoe regarded as a compounding of guilt Adam's attempt "to shift his early Crime,/ And think accusing her, *wou'd excuse him*."[30] And elsewhere he approves the principle that "*a lame Defence of a bad Cause, makes that bad worse*."[31]

It might seem legitimate to infer that whenever his heroines resort to similar evasions, Defoe regards them as doubly culpable and means us to do so as well. Those who find *Moll Flanders* and *Roxana* works of consistent irony will so inter-

[29] *Applebee's Journal*, Dec. 5, 1724 (Lee, III, 339); cf. *Some Remarks On the First Chapter in Dr. Davenant's Essays* (1704): "How easy 'tis for Men of Wit to give anything a fair Face," Defoe exclaims, "and by a happy turn of Language call things of contrary Subjects by the same Name" (p. 2).

[30] *Jure Divino*, octavo edn. (1706), sig. [N3^v]. In one of his earliest poems Defoe notes that Adam's descendants are "Fonder to Plead Excuses Than Obey/ And Glad of all Pretences To Delay/ Till Loading Guilt afresh/ Delayes To Hardned Obstinacy Come" (*Meditations*, p. 12).

[31] *Applebee's Journal*, Aug. 26, 1721 (Lee, II, 421): the "Casuist" who lays down this principle is "receiv'd with Applause" by the "Problematick Society."

pret the casuistical manoeuvering in both books; on their reading, the forensic skill of both heroines serves to confirm rather
than qualify their guilt. Such a view seems to me at best a
half-truth, for it assumes that Defoe keeps steadily in mind
the badness of his heroines' causes, and that to emphasize their
guilt he assigns them lame defenses. The main difficulty with
this is obvious: Defoe often endows his heroines with so much
of his own argumentative power, and enters into their plead-
ings with so much imaginative zest, that their defenses are
anything but lame. Not that Defoe's zealous exertions in behalf of a character prove that he believes her innocent, any
more than the ingenious and impassioned pleas of a trial
lawyer reveal his private opinion of a client's case. I have noted
that Moll and Roxana defend various positions which Defoe
himself attacks on other occasions. Nevertheless, these other
occasions are in some sense irrelevant to the novels. Pronouncements made in other contexts can tell us a great deal
about how Defoe would ordinarily have regarded his fictional
characters, and may even indicate the values which he set out
to uphold through ironic narratives. Yet in actually reading
the novels one is seldom aware of an ironist behind the scenes,
manipulating the self-betrayals of the guilty with cool detachment. Rather, one is struck by an extraordinary empathy between author and character, amounting to a virtual oblitera-
tion of any distinct authorial presence. In this respect (as in
others) Defoe's writings are more akin to Richardson's than
Fielding's. In his prefaces and at certain other points, the
author may stand at a critical distance from his characters, yet
the impression given by the texts is generally one of intense
imaginative absorption, even—or perhaps especially—in the
careers of those stigmatized in prefaces as criminals and sinners.

To put the problem another way, the thesis of this study
might have been that Defoe was in full and unremitting intellectual control of the deeds and utterances of his characters,

and that when his heroines do or say something that flouts the moral principles he espoused elsewhere, the resulting discrepancy is deliberately ironic. More specifically, I might have contended that whenever a Defoe character practices casuistry *in malo*, the implicit contrast with casuistry *in bono* constitutes a calculated irony. Those who interpret Defoe's novels in this way do so with the laudable object of defending his moral insight and artistry against gainsayers, for in the present climate of critical opinion, to identify an author as an ironist is ipso facto to honor him. But this line of defense does not seem to me altogether appropriate or convincing in Defoe's case. For him to have been in complete sympathy with either of his heroines—particularly Roxana—he would have had to silence or circumvent his own conscience more fully than he ever appears to have done. But for his attitude toward his heroines to have been as unwaveringly rational and detached as some commentators have suggested, he probably would have had to write novels more nearly resembling his conduct manuals.

A variant of this ironic interpretation, suggested by an important recent study of *Paradise Lost*,[32] might run as follows. Defoe does not intend that we should instantly see through the sophistry of his heroines. If we were to find their arguments transparent, this ironic perception might amuse us, and gratify our intellectual vanity. But it would allow us to feel complacently superior, and far from edifying us, it would foster in us the very pharisaism that we find grotesque in Moll and Roxana. Instead of this, Defoe wants us to be "taken in"; his object is to make us recognize our essential kinship to Moll and Roxana, our vulnerability to self-serving rhetoric —our own and that of others—and the precariousness of the virtue that we congratulate ourselves upon. On this view,

[32] See Stanley E. Fish, *Surprised by Sin: The Reader in Paradise Lost* (New York, 1967).

Roxana

Defoe takes great pains to make his heroines' arguments persuasive, but he is no "Mollist" himself. He knows that Moll is less savory than she seems, and wants us to come to the same ultimate conclusion, but not until we have been forced to acknowledge our complicity in her guilt. This thesis would preserve the image of Defoe as a consistent conscious ironist; at the same time, it would seem to account for a fact which some ironic interpretations have tended to minimize or overlook—the fact that many sensitive readers have closely identified with Moll, rather than patronizing her with amused detachment.

I find this thesis attractive, but I am dubious of it. Again there is the question of authorial control: *is* Defoe as unequivocally "outside" his characters, as secure against collusion, as this reading would imply? One wonders. Even more troublesome is the affective problem. Do we indeed come to regard Moll as having been deceptive (or self-deceived) all along? Some of her pleas (e.g. at the time of her first theft) not only elicit our immediate sympathy, but stand up to more considered scrutiny, and some of her self-indictments as penitent narrator are at least as severe as any judgments we are likely to pass on her, at the time or in retrospect. Nor is it true, to speak more generally, that the longer one contemplates Moll the cooler towards her one necessarily grows. One of Defoe's achievements is to have shown that positive sympathies and negative moral judgments need not be in inverse proportion, let alone mutually exclusive. It is therefore possible that rereading *Moll Flanders* can confirm both responses, rather than strengthening one at the expense of the other.

The thesis proposed here does not rule out irony, but questions the dominant role assigned it in some recent studies of Defoe's fictional techniques. Neither Defoe nor the reader, in my opinion, stands so comfortably aloof from even the most blameworthy of his characters as such studies would suggest.

Roxana

My discussion of *Moll Flanders* has accordingly stressed Defoe's ability to remain imaginatively at one with the heroine,
and to keep the reader sympathetic in the very act of judging
her; I have contended that Moll's casuistical apologetics are
seldom simply self-deflating, and often prove to be thoroughly
disarming. In the case of *Roxana*, however, I have maintained
that sympathy and judgment tend to oscillate, rather than
coming into play at once; and although I have called attention to certain features of the book that offset the horror or
contempt which we might otherwise feel for her, I have held
that Roxana's ultimate fate is to be estranged from her readers as well as from the people and places that sustain her
within the story. I have cited passages in both books which
could be regarded (and may have been intended) as illustrations of the principle that *"Whores . . . never want Excuse,"*
or as examples of "how industriously . . . Men defend/ The
Faults on which their Interest does depend."[33] But I have
tried to show that the candor of these heroines, as well as
the solid merits of many of their pleas, force us to mitigate
the tone, and to some extent the very substance, of our ver-
dicts. At certain moments our very right to pass judgment is
called in question, but more often we are induced to give up
the rigorous and lofty spirit in which respectability tends to
judge turpitude. To enter into the reasonings of Defoe's characters is not to abandon moral judgment but to humanize it;
our capacity for judging others as we would wish to be judged
is greater, for we have momentarily been those others.

[33] *The True-Born Englishman* (1701), in *A True Collection*, p. 26;
More Reformation (1703), in *A Second Volume*, p. 48.

Appendix: Fiction and Mendacity

THROUGHOUT his writings, Defoe demonstrates that truth is seldom pure and never simple. From his day to our own, those who believe in pure and simple truths have therefore branded him a liar. This view has been particularly prevalent since 1869, when William Lee published evidence of Defoe's duplicity as a political journalist in the reign of George I; it was adopted by most later Victorian critics, and was strongly reinforced by Leslie Stephen, who used it to explain Defoe's success at giving fiction an air of truthfulness.[1] Despite the subsequent discovery that such works as *The Apparition of Mrs. Veal*, which Stephen saw as a total fabrication, were based on actual happenings, and despite increased critical interest in Defoe's theory of fiction, the earlier view of Defoe as a brilliant liar persists. This view is not so much

[1] William Lee, *Daniel Defoe: His Life and Recently Discovered Writings*, 3 vols. (1869), I, v-xx and *passim*. Stephen says that Defoe "had the most amazing talent on record for telling lies," and that "without abandoning every principle of morality, we cannot deny that [he] descended into very dirty practices." Stephen states "with profound regret" that Defoe "plainly condescended to become something little better than a spy," and although he "may have succeeded in blinding himself by plausible casuistry," it is "simply surprising" for critics to defend his "baseness" (*Hours in a Library* [1874], pp. 4, 42-43). Early in this century William P. Trent found himself in a similar plight: "My belief in [Defoe's] integrity was shattered, and I regretfully yielded to the conviction that his journalistic rivals knew his character and his ways far better than any of his biographers" ("Bibliographical Notes on Defoe," *The Nation*, 84 [1907], 515). For a survey of critical opinion on this question, see Charles E. Burch, "Defoe's British Reputation 1869-1894," *E.S.*, LXVIII (1934), 410-423, esp. pp. 413, 419.

false as meaningless: it is based on criteria of truth too literalistic to be useful in discussing fiction, and in any case far cruder than those Defoe actually adapted from traditional casuistry. The casuistical tradition afforded him both a rationale for writing fiction, and an approach to questions of truthfulness that enriched the fiction itself. Here I shall sketch briefly Defoe's views on mendacity, their casuistical background, and their implications for his theory and practice of fiction.

In the seventeenth-century pulpit, discussions of truth and falsehood were based on various Biblical texts, none of which was more popular than Matthew 10:16—"Be ye wise as serpents, and harmless as doves."[2] Early in the century, the recurrence of this theme owed as much to its rhetorical possibilities as to the ethical principles that it embodied.[3] But as the century

[2] See Thomas Adams, "The Good Politician Directed," in *Works*, ed. Thomas Smith, 3 vols. (Edinburgh, 1861-62), II, 24-35; John Downe, "The Dove-Like Serpent," in *Certaine Treatises . . . Published at the instance of his friends* (Oxford, 1633), sigs. oo-[qq⁴ᵛ]; Thomas Vane, *Wisdome and Innocence, Or Prudence and Simplicity, In the Examples of the Serpent And the Dove, Propounded to our imitation* (1652); Barten Holyday, "Of the Serpent and the Dove," in *Motives To A Good Life: In Ten Sermons* (Oxford, 1657), pp. 157-80; Jeremy Taylor, Sermons 20-24 in *Whole Works*, ed. Reginald Heber, rev. Charles P. Eden, 10 vols. (1850), IV, 573-632; and Edmund Calamy, *The Prudence of the Serpent and Innocence of the Dove* (1713). Among secular works, see Balthasar Gracian, *The Art of Prudence* (1702), Maxim 243, in which one is urged to "Let the cunning of the Serpent, go hand in hand with the simplicity of the Dove." (A copy of this work may have been in Defoe's library: see *Librorum . . . Danielis De Foe, Gen. Catalogus* [1731], p. 31, item 1187).

[3] For the changes that could be rung on the figures of antithesis and chiasmus, and on the respective attributes of serpent and dove, see especially Adams, "The Good Politician Directed." In "The Dove-Like Serpent," on the other hand, Downe protests that "although it be no difficult matter to finde out many witty resemblances betwixt the nature of a Serpent and a wise Christian, yet I leaue them all to such as loue such witty impertinences" (sigs. oo3-[oo3ᵛ]).

advanced, divines concentrated more on the practical implications of Christ's double injunction; they argued that the task of the virtuous man is to reconcile, in his words as well as his deeds, claims that are (or seem to be) as opposed as those of serpent and dove. As one might expect, the serpent was usually discussed at greater length and with greater zest than the dove. Preachers found scope for vigorous homiletics, however, in discussing man's disregard for dovelike sincerity.[4] The alternative to simple candor is often represented as sheer chaos, or as a Hobbist state of nature one step short of chaos.[5] Defoe himself was to exclaim, in a "Hymn to TRUTH," that

> *All's Brute without it*, horrid and deprav'd,
> The World *a Stage* of Violence and Blood,
> *Big* with Destruction, *Brooding* Monstrous Crimes,
> Insulting Heaven, and ripening apace
> *To Dissolution*, the Effect of Sin;
> Bright Truth alone, makes the Disorder'd Globe
> A Habitable Clime; and *when that fails*,
> The World must cease, her stated Time is come.[6]

[4] See the attacks on contemporary iniquities in Adams, "The Good Politician Directed," pp. 31-32, 34, and in Downe, "The Dove-Like Serpent," sigs. qq³-[qq⁴ʳ].

[5] Thus Jeremy Taylor says of "Christian Simplicity" that "its contrary . . . destroys society, and it makes multitudes of men to be but like herds of beasts, without proper instruments of exchange, and securities of possession, without faith, and without propriety" (*Whole Works*, IV, 625). Cf. Jeremy Collier, "Of Lying," in *Essays Upon Several Moral Subjects*, Part IV, 2nd edn. (1725), p. 135: "Unless People were ty'd by their Words, the World would run strangely to Ruin: If we had no Way of collecting each other's Meaning, Trust must fail, and Commerce be maim'd, and Society disband in a great Measure."

[6] *Review*, facsimile ed. Arthur W. Secord, 22 vols. (N.Y., 1938), II (Feb. 27, 1705), 4. Twenty years later Defoe was to observe rather more cynically that "all the ordinary communication of life is now full of lying, and what with table-lies, salutation-lies, and trading-lies, there is no such thing as every man speaking truth with his neigh-

Appendix

Blank verse tended to bring out a hyperbolic strain in Defoe, but we need not rely on such rhapsodic passages to determine his views on truth and falsehood, since he frequently discussed political, religious, and economic questions in terms of conflicts over honesty.[7] It may be that he was not prompted to write on such issues by moral considerations alone; but whether we regard his initial impulse as disinterested and patriotic or mercenary and partisan, it is significant that his constant strategy is to express, and to generate in his readers, a revulsion toward dishonesty.

Defoe does not limit the concept of honesty to questions of truthfulness, however, either in these pamphlets or in other

---

bour" (*The Compleat English Tradesman*, 2 vols. [1727], I, 235). Cf. also *The Candidate: Being a Detection of Bribery and Corruption As it is just now in Practice all over Great Britain* (1715), p. 57: "The World's all Fraud,/ Knavery's the General Trade, He that's not in't/ Is unemploy'd"; *The Commentator*, No. xxxvii (May 9, 1720); and *Serious Reflections*, in *Romances and Narratives*, ed. George A. Aitken, 16 vols. (1895), III, 97. The *Spectator* had complained, "Our Language is running into a Lie; . . . Men have almost quite perverted the use of Speech, and made Words to signify nothing; . . . the greatest part of the Conversation of Mankind is little else but driving a Trade of Dissimulation" (No. 103 [June 28, 1711], ed. Donald F. Bond, 5 vols. [Oxford, 1965], I, 431). Cf. also Tom Brown, *Amusements Serious and Comical*, ed. Arthur L. Hayward (1927), p. 83.

[7] Defoe insisted, for example, on putting the question of Occasional Conformity in these terms: although he resented the injustice of barring Dissenters from public office, he was scandalized by the practice of taking the sacrament as a political qualification, and condemned it as flagrantly dishonest. (See *An Enquiry into the Occasional Conformity of Dissenters* [1698] in *A True Collection of the Writings of the Author of the True Born English-man* [1703], p. 315, where Defoe attacks *"playing-Bopeep"* with God Almighty"; cf. *A Letter to Mr. How* [1701] in *A True Collection*, pp. 342-43.) Similarly, the heart of Defoe's charges against Sacheverell and his fellow High-Fliers was that they lied: just as their predecessors had deluded and betrayed James II with protestations of absolute non-resistance, so the Tories of Queen Anne's reign, amidst deceitful and groundless clamors of the Church in danger, were furthering ends of their own. (See *Review*, I [Dec. 16, 1704], 341, and especially III [Apr. 8, 1706] 169-76.)

books where honesty is discussed at greater length.[8] Nor does
he regard the problem of truthfulness itself as exclusively verbal. He shares the belief of one seventeenth-century divine
that "persons may act, as well as speak a lie; for words are
but the mode of expressing our apprehensions, which may as
strongly be signified by actions; for instance, the man that
lives as if he had the estate he knows he has not; or was what
indeed he knows he is not, doth as truly lie, as if he was
continually to express it by words; if it be done with a design
to injure and deceive others."[9] In the *Little Review*, Defoe
prints the case of a poor tradesman who in the course of
business has "*unhappily taken at several Times one Pound
thirteen Shillings, in Counterfeit Money*," but whose "*Conscience wou'd not permit* [*him*] *to pay it away*" to others. His
first reason for not doing so is that "I pretend to give that
for good, which I know is naught; and so do, in effect, Lye."[10]
Similar cases of nonverbal lying arise in Defoe's writings on
trade, and more complex ones are common in the fiction.

To turn more directly to Defoe's notion of what constitutes

[8] See *The Compleat English Tradesman*, I, 226-57, and *Serious
Reflections*, in *Romances and Narratives*, III, 16-66.
[9] *The Religious Tradesman* (Trenton, 1823; a reprint of Isaac Watts's
1747 revision of Richard Steele's *The Tradesman's Calling*, 1684), p.
123. Cf. Jeremy Taylor, *Ductor Dubitantium* (1660), in *Whole Works*,
X, 128-30. In *The Compleat English Tradesman*, Defoe says that "A
Tradesman should be wise as the Serpent, but he should be innocent,
that is, *Honest* too as the Dove; he should have the Wisdom of the
Serpent, but not the Cunning, the Craft, the Sharping, the Biting of
the Serpent" (II, 66).
[10] *Review*, II (July 27, 1705), 63; cf. Steele's remark that "you ought
not to pay coin that is defective in goodness or value, but plainly tell
them your suspicion of it; for otherwise you deceive them in deeds,
if not in words" (*The Religious Tradesman*, p. 133). Cf. also Defoe's
Compleat English Tradesman, I, 241-48; *Serious Reflections*, pp. 48 f.
In *The Young Man's Guide through the Wilderness of this World to
the Heavenly Canaan* (1670), Thomas Gouge calls this practice "a
branch of deceit" (*Works* [Whitburn, 1798], p. 408). Cf. also Collier,
Essays, p. 35.

a lie, we may begin by examining one of his letters to Harley, in which he argues that "as a Lye Does Not Consist in the Indirect Position of words, but in the Design by False Speaking, to Deciev and Injure my Neighbour, So Dissembling does Not Consist in Puting a Different Face Upon Our Actions, but in the further Applying That Concealment to the Prejudice of the Person." Not content with abstract definitions, he goes on to pose the following imaginary case: "I Come into a persons Chamber, who on a Surprize is Apt to Fall into Dangerous Convulsions. I Come in Smileing, and Pleasant, and ask the person to Rise and Go abroad, or any Other Such question, and Press him to it Till I Prevail, whereas the Truth is I have Discoverd the house to be On Fire, and I Act thus for fear of frighting him. Will any Man," he asks, "Tax me with Hypocrisye and Dissimulation?" Defoe's next step is to draw support from scripture: "This is the Dissimulation I Recomend, which is Not Unlike what the Apostle Sayes of himself; becoming all Things to all Men, that he might Gain Some" (I Cor. 9:22). Having appealed both to experience and to authority in support of his argument, he concludes with a paradoxical restatement of it: "This Hypocrise," he declares, "is a Vertue."[11]

This passage reveals Defoe's talent for adopting various roles in the interest of political intrigue, which is a short step from the kind of role-playing he was to pursue in his fiction during the next two decades. In addition to an obvious relish

---

[11] *Letters*, ed. George Harris Healey (Oxford, 1955), pp. 42-43; see also p. 159. Cf. Pope's Epistle to Lord Bolingbroke, ll. 31-34:

> Sometimes, with Aristippus, or St. Paul,
> Indulge my Candor, and grow all to all;
> Back to my native Moderation slide,
> And win my way by yielding to the tyde.

("The First Epistle of the First Book of Horace Imitated," *Imitations of Horace*, Twickenham Edition, ed. John Butt [New Haven, 1961], p. 281).

for such role-playing, however, there is a clear concern for its intent and consequences. Defoe's readiness to assume a Pauline stance may indicate how far presumption and complacency could carry him in rationalizing shady doings;[12] it may seem reminiscent of Mr. Hold-the-World in *Pilgrim's Progress*, who exclaims "Let us be wise *as Serpents*," and forgets the rest of the verse. But two other features of the passage deserve equal notice: namely, Defoe's awareness of the moral implications, however uncomfortable, of everything he said and did, and his habit of assessing specific actions in the light of various ethical norms. To put it another way, such passages certainly furnish evidence of Defoe's ingenuity in putting the best construction on his own dubious conduct—his skill at casuistry *in malo*; but they also reveal his ability to examine a given ethical question in the multiple perspectives of theory, authority, and experience—his skill, in short, at casuistry *in bono*.

As for the substance of the letter to Harley, it is significant

[12] Another Pauline tag, attached to Stephen Marshall in the mid-seventeenth century, may seem more appropriate to Defoe; Marshall is said to have been "of so souple a soul, that he strained not a joynt, nor sprained a sinew, in all the alteration of times, and that his friends put all on the account, not of his inconstancy but prudence, and who in his own practice reconciled the various lections of the precept, Rom. 12:11, 'Serving the Lord and the Times'" (*Memoirs of the Life of Mr. Ambrose Barnes*, ed. W.H.D. Longstaffe, Surtees Society Publications, Vol. L [1867], p. 169). Comparable Pauline precedents (Acts 28:11 and 19:10) are cited by Perkins in the chapter "Of Prudence" in *The Whole Treatise of the Cases of Conscience* (1617), p. 116. Nearer to Defoe's own day, Roger L'Estrange observes that "We are . . . taught in some Cases to Yield to Times and Occasions; but with a Saving still, to Honour, and to Conscience. A Wise Man and an Honest Man will always mean the same Thing; but he's a Fool that always says the same thing. . . . there are certain Ways, Cases, and Occasions, wherein Disguises, and Artificial Evasions are in some Measure Allowable, provided only that there be No Scandalous, or Malicious Departure from the Truth" (*Fables, of Aesop and Other Eminent Mythologists*, 6th edn. [1714], p. 54).

that Defoe should assign to malice a crucial role in his definitions both of lying—"the Design by False Speaking, to Deciev
and Injure my Neighbour"—and of dissembling—"Concealment to the Prejudice of the Person." This emphasis on hos-
tile intent has important aesthetic as well as moral consequences: it not only underlies a distinction between lying and
legitimate deception which, as we shall see in a moment, is
central to Defoe's theory of fiction, but it introduces a factor
notably absent from many earlier definitions of lying. At the
beginning of the seventeenth century, William Perkins had
declared simply that "Lying is, when a man speaketh otherwise th[a]n the truth is, with a purpose to deceiue";[13] a century later Jeremy Collier gives his definition a more Lockean
turn, but similarly omits any mention of malicious purpose.
Lying, Collier says, is "a Disagreement between the Speech
and the Mind of the Speaker: When one Thing is declar'd,
and another meant, and Words are no Image of Thoughts."[14]
On the other hand, Defoe's contemporary John Hartcliffe remarks that "*Mendacia animo constant*; we then *Lye*, when
wittingly we broach a Falshood for some evil End."[15] And a

[13] *A Direction for the Governement of the Tongve According to
Gods Word*, in *Workes*, I, 443. Thomas Gouge defines a lie as "a
deceitful expression of one's mind against his mind: or, it is a speaking an untruth wittingly and willingly, with a purpose to deceive"
(*The Young Man's Guide*, in *Works*, p. 436). William Ames says "A
lie is properly a testimony whereby one pronounces otherwise than is
in his heart" (*The Marrow of Sacred Divinity* [1638], quoted in George
L. Mosse, *The Holy Pretence: A Study in Christianity and Reason of
State from William Perkins to John Winthrop* [Oxford, 1957], p. 71).

[14] *Essays*, p. 133; cf. also pp. 181-84. In a similarly Lockean vein,
Collier maintains that we are under the highest obligation "to make the
Sign bring up a correspondent Idea, and answer the Thing 'twas in-
tended to signify" (p. 135).

[15] "Of Veracity," in *A Compleat Treatise of Moral and Intellectual
Virtues*, 2nd edn. (1722), pp. 136-37. A copy of this work is listed in
the Defoe-Farewell library catalogue (*Librorum . . . Danielis De Foe,
Gen. Catalogus* [1731], p. 25, item 935). Defoe himself occasionally

generation earlier, Samuel Pufendorf had maintained that no man can be "properly said to *lye*, but he who with evil Intention, and pre-conceiv'd Malice, tells another what is really different from his Sentiments or Resolutions, either to prejudice or to delude him."[16] Defoe's stress on injurious intent is therefore distinctive but not unique; nor can it be dismissed as a piece of ad hoc Machiavellianism,[17] since it had been anticipated in the works of eminent laymen and divines of the previous century, and was to be put to good use elsewhere when Defoe came to defend fiction.

We have seen that Defoe defends hoodwinking the kind of person who "on a Surprize is Apt to Fall into Dangerous Convulsions." Even though the man's house is on fire, Defoe feels that it is best to come in "Smileing, and Pleasant," so as to gain his charitable object. The illustration may be taken as a paradigm for his justification of fiction, which involves the attainment of laudable ends in a manner adapted to the capacities (or rather the incapacities) of readers. Even if it does not throw them into "Dangerous Convulsions," unvarnished truth may antagonize them, perplex them, or (what is worse) simply bore them. The depraved taste of the reading public, like a proneness to epileptic fits, calls for dexterous

omits malicious intent from his definition of lying; in *Conjugal Lewdness* (1727), he speaks of "a Protestation, with a design to deceive, which by the Way, is the very Essence of a Lye" (p. 191).

[16] *Of The Law of Nature and Nations*, trans. Basil Kennett, 4th edn. (1729), p. 316. Jeremy Taylor quotes Melancthon as holding that "to lie is to deceive our neighbour to his hurt" (*Ductor Dubitantium*, in *Whole Works*, x, 102).

[17] See Maximillian E. Novak, "Defoe's Theory of Fiction," *SP*, LXI (1964), 663: "We can be certain that Defoe was fully aware of the Jesuitical overtones of his remarks to Harley." But English writers attacked the Jesuits for putting equivocation and dissimulation to mischievous uses; in the service of a "just cause," Protestant authors found such devices legitimate. See the quotations from Henry Mason, *The New Art of Lying Covered by the Jesuits under the Vaile of Equivocation* [1634], pp. 5-6, in Mosse, *The Holy Pretence*, pp. 45-46.

and insinuating management: certain truths must be incul-
cated indirectly, by means of *un*truths. Defoe supports this
position by applying to the reading public at large arguments
traditionally used to justify the deception of children and madmen. Samuel Pufendorf had said of children that "for as much
as through the weakness of their Reason, and the strength of
their Passions, they have scarce any Relish for plain Truths,
therefore 'tis convenient to instruct them by Fables . . . till
such time as they grow weary of Trifles, and are able to
apprehend and to value the real Solidity of things. And thus
we address to them by Fiction and Disguise, not to sport with
their Ignorance, or to procure their Harm; but only because
they cannot well be applied to in any more serious Method of
Information."[18] Generations of casuists, weighing the circumstances in which deception is legitimate, had come to the same
conclusion. Moreover, they had anticipated Defoe's broader
application of this doctrine, by defending well-intended fictions
of all kinds on the same grounds. Immediately after justifying the lawfulness of constructively deceiving children and
madmen, Jeremy Taylor endorses "inventing a witty fable, or
telling a false story to gain ground upon him that believes a
false opinion, and cannot any other way so easily be confuted."[19] Similarly, Defoe holds that so long as fiction is not

[18] *Of The Law of Nature and Nations*, p. 325. John Hartcliffe observes that "The best of us all are sometimes forced to make use of
By-ways when the High-way is beset with Thieves; when we deal
with *Children*, with *Fools*, with *sick Persons*, with our *Enemies* in
the Field . . . yea with our familiar friends, we are compell'd to make
use of Art and Sleights, to cozen them for their Benefit" (*A Compleat Treatise*, p. 144). Richard Baxter uses the same argument in the
Christian Directory, and concludes that "such a charitable deceit . . .
can be no sin" (*Practical Works*, ed. William Orme, 23 vols. [1830],
III, 514).

[19] *Ductor Dubitantium*, in *Whole Works*, x, 104; Taylor's general
thesis is that if a man "intends to profit and to instruct, to speak probably and usefully, to speak with a purpose to do good and to do no

designed to "Deciev and Injure" the reader, but to delight and edify him, it cannot be branded lying; on the contrary, it can be defended as an "honest Cheat."[20] Defoe did not originate this concept: the equivalent (and perhaps more familiar) paradox of the *dolus bonus* or "pious fraud" had long been debated by divines, and other authors had pleaded for the legitimacy of fiction on similar grounds.[21] The first critic of *Robinson Crusoe* nevertheless protested to Defoe that "the Design of the Publication of this Book was not sufficient to justify and make Truth of what you allow to be Fiction and Fable; what you mean by *Legitimating, Invention*, and *Parable*, I know not; unless you would have us think, that the manner of your telling a Lie will make it a Truth."[22] Defoe

---

evil, though the words have not in them any necessary truth, yet they may be good words" (x, 102). Such beneficent deceptions were often classified as "officious lies": see Gouge, *The Young Man's Guide*, p. 436; the *Spectator*, No. 234 (Nov. 28, 1711), II, 410.

[20] Defoe uses this phrase in the *Review*, where he argues that by entertaining readers with the livelier, nonhistorical, but "every Jot as useful" material at the end of each paper, he may manage to "wheedle" them into considering the serious truths in the body of the *Review* (*Supplement*, 1 [Sept., 1704], 5).

[21] Perkins had maintained that there is "a kinde of deceit called *dolus bonus*, that is, *a good deceit*"; see his *Commentarie or Exposition vpon . . . Galatians, Workes*, II, 183. Evidence that this view was widely shared is assembled by George L. Mosse in *The Holy Pretence*, pp. 50-51 and *passim*. Nathaniel Hardy pithily sums up the opposing view when he says, "There are some indeed who tell us of *piæ fraudes*, a godly dissimulation, I like well the Christian, but not the Sir name, and I wonder how any dare joyne them together, when the parties are not agreed" (*Wisdomes Counterfeit: or Herodian Policy* [1656], p. 21).

[22] Charles Gildon, *The Life and Strange Surprizing Adventures of Mr. D..... De F..* (1719), ed. Paul Dottin as *Robinson Crusoe Examin'd and Criticis'd* (London and Paris, 1923), p. 113. Cf. also a contemporary reference to "the little Art he is truly master of, of forging a Story, and imposing it on the World for Truth" (*Weekly Journal and British Gazetteer*, Nov. 1, 1718, quoted in Lee, *Daniel Defoe*, I, 282).

Appendix

does not claim, however, that good intentions suffice to trans-
form falsehood into truth, but merely that a distinction must
be made between wholesome and pernicious falsehoods, and
that only the latter should be called lies. Thus his theory of
fiction does not really rest, as one recent critic maintains, on
a "defense of lying," but rather on a traditional distinction
between lying and beneficial deception.[23]

By the same token, Defoe makes no moral issue of the un-
truthfulness of his characters when the element of injury is
absent. This can be seen in *The Farther Adventures of Robinson Crusoe*, when the caravan bound from Peking to Moscow
comes to the great wall of China. "I stood still an hour to look
at it on every side, near, and far off," says Crusoe, "and the
guide of our caravan, who had been extolling it for the wonder
of the world, was mighty eager to hear my opinion of it. I
told him it was a most excellent thing to keep off the Tartars,
which he happened not to understand as I meant it, and so
took it for a compliment; but the old pilot laughed. 'O seignior
Inglese,' says he, 'you speak in colours.' 'In colours!' said I;

[23] Novak, "Defoe's Theory of Fiction," p. 663. Defoe expresses this
distinction most emphatically in *A New Family Instructor* (1727):
"a Fiction or a Romance," he says, "told only with Design to deceive
the Reader, bring him to believe, that the Fact related was true, and
delight him with a Falshood instead of a History, must be . . .
criminal and wicked, and *making a Lye* . . . and was made still more
so, by how much it was more or less design'd to deceive prejudicially,
and to the Hurt of the Person, as particularly where it was calculated
to recommend Vice, discourage Virtue, debauch the Ears and Minds
of Youth, raise loose and vain Conceptions of Things in the Thoughts,
and the Like"; notice the shift in focus from deception to *prejudicial*
deception. In the paragraph that follows, Defoe goes on to defend
"Fables, feigned Histories, invented Tales, and even such as we call
Romances" as "the most pungent Way of writing or speaking" when
they are devoted to "enforcing sound Truths; making just and solid
Impressions on the Mind; recommending great and good Actions," and
so on. There is no pretence that such worthy objects make fictions true,
but by having "the End directed right," fictions are freed from the
stigma of *"making a Lye"* (pp. 51-53).

'what do you mean by that?' 'Why, you speak what looks white this way, and black that way—gay one way, and dull another way. You tell him it is a good wall to keep out Tartars; you tell me, by that, it is good for nothing but to keep out Tartars, or it will keep out none but Tartars. I understand you, seignior Inglese, I understand you,' says he, 'but seignior Chinese understand you his own way.' "[24] The rich possibilites of "speaking in colours" had long been recognized, even by grave Puritan divines,[25] and were to be exploited more fully by later writers of fiction.[26] But Defoe's ventures in this

[24] *Farther Adventures*, in *Romances and Narratives*, ii, 267; cf. the potentially tragic encounter between a soldier and a countryman, which turns instead to comedy, in *Memoirs of the Church of Scotland* (1717), pp. 247-48, and Defoe's charges against the Turkey Company in *The Case Fairly Stated between the Turky Company and the Italian Merchants* (1720), p. 4: "I am loth to call it Shuffling . . . but Necessity obliges me to say, That what they offer, evidently looks one Way but means another." Panurge's judgment on the walls of Paris is more robust but no wittier than Crusoe's on the Great Wall of China: "Oh, how strong they are! They're just the thing for keeping goslings in a coop. By my beard, they are pretty defences for a city like this. Why, a cow could knock down more than twelve foot of them with a single fart" (*The Histories of Gargantua and Pantagruel*, Book ii, Chapter 15). On the meaning of the phrase "speaking in colours," see *OED*, colour, sb. 11b, "A fiction, an allegory," and the phrases (12d) involving disguise and dissembling. In *An Apology for the Army* (1715), Defoe asks "what Colours so gross, what Lies so palpable, as not to be imposed on *home-spun Clowns*?" (p. 6).

[25] E.g. William Perkins, "Of Truth," in *A Direction for the Governement of the Tongve, Workes*, i, 443: "report is made of a rich man that had two chests: the one whereof he called *all the world*, the other his *friend*. In the first he putteth nothing: in the second he putteth all his substance. When his neighbour came to borrow money, he vsed to answer, Truely I haue neuer a pennie in all the world, meaning his emptie chest, but I will see (saith he) what my friend can doe."

[26] In the *Pickwick Papers*, to take a single example, Sam Weller's humor has a similar basis when his testimony at Pickwick's trial is interrupted by a shout from the gallery: "The little judge turned to the witness as soon as his indignation would allow him to speak, and

direction—seldom boisterous, yet often full of austere humor—
are more frequent than is usually recognized, and help to keep
even his most matter-of-fact characters from seeming merely
stolid.

In the seventeenth and early eighteenth centuries, no group
in England took more literally than the Quakers Christ's bid-
ding, "Let your communication be Yea, yea; Nay, nay: for
whatsoever is more than these cometh of evil" (Matth. 5:37).
In Defoe's writings, however, Quakers are masters of amphibology and circumlocution. It was not until the 1720's that he
created his two most remarkable Quaker characters, in *Captain
Singleton* and *Roxana*. But in several pamphlets that appeared
between 1715 and 1719 he had written satirically on religious and
political topics in the guise of a Quaker, and in all these works
the question of truthfulness is central. In the pamphlets, the
serpentine side of the Quaker spirit remains covert, as Defoe
adopts an air of completely dovelike candor.[27] His "seasonable

said, 'Do you know who that was, sir?' 'I rayther suspect it was my
father, my lord,' replied Sam. 'Do you see him here now?' said the
judge. 'No, I don't, my lord,' replied Sam, staring right up into the
lantern in the roof of the court." Later in the book, Pickwick is shown
his cell in the Fleet Prison: " 'You wouldn't think to find such a room
as this in the Farringdon Hotel, would you?' said Mr. Roker with a
complacent smile. To this Mr. Weller replied with an easy and un-
studied closing of one eye, which might be considered to mean either
that he would have thought it, or that he would not have thought it,
or that he had never thought anything at all about it, as the observer's
imagination suggested."

[27] See *A Seasonable Expostulation with, and Friendly Reproof unto
James Butler, Who, by the Men of this World, is Stil'd Duke of
O——d, Relating to the Tumults of the People*, 2nd edn. (1715); *A
Friendly Epistle By Way of Reproof From one of the People called
Quakers, To Thomas Bradbury, A Dealer in many Words* (1715); *A
Declaration of Truth to Benjamin Hoadly, One of the High Priests
of the Land, And Of the Degree whom Men call Bishops, By a Min-
istring Friend, who writ to Tho. Bradbury, a Dealer in many Words*
(1717); and *A Friendly Rebuke to one Parson Benjamin; Particularly*

expostulations" and "friendly reproofs" purport to be utterly guileless. Yet once he has established himself as a plaindealing lover of truth, motivated solely by public spirit and charity towards his victim, Defoe is able to be merrily abusive. In a typical "friendly epistle," addressed to "James Butler, Who, by the Men of this World, is Stil'd Duke of O——d," Defoe's Quaker spokesman assumes that Ormond is a simple, honest man like himself, but that he is being exploited and duped by wily counsellors. Defoe poses as a dove the better to play the serpent; the effect depends upon his seeming totally naïve and forthright in his conception of honesty.

On the other hand, Roxana's landlady in the Minories combines the dove and the serpent in a fashion that Defoe evidently regarded as more typical of contemporary Quakers. Roxana introduces her as "a most courteous, obliging, mannerly Person; perfectly well-bred, and perfectly well-humour'd. . . . so grave, and yet so pleasant and so merry, that 'tis scarce possible for me to express how I was pleas'd and delighted with her Company"; moreover, Roxana finds her "a Woman of Understanding, and of Honesty too," and what interests us is the curious nature of this honesty.[28] Her unwillingness to tell outright lies is shown almost at once. When the Dutch merchant comes to her house to see Roxana, who wishes to postpone the encounter, Roxana orders her to deny that she is there. "That I cannot do, *says she, because it is not the Truth*," and on several later occasions Roxana has further proof that "the honest QUAKER, tho' she wou'd do any-thing

---

relating to his Quarrelling with his Own Church, and Vindicating the Dissenters (1719). Some Farther Account of the Original Disputes in Ireland (1724) is cast in the form of a discourse with "a sensible and intelligent Person, *one of the People call'd Quakers* . . . who came lately from *Dublin*" (p. 3) but the Quaker is used as a straightforward truth-teller rather than as a taunter of one or another worldling.

[28] *Roxana*, ed. Jane Jack, Oxford English Novels (1964), pp. 210-11, 213.

else for me, wou'd not LYE for me."[29] Nevertheless the distinction is a very fine one between the Quakeress's equivocations in Roxana's behalf and downright lying.

In the following scene, for instance, the landlady is being questioned about her lodger by Roxana's unacknowledged daughter. When the girl asks, "Has she not a Maid nam'd *Amy?*" Roxana tells us that *"the honest* QUAKER *was nonpluss'd, and greatly surpriz'd at that Question"*: "Truly, *says she,* the Lady——has several Women-Servants, but I do not know all their Names. But her Woman, her Favourite, *adds the Girl*; is not her Name *Amy?* Why truly, *says the* QUAKER, *with a very happy Turn of Wit,* I do not like to be examin'd; but lest *thou* should'st take up any Mistakes, by reason of my backwardness to speak, I will answer *thee* for once, That what her Woman's Name is, I know not; but they call her *Cherry.* N.B. *My Husband gave her that Name in jest, on our Wedding-Day, and we had call'd her by it ever after; so that she spoke literally true at that time."*[30] It is very characteristic of Defoe to have *"the honest* QUAKER" introduce her statements with "truly," "why truly"; this *"Turn of Wit"* is as happy as the others he ascribes to her. She does *not* know the names of all her lodger's servants; she does *not* like to be examined; she *has* heard Amy called Cherry: all this is, as Roxana says, *"literally true."* Whether it is true in any but a narrowly literal sense is a different matter; yet her predicament is a difficult one. Unlike the servants and bawds of clas-

[29] *Roxana*, pp. 222, 282. Roxana herself is far less strict in her conception of what is and is not a lie, though she too prefers to avoid bald untruths: see pp. 294-95.

[30] *Roxana*, p. 305; cf. Perkins, *A Direction for the Governement of the Tongve, Workes,* I, 449: "An asseueration is a forme of speech, wherby one doth vehemently affirme or denie any thing: as when a man shall say; *Verily, in truth, in very truth, without all doubt, &c.* These and such like are not to be vsed at euery word; but then onely when a truth of great importance is to be confirmed."

sical comedy and rogue literature, the Quakeress embodies the
dove as well as the serpent, although (like Amy) she proves
to be far more ophidian than columbine.

Another such scene occurs when Roxana has fled to Tun-
bridge; the girl seems about to pursue her there, and the landlady is intent on throwing her off the scent:

> The QUAKER, with as much Caution as she was Mistress
> of, *not to tell a downright Lye*, made her believe she
> expected to hear of me very quickly; and frequently *by
> the by*, speaking of being Abroad to take the Air, talk'd
> of the Country about *Bury*, how pleasant it was; . . .
> How the *Downs* about *Newmarket* were exceeding fine;
> and what a vast deal of Company there was, now the
> *Court* was there; till at last, the Girl began to conclude,
> that *my Ladyship* was gone thither; for, *she said*, She
> knew I lov'd to see a great-deal of Company. Nay, *says
> my Friend, thou* tak'st me wrong, I did not suggest, *says
> she*, that the Person *thou* enquir'st after, is gone thither,
> neither do I believe she is, *I assure thee*: Well, the Girl
> smil'd, and let her know, that she believ'd it for-all that;
> so, to clench it fast, Verily *says she, with great Serious-
> ness, Thou* do'st not do well, for *thou* suspectest every-
> thing, and believest nothing: I speak solemnly to *thee*,
> that I do not believe they are gone that Way; so if *thou*
> giv'st *thyself* the Trouble to go that Way, and are dis-
> appointed, do not say that I have deceiv'd *thee*.[31]

[31] *Roxana*, pp. 309-10; cf. Baxter's answer to the question, "Is it
lawful by speech to deceive another, yea, and to intend it? Supposing
it be by truth?" "It is not," he maintains, "a sin in all cases, to contribute towards another man's error or mistake. For . . . there are
many cases in which it is no sin in him to mistake, nor any hurt to
him: therefore to contribute to that which is neither sin or hurt, is
of itself no sin" (*Christian Directory*, in *Practical Works*, III, 512; cf.
also Pufendorf, *Of The Law of Nature and Nations*, p. 316, and Taylor,
Ductor Dubitantium, in *Whole Works*, x, 106-10.)

The most striking thing about this passage is perhaps the way truths are used to foster untruths: with "Verily" in her mouth and *"great Seriousness"* in her manner, the Quakeress acts with a design to deceive—to "clench fast" the girl's mistake, which she has deliberately induced.[32] According to Perkins she is guilty of lying, but for Defoe, as we have seen, the crucial question is whether the deception has an injurious intent. The answer in this case would appear to be that malice is absent—the Quakeress feels she is acting in the girl's best interests as well as Roxana's—so that this particular untruth may not deserve the stigma of *"a downright Lye."* Another mitigating factor is that the girl herself seizes on the Quakeress's allusions to Newmarket, and wrongly concludes that Roxana is there, although the Quakeress has actually said no such thing. However dubious we may find it, the Quakeress seems to accept Richard Baxter's doctrine that one can legitimately speak to others in such a way that "through some weakness of their own they will misunderstand," and that in such cases "the hearer sometimes is the deceiver of him-

---

[32] This paradoxical situation is the basis of a joke discussed by Freud: "Two Jews met in a railway carriage at a station in Galicia. 'Where are you going?' asked one. 'To Cracow,' was the answer. 'What a liar you are!' broke out the other. 'If you say you're going to Cracow, you want me to believe you're going to Lemberg. But I know that in fact you're going to Cracow. So why are you lying to me?'" (*Jokes and their Relation to the Unconscious* [1905], in *Complete Psychological Works*, ed. James Strachey [1960], VIII, 115.) As Pufendorf observes, "The very speaking what is true may sometimes create and constitute a *Lye:* which not only happens when a Person affirms the Truth with the Air and Address of a *Lye,* and by his Manner, his Gestures, and his Actions . . . makes his Hearers believe the contrary to what he delivers . . . but it chiefly takes place in those, who by a Practice of frequent Lying have depriv'd themselves of all Credit and Belief" (*Of The Law of Nature and Nations,* p. 321). Cf. also *The Double Dealer,* v, i: "No Mask like open Truth to cover Lies,/ As to go naked is the best disguise" (William Congreve, *Complete Plays,* ed. Herbert Davis [Chicago, 1967], p. 190).

self, and not the speaker, when the speaker is not bound to reveal any more to him."[33]

The question of truthfulness is also a significant feature in Defoe's portrayal of the Quaker in *Captain Singleton*. Singleton describes William Walters, who accompanies him as "privy counsellor and companion" during most of his piratical voyage, as "a wise and wary man," to whom "all the prudentials of my conduct had for a long time been owing."[34] Singleton also finds him "a very honest fellow": William's prudence is obvious, but the problem is whether he sacrifices the dove's innocence to the serpent's wisdom. Once again the issue is not solely one of verbal honesty; also in question is William's sincerity in practicing the Quaker principle of nonviolence. On the whole, we are made to feel that the innocence he preserves is little better than what Singleton calls a "quaking quibble," a connivance at crime that shares its profits without its risks.[35] But this may be to put the matter in too severe a light, since Defoe seems to find William's dissimulation more comical than sinister.[36]

At any rate, William Walters plays an important part in several scenes that hinge on verbal truthfulness. Late in the

[33] *Christian Directory*, in *Practical Works*, III, 510.

[34] *The Life, Adventures and Pyracies of the Famous Captain Singleton*, in *Romances and Narratives*, x, 192, 288, 302.

[35] *Captain Singleton*, p. 176; for Defoe's somewhat more rigorous comments on an analogous moral posture, see his discussion of Jonathan Wild's practice of helping the victims of theft to recover their goods, in *The Life and Actions of Jonathan Wild, Romances and Narratives*, XVI, 249.

[36] Paul Dottin's impression strikes me as sound: "Ce n'est certes pas un personnage recommandable, mais il n'a rien de Tartufe, et sa franchise un peu cynique désarme nos rigueurs" (*Daniel De Foe et ses Romans* [Paris and London, 1924], p. 638). Cf. also Frank W. Chandler, *The Literature of Roguery*, 2 vols. (Boston, 1907), II, 289. In my opinion, the humor of Defoe's portrait is partly lost if we think of Walters as a *"renegade* Quaker" (Maximillian Novak, *Defoe and the Nature of Man* [Oxford, 1963], p. 147).

story the ship is driven aground on Ceylon; the next day some natives appear under a flag of truce, and beckon the crew ashore. Singleton naïvely intends to go, but is dissuaded by Quaker William, who is familiar with stories of Ceylonese perfidy.[37] The next day an old Dutchman is sent to lure the Englishmen to their doom, but in the parley that follows, William is a match for the "double-tongued" man. When the Dutchman declares that the king of Ceylon "invites you to come on shore, and has ordered you to be treated courteously and assisted," William asks, "dost thou believe the king . . . means one word of what he says?" "He promises you by the mouth of his great general," replies the Dutchman. "I don't ask thee what he promises, or by whom; but I ask thee this: Canst thou say that thou believest he intends to perform it?" "How can I answer that? How can I tell what he intends?" "Thou canst tell what thou believest." "I cannot say but he will perform it; I believe he may."[38] This fragment of the dialogue suggests the Dutchman's style of equivocation, and William's way of parrying it. The Dutchman's speech is clearly designed "to Deciev and Injure"; he himself is largely exonerated, however, since he is acting under duress, perfunctorily and unwillingly, as the remainder of the dialogue indicates.[39]

[37] Robert Knox's narrative of his twenty years on the island (summarized in *Captain Singleton*, pp. 271-83) had made Ceylon notorious for treachery toward Europeans: see *An Historical Relation of Ceylon*, ed. James Ryan (Glasgow, 1911).

[38] *Captain Singleton*, pp. 258-59; on the ethical status of such promises, see *The Compleat English Tradesman*, I, 238: "There is a distinction to be made between wilful premeditated lying, and the necessity men may be driven to by their disappointments, and other accidents of their circumstances, to break such promises, as they had made with an honest intention of performing them." Thus Defoe concludes that "He that breaks a promise, however solemnly made, may be an honest man: but he that makes a promise with a design to break it, or with no resolution of performing it, cannot be so." The king of Ceylon clearly belongs in the latter category.

[39] Defoe had considered a predicament similar to the Dutchman's in

It should also be noted that when William asks him whether he believes the Ceylonese king intends to carry out his promises, the Dutchman replies, "How can I answer that? How can I tell what he intends?" Both the Dutchman and William himself know that the king has no intention of keeping his word, but William does not challenge the veracity of this answer, nor does Defoe. The grounds on which such an answer can be called truthful are suggested by Nathaniel Hardy: "Indeed we must distinguish between concealing truth, & speaking falshood, it is one thing *cum silendo absconditur verum*, to keep in a truth, another, *cum loquendo promittitur falsum*, to belch out a lye. I am not bound to say all I thinke, and yet I must thinke all I say; the tongue is but the hearts herauld, and must proclaime the senders message; he that speaketh all he knowes is not wise, but he that speaketh what he does not meane is not honest. I would not have my heart too near my mouth, lest I speak rashly, nor yet too farre from my tongue, lest I speak falsely."[40] In the present case the

---

the *Little Review*, where the question had arisen "Whether a Servant may lawfully tell a Lye for his Master?" Defoe's advice had been that "If his Master will have him Lye, let him tell it as a Lye"—i.e. in such a way that the hearer will be sure to infer the true state of things. To reveal the truth in this manner requires, however, the same ingenuity which Defoe's characters more often employ to conceal it; see *Little Review*, II (July 6, 1705), 39.

[40] *Wisdomes Counterfeit*, pp. 21-22; cf. Arthur Warwick, *Spare Minutes: Or Resolved Meditations, and Premeditated Resolutions* (ca. 1630): "To speak all that is true, is the property of fools; to speak more than is true, is the folly of too many. . . . I may sometimes know what I will not utter, I must never utter what I do not know. I should be loth to have my tongue so large as my heart, I would scorn to have my heart less than my tongue. For if to speak all that I know, shows too much folly; to speak more than I know, shows too little honesty" ([1890], p. 187). Cf. also *The Religious Tradesman*, p. 136; Pufendorf, *Of The Law of Nature and Nations*, p. 316; and the Athenian Society's response to the question "*If 'tis convenient to speak the* Truth *at all Times?*": "Undoubtedly its not *convenient*, but the meaning I suppose

Appendix

Dutchman may be speaking honestly, not only by keeping in a truth instead of belching out a lie, but by keeping it in with so transparent an evasion that his hearer can readily deduce it for himself, as William of course does.

"Rational Creatures," Defoe says in the *Review*, "are no otherwise rational than by being Capable of Judging, Arguing, and Determining of Truth, and Falsehood":[41] truthfulness is not automatic, dovelike innocence but involves an exercise of judgment. It is significant that elsewhere in the *Review* Defoe should put in the mouth of a madman the assertion that "Truth, should always be spoken like itself, plainly and honestly, or else it really is not Truth,"[42] since only madmen, in his opinion, could follow so literally the injunction to dovelike simplicity; all others must temper it with serpentine wisdom, and the function of rationality—indeed of moral judgment in general—is to determine how much serpentine wisdom is admissible. Nor can the just proportions of dove and serpent be laid down in any comprehensive formula, since circumstances alter cases. Since malice is the *sine qua non* of lying, one can be untruthful yet a *"virtuous* hypocrite," the author of *"honest* cheats."

---

is, Whether it be *necessary*: We answer, its neither *one* nor *t'other*. 'Tis undoubtedly *necessary* never to speak an *Untruth*; but the contrary holds not, that we always must *speak Truth*, since there's a *Medium* of *Negation,* something that's neither one nor t'other, namely, *not speaking at all"* (*Athenian Mercury*, ii, i, 14).

[41] *Review*, vi (Mar. 31, 1709), Edinburgh 2.
[42] *Review*, v (June 26, 1708), 156.

Index

Index

Defoe, Daniel (*cont.*)
Apology for the Army, An, 202; *Apparition of Mrs. Veal, The*, 190; *Applebee's Journal*, 39, 46, 90, 105, 123, 128, 146, 159-60, 174, 184, 185; *Augusta Triumphans*, 124; *Candidate, The*, 193; *Captain Singleton*, 144-45, 177, 184, 203, 208-11; *Case Fairly Stated between the Turky Company and the Italian Merchants, The*, 202; *Charity Still a Christian Virtue*, 104; *Colonel Jack*, 22, 32, 42, 82-110, 150, 158-59, 161, 177-78, 184; *Commentator, The*, 18, 92, 96, 158-59, 178, 193; *Compleat English Gentleman, The*, 42, 66, 86, 88, 150; *Compleat English Tradesman, The*, xii, 92, 111-13, 141, 150, 192-94, 209; *Conjugal Lewdness*, xii, 29, 40, 124, 137, 142, 146-47, 198; *Consolidator, The*, 55; *Declaration of Truth to Benjamin Hoadly, A*, 203; *Defoe's Answer, To Dyer's Scandalous News Letter*, 178; *Due Preparations for the Plague*, 65, 76, 79; *Dyet of Poland, The*, 178; *Effectual Scheme for the Immediate Preventing of Street Robberies, An*, 178; *Enquiry Into the Case of Mr. Asgil's General Translation, An*, 184; *Enquiry into the Occasional Conformity of Dissenters, An*, 4, 193; *Essay on the History and Reality of Apparitions, An*, 122, 154; *Family Instructor, The*, xii, 33, 35, 39, 43; *Farther Adventures of Robinson Crusoe, The*, 37, 87-88, 93, 122, 201-202; *Friendly Epistle By Way of Reproof . . . To Thomas Bradbury, A*, 203; *Friendly Rebuke to one Parson Benjamin, A*, 203; *Hint to the Blackwell-Hall Factors, A*, 175; *Jonathan Wild, The Life and Actions of*, 208; *Journal of the Plague Year, A*, 32, 51-81, 109-10, 160; *Jure Divino*, 185; *Just Complaint of the Poor Weavers, The*, 111; *King of Pirates, The*, 182-83; *Lay-Man's Sermon upon the Great Storm, The*, 82; *Letter to Mr. How, A*, 113, 184, 193; *Letters*, 7, 195-97; *Meditations*, 178, 185; *Memoirs of the Church of Scotland*, 202; *Mercurius Politicus*, 111-12; *Mist's Journal*, 11, 54, 66; *Mock Mourners, The*, 178; *Moll Flanders*, v, 17, 24-25, 32-33, 41, 62, 90, 93-94, 96, 102-103, 106, 108, 111-64, 179, 181, 184f; *More Reformation*, 124, 189; *New Discovery of an Old Intreague, A*, 178; *New Family Instructor, A*, 33, 201; *New Test of the Church of England's Loyalty, A*, 122; *Not[tingh]am Politicks Examined*, 70; *Perjur'd Free Mason Detected, The*, 123; *Political History of the Devil*, 128, 153; *Reformation of Manners*, 178, 184; *Religious Courtship*, xii, 23, 33-50, 88, 184; *Remarks on the Bill to Prevent Frauds Committed*

214

Index

Defoe, Daniel (*cont.*)
  by Bankrupts, 174; *Review*, 12,
  19-20, 22, 26, 28, 33, 46-47,
  80, 111, 113, 119, 122, 126,
  135-36, 139, 142, 145, 150,
  177, 192-94, 200, 210-11;
  Robinson Crusoe, v, 4-5, 51-52,
  93-95, 102, 136, 143, 150, 160-
  61, 182, 184, 200; *Roxana*, v,
  19, 22, 24-25, 32-33, 62, 90,
  93, 96, 102, 106, 111, 122-23,
  143, 156, 165-89, 203-207;
  *Seasonable Expostulation with,
  and Friendly Reproof unto
  James Butler, A*, 203; *Serious
  Reflections*, 61, 111, 123, 141,
  144, 150, 178, 193-94; *Some
  Further Account of the Original
  Disputes in Ireland*, 204;
  *Some Remarks on the First
  Chapter in Dr. Davenant's
  Essays*, 171-72, 185; *Spanish
  Descent, The*, 178; *Storm,
  The*, 178; *True-Born English-
  man, The*, 189; *Voyage of
  Don Manoel Gonzales, The*,
  92; *Whitehall Evening Post*,
  145; *Ye True-Born* Englishmen
  Proceed, 178
De Quincey, Thomas, 5, 47-48, 89
dialogue, 36-37, 46, 49, 169
Dickens, Charles, 202-203
divorce, 28-29
Dobrée, Bonamy, 52-53, 127, 130
Donne, John, 76, 81
Donovan, Robert, 135
Dottin, Paul, 28, 58, 171-72,
  179, 208
Downe, John, 191-92
duelling, 88-90
Dunton, John, xxi, 9f, 37, 102;
  Life and Errors, 10, 12;

Whipping Post, 28; see
  Athenian Mercury

Eliot, George, 1
equivocation, 45-46, 201f
expediency, vii, 23, 64

Fielding, Henry, 130, 156, 186
Fish, Stanley E., 187-88
Franklin, Benjamin, 34
Freud, Sigmund, 131, 207

gentility, 86f, 163
George, M. Dorothy, 101, 105
Gildon, Charles, 10, 13, 200
Girdler, Lew, 13
Gouge, Thomas, 194, 197, 200
Gracian, Balthasar, 191

Hall, Joseph, xi, 11, 14, 16, 17,
  20, 23, 26, 29, 30-31, 41, 89,
  119, 134, 137, 141, 142, 146,
  160
Hardy, Nathaniel, 200, 210
Hartcliffe, John, 197, 199
Hazlitt, William, 85
Heptameron, The, 134
Herbert, George, 6
Herrick, Cheesman A., 101
Heywood, Oliver, 7
Hill, Peter Murray, 9
Holyday, Barten, 191
honor, 86f, 180-81
Hunter, J. Paul, 61

incest, 14-15, 117, 122-23, 134-35
inclination, 2, 137, 138, 145
intentions, 51, 106, 118, 122-24,
  138
irony, vii, 22, 67, 75, 78, 91,
  108-09, 114, 130, 135, 142,
  156, 180-81, 186-89

Index

216

Index